Principles of Turkish Administrative Law

Ahmet Yayla and Nihal Özkardeş

Principles of Turkish Administrative Law

PETER LANG

Lausanne - Berlin - Bruxelles - Chennai - New York - Oxford

Library of Congress Cataloging-in-Publication Data
A CIP catalog record for this book has been applied for at the
Library of Congress.

Bibliographic information published by the Deutsche Nationalbibliothek.
The German National Library lists this publication in the German National
Bibliography; detailed bibliographic data is available on the Internet
at http://dnb.d-nb.de.

ISBN 978-3-631-89898-7 (Print)
E-ISBN 978-3-631-89906-9 (E-PDF)
E-ISBN 978-3-631-90606-4 (E-PUB)
10.3726/b21056

Published by Peter Lang GmbH, Berlin, Deutschland

info@peterlang.com - www.peterlang.com

This publication has been peer reviewed.

In memory of our beloved people we lost in the Kahramanmaraş Earthquake

Preface

Turkish administrative law is a complicated area of law which students have struggles with during their undergraduate education. The reasons thereof may be seen in the fact that this branch of law is not codified even though there are some attempts on this regard. Practitioners are lost in excessive number of laws, which regulate specific powers or obligations of administration, but lack the general principles. In such an environment, we have noticed that it is hard for non-Turkish-speaking people to understand administrative law, which is mostly developed through decisions of administrative courts which is even hard for Turkish-speaking people to understand. We hope that this book helps non-Turkish-speaking students, practitioners and theoreticians who wish to learn general principles of Turkish administrative law.

We would like to thank Law Faculty community of University of Bahçeşehir who have given the sincerest support during the study on the draft of this book. We would especially like to thank our dean Prof. Emre GÖKYAYLA, who has provided a peaceful and encouraging environment that supports the community in all academic activities.

We are beyond grateful for the enthusiasm and dearest support of Dr. Deniz MERAKLI YAYLA.

We would also like to thank Peterlang Group, and specifically Esra Bahşi and Kalyani Kanekal who have always been there for all of our questions.

Contents

Abbreviations

AN	Application number
APC	Administrative Proceedings Circuit
C.	Circuit
CC	Constitutional Court
CJD	Court of Jurisdictional Disputes
D.	Decision
DAC	District Administrative Court
DG	Decision Gazette
EPDK	Energy Market Regulatory Authority
IA	Individual Application
İLR	İstanbul Law Review
İSKİ	İstanbul Water and Canalization Administration
JALAS	Journal of Administrative Law and Administrative Sciences
MHAC	Military High Administrative Court
M.	Merits
no.	number
OG	Official Gazette
OIZ	Organized Industrial Zones
p.	page
par.	paragraph
SC	State Council
SCPSCAC	SC Plenary Session of the Chambers for Administrative Cases
SE	Suspension of Execution
Sec.	Section
SGD	Security General Directorate
TBMM	Grand National Assembly of Turkey
TEİAŞ	Turkish Electricity Transmission Corporation
V	Volume

Introduction

From the viewpoint of historical development process, we may state that there are two systems governing administration. The distinction on these systems emerges on whether a separate administrative law regime is adapted. Within the scope of common law, administration is scrutinized by general courts and disputes are resolved within the scope of general provisions which are also applied to private law persons. On the other hand, in administrative regime systems, which firstly arose in France, administration is subject to a separate branch of law and disputes concerning administration is scrutinized by a separate branch of judiciary.[1] Turkey is one of the states which has a separate branch of judiciary, and which adopted a separate administrative law branch, which is also the subject of this book.

Generally speaking, the basic idea of Turkish administrative law is that administration serves to the public interest. Due to the obligations of public interest, it is also granted with superior rights compared to private law persons. Therefore, Turkish administrative law tries to establish the way in which public interest will be realized and the protection of private law persons confronting the "powerful" administration.

From this perspective, in the first section named "Public Force: Organization, Personnel and Property," we will touch upon the organization, personnel and property of administration which are the tools that administration has while serving for public interest. In this section, within the subject of "The Notion of Administration" we intend to write on the basic principles governing administration, namely where the administration is situated in the organization of the state and its stance before judiciary and legislature. In this subject, firstly, we will explain "the principle of legal administration," which rules administration to be regulated by laws (namely, legal codes of legislature). Secondly, we will touch upon "public corporate bodies," which together forms the administration, and specifically how these bodies are established and specified. Thirdly, we will handle the principles of centralization and decentralization, which govern Turkish administrative organization and function according to the Turkish

1 Hayrettin Yıldız, "İdare Hukukunun Kısa Tarihçesi [Short History of Administrative Law]," *Ankara Hacı Bayram Veli Üniversitesi Hukuku Fakültesi Dergisi* 22, no. 4 (2008), 200, https://dergipark.org.tr/tr/download/article-file/685872.

Constitution. Fourthly, we will explain the principle of integrity of administration, which is laid down in Turkish Constitution. We will detail the mechanisms such as hierarchy and administrative tutelage which serve to provide administrative integrity. Lastly, we will explain the legal status and regime of independent regulatory authorities as a different organization from the perspective of integrity of administration.

In the first section, secondly, we will elaborate the subject of "public employees," specifically by dealing with the fundamental principles governing the subject, disciplinary regime and legal and criminal liability of public employees.

Lastly, in the first section, we will explain the regime of "public properties." We will focus on the subjects of how public property emerges, the types of public properties according to the aim of allocation, legal regime of public properties, usage of such properties and how administration can acquire such properties.

In the second section named "Activities of Administration," we will assess two main activities of administration, which are police and public service. Within the scope of police, we will specifically touch upon the notion of "public order" and its elements, which the activity of police aims to protect. Thereafter, we will assess essential distinctions regarding policing (such as general and special police, judicial and administrative police), policing procedures as freeness, notification, permission, prohibition and lawfulness of policing acts and actions pursuant to Turkish Constitution.

Within the scope of the subject of "public service," at first, we intend to explain the principles of public service as the principles of continuity, regularity, adaptation, equality, impartiality and gratuitousness. Secondly, we will explain how public service can be established. Thirdly, we will detail operating procedures of public service through which we will explain the person who will carry out the service, with which monetary resource and personnel.

In the third section named "Acts of Administration," we intend to assess unilateral acts of administration (administrative acts) and bilateral or multilateral acts of administration (administrative agreements). Firstly, within the subject of "administrative acts," features of administrative acts will be handled. These features may be seen as the evidence of public force that administration benefits. Secondly, we will touch upon the types of administrative acts. Thirdly, we will detail the elements of administrative acts, which judiciary applies when determining on the lawfulness of administrative acts. Fourthly, termination of administrative acts and lawfulness of such terminations will be explained. Lastly, judicial review of administrative acts which are null and void will be handled, since such review differs from the (ordinary) unlawful administrative acts.

In the third section, secondly, we will touch upon agreements of administration, specifically focusing on how an agreement of administration may be seen as an "administrative agreement," types, termination and important principles of such agreements and lastly private law agreements of administration.

Lastly, in the fourth section named "Administrative Liability," we intend to assess how and when administration may be held liable due to its damages. In this section, we will specifically focus on the general conditions of liability, types of liability namely fault-based and absolute liability, compensation liability of public employees and factors effecting administrative liability.

Section I: Public Force: Organization, Personnel and Property

Abstract

By using public force, administration establishes unilateral and executable acts, benefits from the presumption of legality and is secured more than private law persons concerning their property, personnel, receivables and debts. While the idea behind this public force is the provision of public interest, administration nevertheless may violate the rights of persons who are clearly "weaker" compared to the "powerful" administration. Thus, a mechanism is needed to protect the rights of persons and ensure that administration acts lawfully. In this sense, administrative law emerges as an "opponent" branch of law, which constantly tries to push administration to the "lawful side." Within this scope, to guarantee a "lawful" administration, administration is under the supervision of judiciary and is established by legislature.

In this section, we aim to "concertize" the abstract notion of "administration" which possesses public force to the aim of public interest. Truly, administration appears as an "organization," with "employees" who use public force over persons in real and possessing "property" aimed at public interest. The organizational structure of administration comprises a community of public corporate bodies, which are separate from each other, but also integrated. In order for these public corporate bodies to carry out services, they need employees and properties which are governed with a different regime.

Keywords: principle of legal administration, public corporate body, public employee, public property, the principle of integrity of administration, administrative tutelage, hierarchy

1. The Notion of Administration

When handling Administrative Law, it is required to ask the question of "what is administration" at first. Administration is—or at least gives the impression of—a power or a force. Examples such as school administration indicating to some students that they cannot enroll to specific courses, police officer stopping people and asking for identification, municipality expropriating a person's garden house within some conditions are a few of instances where the administration possesses or gives the impression to possess such a power or force.

The impression of a power or a force unavoidably calls to mind the question of whether the notions of "state" and "administration" are identical. Since the notion of state also associates with a force or power, is administration tantamount to state? Within this regard, if we start by defining the state, a set of different definitions would be at hand since this definition varies from person to person. Therefore, it is not possible to conclude certainly that one definition is more accurate over the others.

However, it is true that the state emerged from the need of people to live together. It may be possible to designate the occurrence and development of the state and the dynamics associated with it from a historical point of view. However, this identification would be subject to different studies and disciplines. Rather than an approach from the historical development, from the viewpoint of Administrative Law, the state can be designated pursuant to positive law. Pursuant to the article 6 of the Turkish Constitution; "Sovereignty belongs to the Nation without any restriction or condition. The Turkish Nation shall exercise its sovereignty through the authorized organs, as prescribed by the principles set forth in the Constitution." These prescribed authorized organs are also laid down in the Constitution:

"**ARTICLE 7-** *Legislative power is vested in the Grand National Assembly of Turkey on behalf of Turkish Nation. This power shall not be delegated.*"

"**ARTICLE 8-** *Executive power and function shall be exercised and carried out by the President of the Republic in conformity with the Constitution and laws.*"[2]

---

2 With the last constitutional amendment, expression of "and council of ministers" is removed from the article. Before the constitutional amendment (with the Law dated 21.01.2017 numbered 6771), the Constitution of the Turkish Republic envisaged a parliamentary system. Accordingly, article 8 of the Constitution titled "Executive power and function" laid down that executive power and function shall be exercised and

"**ARTICLE 9**- *Judicial power shall be exercised by independent and impartial courts on behalf of the Turkish Nation.*"[3]

As seen, the state comprises of "legislature," "executive" and "judiciary."

Then what is the state in the lives of individuals? To receive education as well as being obliged to abide by the rules throughout the education; to receive health care as well as waiting in the corridor of a hospital for a doctor who does not show up; to receive protection as well as being conscripted for military service at a certain age and so forth. In brief, from the perspective of individuals, while state provides us with some services, sometimes it also restrains our fundamental rights and freedoms.

Is it the legislature that makes us live as such? On one side, there are decision makers and on the other side, there are implementers. The ones that are directly in relation with us are the implementers. The decisions of legislature, executive and judiciary do not generally affect us unless they are implemented.[4] The mechanism called "administration" —is the one that implements those decisions.

We have mentioned that the state is comprised of "legislature," "executive" and "judiciary." At this point, we should also sort out where the mechanism of administration is located within these powers. Administration is laid down in the section related to the executive in the Constitution. Therefore, administration is located within the executive. In that case, are the president, ministers and deputies of the president included in the administration?

After the last constitutional amendment dated 2017 answering this question rather seems troublesome by just reviewing the related norms of the Constitution for two reasons. Namely;

1. Before the constitutional amendment, under the title of administration in the Constitution, administrative judicial review was laid down and the acts solely taken by the president was excluded from the review of administrative judiciary.[5] With regard to this provision, since the president was referenced in the

---

carried out by the President and Council of Ministers. Therefore, the executive was two-headed.

3 The expression of "impartial" is also attached in the article with the constitutional amendment dated 2017.

4 Lütfi Duran, *İdare Hukuku Ders Notları* [*Administrative Law Lecture Notes*] (İstanbul: İstanbul Üniversitesi Yayınları, 1982), 8–9. The writer highlights that the jurisdiction also lacks the ability to directly implement its own rulings. See Duran, *İdare Hukuku Ders*, 4.

5 We have mentioned in the footnote 1 that the executive was two headed before the constitutional amendment. Article 105 of the Constitution stated that the decisions of

section related to administrative judicial review, it was concluded implicitly that the president was within the administration.

However, as a consequence of the constitutional amendment, the president is no longer mentioned in the section related to administrative judicial review. In the meantime, in the related section (article 125/4), it is laid down that no judicial ruling shall be passed which restricts the exercise of the executive function in accordance with the forms and principles prescribed by law, which has the quality of an administrative action and act, or which removes discretionary powers. From the antonym of this provision, it is understood that the administrative jurisdiction (Administrative Courts, District Administrative Courts and State Council [SC]), which has the power to review administration has the power to review executive, provided that it does not restrict the exercise of executive function or remove discretionary powers. Therefore, pursuant to this provision, it may be accepted that the executive and the president are also within the "administration."[6]

2. It may be concluded that the president, ministries and public corporate bodies are within the administration since these are mentioned to have the power to issue bylaws. This is because "bylaw" is an administrative act. However,

---

the president shall be countersigned by the Prime Minister or related ministers and that the ministers are responsible for such decisions. However, the article also prescribed the exception by excluding the decisions which the laws or the Constitution allows them to be taken solely by the President. See Kemal Gözler, *İdare Hukuku* [*Administrative Law*], Volume I (Bursa: Ekin Basım Yayın Dağıtım, 2019), 338–339. For a review on the constitutional developments of Turkish Republic, see Şule Özsoy Boyunsuz, "Regime Cycles, Constitution Making, and the Political System Question in Ottoman and Turkish Constitutional Developments," in *The Failure of Popular Constitution Making in Turkey*, ed. Felix Petersen and Zeynep Yanaşmayan (Cambridge: Cambridge University Press, 2020), 84–117.

6 Akyılmaz, Sezginer, and Kaya state that it is impossible to think the administration separate from the President. The authors indicate that while the President constitutes the *administrative-political* perspective of the public service, general administration constitutes the *technical* perspective. Bahtiyar Akyılmaz, Murat Sezginer, and Cemil Kaya, Türk *İdare Hukuku* (Ankara: Savaş, 2022), 82. The authors use the term "general administration" to refer the central administration which does not possess a separate personality other than the State. See Akyılmaz, Sezginer, and Kaya, *Türk İdare Hukuku*, 190, footnote 190; Gözler indicates that after the last constitutional amendment, the President has become the most important organ of the administration. Gözler, *İdare Hukuku V. I*, 36.

it should be indicated that to come to a conclusion by solely the title of an act will not be a strong inference legally.

From this point of view, it is an object of interest if a second approach is possible. It may be possible to make a conclusion with an approach related to the context of the acts taken by the institutions of the executive. This is because, in the article 125 of the Constitution, under the title of "administration," both administration with its organic sense and material sense (which refers to "administrative acts") are mentioned.

In case that an act is related to "daily public services" (including acts undertaken by the state to protect the public order), it may be concluded that an administrative act is in question. As a natural consequence, if the maker of the act is the executive, the office will be accepted to be within the administration for that act. Furthermore, an act of legislative power and judiciary may also be "administrative" in essence. This subject will be discussed in the chapter relating to administrative acts.

In light of these explanations, we may conclude that the president, ministries and deputies of the president are within the administration. However, it would not be accurate to conclude that "executive" and "administration" are identical[7] due that there are acts called "acts of government" which pertain to the executive. To make a decision to declare state of emergency,[8] to conclude treaties with foreign states, equal treatment in return[9] (in response to the decisions implemented to Turkish citizens in foreign states, implementing a decision to the citizens of that state in Turkey; for instance, seizing the goods that belong to Syrian citizens after the seizure of the goods belonging to Turkish citizens in Syria), to deport the folk from a place in the borderline for purposes related to security,[10] to naturalize a person, deprive of citizenship[11] are a few examples to the acts of government. These are conducted to protect the superior interests of the state and the nation rather than providing the daily needs of the community.[12] This type of acts are not subject to judiciary review. To put it another way, bringing action over the acts of government before administrative judiciary is not possible,

7 Pierre Delvolve, *Droit Administratif* (Paris: Dalloz, 2014), 12–13.
8 Gözler, *İdare Hukuku V. II*, 1080.
9 Ragıp Sarıca, *İdari Kaza [Administrative Jurisdiction]* (İstanbul: Kenan Matbaası, 1942), 47.
10 Sarıca, *İdari Kaza*, 51.
11 Yahya Kazım Zabunoğlu, *İdare Hukuku* (Ankara: Yetkin, 2012), 711.
12 Gözler, *İdare Hukuku V. I*, 49.

otherwise administrative judiciary shall refuse to hear such a case.[13] It should be noted that the existence of "acts of government" which are not subject to judiciary review is criticized in a state governed by rule of law in which recourse to judicial review shall be available against all actions and acts of administration.[14]

Surely, there are further institutions within the administration. Notwithstanding that it is not possible to indicate each one of them, we may give some examples of such institutions: universities, municipalities, public hospitals, general directorate of security, general directorate for highways, capital markets board, competition board and so forth.

However, the very notional existence of these institutions does not affect our lives. What affects us are the persons who work in this mechanism. In reality, we coincide with real persons and deal with them under the name of administration. For instance, one of these persons may replace our place during an exam or may not allow us to leave the exam room for a certain time. As seen, these persons may restrict our fundamental rights and freedoms. That is, the thing that appears as a force or authority over us is actually the real persons who implement the rules.

Why are not we equal to those persons? This is simply because they use sovereignty which belongs to the abstract notion called state. The authority to use this sovereignty is granted to the offices which they represent for the purposes of providing public service and public interest. Within this scope, the Constitution (article 128) states: "The fundamental and permanent functions required by the public services that the State, state economic enterprises and other public corporate bodies assigned to perform in accordance with principles of general administration, shall be carried out by public servants and other public employees."

As seen, from a realistic perspective, administration is nothing more than persons just like us who work in the institutions within the mechanism of administration.[15]

---

13 Sarıca, *İdari Kaza*, 51; Gözler, *İdare Hukuku V. II*, 1080.

14 Murat Sezginer, *Ayrılabilir İşlem Kuramı* (Ankara: Yetkin, 2000), 95 ff.; In doctrine, Kaya indicates that this practice is an exception of the principle of constitutional state. Cemil Kaya, "Danıştay İçtihatlarında Hükümet Tasarrufu Teorisinden Devletin Hükümranlık / Egemenlik Hakkı Teorisine [From the Act of State Theory within the Council of State Jurisprudence through to the State Sovereignty Theory]," *Court of Jurisdictional Disputes Journal*, no. 7 (2016): 637, https://dergipark.org.tr/tr/download/article-file/229918.

15 Yıldızhan Yayla, *İdare Hukuku* [*Administrative Law*] (İstanbul: Beta, 2009), 272.

Then, who will protect us from these persons if these use the authority of sovereignty for arbitrary practices rather than public welfare? For instance, who will protect students against the possibility of their lecturer to fail them arbitrarily and prevent them to be graduated? As we have mentioned, even though the administration has the authority to use "public force," a mechanism is needed to prevent the administration from using this authority in an unproportionate and arbitrary manner.

We may begin to answer this question with reference to the article 2 of the Constitution, involving the principle of rule of law:[16]

> The Republic of Turkey is a democratic, secular and social state governed by rule of law, within the notions of public peace, national solidarity and justice, respecting human rights, loyal to the nationalism of Atatürk, and based on the fundamental tenets set forth in the preamble.

Considering that the state is compromised of the legislature, executive and judiciary, the principle of rule of law involves legislature governed by rule of law, executive governed by rule of law and judiciary governed by rule of law. Since the administration is located within executive, the principle of rule of law also includes administration governed by rule of law. Below there is a chart describing the formula of the principle:

<u>Formula:</u> A STATE GOVERNED BY RULE OF LAW → (STATE=legislature, executive, judiciary)

Meaning: 1- Legislature governed by rule of law
2- Executive governed by rule of law
3- Judiciary governed by rule of law

Since the administration is within executive: "ADMINISTRATION GOVERNED BY RULE OF LAW"

Figure 1: State Governed by Rule of Law

At this point, a further question comes into mind: Will legislature, executive and judiciary act consistent with the law just because it is laid down so? What happens if they do not? What is the sanction of such inconsistency? For instance,

16 "the rule of law principle, which is laid down in article 2 of the Constitution and which is a fundamental feature of the Republic of Turkey is one of the most important elements which provide citizens with legal security, which aims administration to abide by law and which prevents public force to be used in a limitless, unproportionate and arbitrary manner." SC 2nd C., M. 2015/7531, D. 2016/1765, 14.04.2016, www.kazanci.com.

when a political party alleges that it can do whatever it wants since it was elected and when it has a sufficient number of deputies in the assembly, can this political party be able to enforce any law it wants? Can these deputies lay down a law freeing torture? These examples show the difference between a "state governed by rule of law" (hereinafter, "state governed by rule of law" will be referred as "constitutional state" to avoid confusion) and a "state of law."

A constitutional state and a state of law differ from each other to a significant extent.[17] A constitutional state is a state which acknowledges rule of law (such as general principles of law) above laws, and which respects human rights. However, within the scope of "state of law," laws may as well be unjust and repressive.[18] The contrary of constitutional state is "police state."[19] Police state is a state which does not consider itself to be obliged to be consistent with law and in which individual rights and freedoms do not exist.[20] Police state and gendarmerie state should not be confused too. Briefly, gendarmerie state is a state in which rights and freedoms are granted; however, the state does not possess social obligations, and only guards the current public order.[21]

Since the Constitution envisages constitutional state, then who will protect us from legislature, executive and arbitrary actions of administration within executive? Judiciary needs to become involved at this point. The State Council, which is the highest court of the administrative judiciary branch, has highlighted that the only guarantee against administration is an efficient judiciary review: "… The only guarantee persons have, against the supremacy and privilege of the administration to act along with public force and power in the relationship it has with other persons, is the existence of an efficient judiciary review."[22]

As seen, judiciary will audit legislature, executive and administration and when they act inconsistent with law, judiciary will sanction them. Then, how is this accomplished? First, in order for judiciary to properly carry out the auditing or reviewing task, legislature and executive should not give orders and directives to it. To put it more simply, it is essential for the judiciary not to be under the

---

17 Bülent Tanör and Necmi Yüzbaşıoğlu, *1982 Anayasasına Göre Türk Anayasa Hukuku* [*Turkish Constitutional Law According to 1982 Constitution*] (İstanbul: Beta, 2020), 116.

18 Tanör and Yüzbaşıoğlu, *1982 Anayasası*, 116.

19 Gözler, *İdare Hukuku V. I*, 135.

20 Yayla, *İdare Hukuku*, 14, footnote 37; Akyılmaz, Sezginer, and Kaya, *Türk İdare Hukuku*, 88.

21 Yayla, *İdare Hukuku*, 14.

22 SC 5th C., M. 2005/5354, D. 2006/3391, 13.06.2006, www.hukukturk.com; SC 5th C., M. 2012/4927, D. 2014/6653, 10.10.2014, www.kazanci.com.

influence of the other two organs. Briefly, judiciary needs to be independent. Independency will result in judiciary to be impartial as well, since being impartial can only be possible by being independent.

On the other hand, judiciary too should not be arbitrary. Otherwise, a regime called "government of judges" may arise. Such a regime and its harms have been witnessed in history.[23]

In that case,

1. Independent judiciary is a necessity to scrutinize political power and legislature.
2. It is obligatory to prevent the political power from prescribing any law it desires and pushing judiciary out by using its majority in the assembly.
3. It is also necessary to prevent judiciary to make decisions arbitrarily.

For these mentioned reasons, it is needed to make rules that will be binding on all organs of the state. The Constitution and constitutional review which are needed to annul a law that is inconsistent with the constitution step in at this point.

Within this scope, first of all, the Constitution should compromise rules regarding legislature, executive and administration to be subject to judicial review. The below-mentioned provisions of the Constitution serve to that purpose:

> "**ARTICLE 11**- The provisions of the Constitution are fundamental legal rules binding upon legislative, executive and judicial organs, and administrative authorities and other institutions and individuals. Laws shall not be contrary to the Constitution."
> "**ARTICLE 8**- Executive power and function shall be exercised and carried out by the President … in conformity with the Constitution and laws."
> "**ARTICLE 129**- Public servants and other public officials are obliged to carry out their duties with loyalty to the Constitution and the laws."
> "**ARTICLE 9**- Judicial power shall be exercised by independent and impartial courts on behalf of the Turkish Nation."
> "**ARTICLE 138**- Judges shall be independent in the discharge of their duties; they shall give judgment in accordance with the Constitution, laws, and their personal conviction conforming to the law."

Part two of the Constitution regarding fundamental rights and duties are also important on this regard in conjunction with article 13:

---

23 Ender Ethem Atay, "Kuvvetler Ayrılığı İlkesi Uyarınca Yürütme Yargı Ayrılığı ve İdari Yargı Denetiminin Niteliği [Separation of Executive and Judiciary and The Characteristics of Administrative Judicial Review Within the Scope of the Principle of Separation of Powers]," in *Danıştay ve İdari Yargı Günü 140. Yıl Sempozyumu* (Danıştay Tasnif ve Yayın Bürosu Yayınları no. 77, Danıştay Matbaası, 2009), 136.

> Fundamental rights and freedoms may be restricted only by law and in conformity with the reasons mentioned in the relevant articles of the Constitution without infringing upon their essence. These restrictions shall not be contrary to the letter and spirit of the Constitution and the requirements of the democratic order of the society and the secular republic and the principle of proportionality.

Accordingly, State Council has ruled that "... The most important feature of a state governed by rule of law is to protect persons' rights and freedoms against public force."[24]

Surely, article 90/end of the Constitution is important to mention:

> International agreements duly put into effect have the force of law. No appeal to the Constitutional Court shall be made with regard to these agreements, on the grounds that they are unconstitutional. In the case of a conflict between international agreements, duly put into effect, concerning fundamental rights and freedoms and the laws due to differences in provisions on the same matter, the provisions of international agreements shall prevail.

The sanctions prescribed in the Constitution also serve to the purpose of the organs to be governed by rule of law. Article 148/1[25] for the legislature and 125/1, 138/end,[26] 137[27] for the executive and administration may be considered within this scope.

---

24 SC 8th C., M. 1998/397, D. 1998/2243, 15.06.1998, www.lexpera.com.

25 "The Constitutional Court shall examine the constitutionality, in respect of both form and substance, of laws, presidential decrees and the Rules of Procedure of the Grand National Assembly of Turkey, and decide on individual applications. Constitutional amendments shall be examined and verified only with regard to their form. However, presidential decrees issued during a state of emergency or in time of war shall not be brought before the Constitutional Court alleging their unconstitutionality as to form and substance."

26 "The organs of legislature and executive and the administration shall comply with court decisions; these organs and the administration shall neither alter them in any respect, nor delay their execution."

27 "If a person employed in any position or status in public services finds an order given by her superior to be contrary to the provisions of by-laws, presidential decree, laws, or the Constitution, she shall not carry out, and shall inform the person giving the order of this inconsistency. However, if her superior insists on the order and renews it in writing, her order shall be executed; in this case the person executing the order shall not be held responsible.
An order which in itself constitutes a criminal offence shall under no circumstances be executed; the person who executes such an order shall not evade responsibility. ..."

Article 125/1 of the Constitution is especially essential for the administration. Pursuant to this article, "Recourse to judicial review shall be available against all actions and acts of administration…"

It is a matter of wonder if recourse to judicial review is truly available against all actions and acts. Article 159 of the Constitution states that the decisions of the Council of Judges and Prosecutors, other than dismissal from the profession, shall not be subject to judicial review. Likewise, article 125/2 of the Constitution states that the acts of promotion and retiring due to lack of tenure of Supreme Military Council shall not be subject to judicial review. In addition, while article 129/3 states that disciplinary decisions shall not be exempt from judicial review, "provisions concerning the members of the armed forces, judges and prosecutors are reserved" in the article 129/4. As seen, recourse to judicial review is not open to all acts. This situation effects the independence of administrative judiciary. Likewise, it may be alleged that article 146, regarding the elections of the members of the Constitutional Court,[28] is a provision which effects the independence of constitutional review.

1.1. Principle of Legal Administration

Article 123/1 of the Constitution states that "administration is a whole with its formation and functions, shall be regulated by law." Within this scope, both the establishment, functions and powers of administration have to be regulated by law. That is to say, the rule includes administration both organically and functionally.[29] The reason behind this rule is that administration is in a superior position compared to other persons and it has the ability to act contrary to other persons' wills. As mentioned above, a mechanism is needed to prevent the arbitrariness of administration which can use public force and therefore can interfere with the other persons' fundamental rights and freedoms. This mechanism, along with administrative judiciary, is legislature elected by the people and constitutional judiciary in case that the legislature issues a law that is illegitimate. If administration was authorized to regulate administration without a law, then a danger—in which administration grants itself with powers arbitrarily and authorizes itself contrary to law—would emerge. Within this scope, the principle of legal administration includes two different meanings: Firstly, all acts and actions

28 According to this article, Constitutional Court shall be composed of 15 members. TBMM will elect three and the President will elect 12 of these members.

29 Gözler, *İdare Hukuku V. I*, 156.

of administration shall base on a law. Secondly, these acts and actions shall not be contrary to the law.[30]

However, with the last constitutional amendment, the regulative area of the President has been increased to a great extent, which also has serious changes in Administrative Law.[31] Accordingly, the President is powered to issue presidential decrees (PD) "on the matters regarding executive power" in the article 104/17 of the Constitution.[32] Therefore, it can be concluded that the President is now authorized with primary regulatory power.[33] In other words, the President can

---

30 Gözler, *İdare Hukuku V. I*, 152.

31 Before the constitutional amendment, presidential decree was regulated in only one provision: "The establishment, organization and working principles, acts of assignment of personnel of General Secretariat of the Presidency shall be regulated by presidential decree." This provision was accepted to be an exceptional provision.

32 In doctrine, some authors criticized the usage of this expression ("on the matter regarding executive power") since it is vague and insufficient to limit the regulative area of PDs. Yavuz Atar, "Cumhurbaşkanlığı Kararnamelerinin Hukuki Rejimi ve Anayasallık Denetimi [Legal Regime and Constitutional Review of Presidential Decrees]," *Anayasa Yargısı* 36, no. 1 (2019): 247; Lokman Yeniay and Gülden Yeniay, "Türk Hukukunda Yürütme Organının Düzenleme Yetkisi ve Cumhurbaşkanlığı Kararnamesi [Regulatory Authority of the Executive Branch and Presidential Decree in Turkish Law]," *Anayasa Yargısı* 36, no. 1 (2019): 129; Akyılmaz, Sezginer, and Kaya, *Türk İdare Hukuku*, 33; Ekrem Ali Akartürk, "2017 Anayasa Değişikliğinin 'Parlamentosuzlaştırma' Etkisi Üzerine [About 'Deparliamentarization' Effect of Constitutional Amendment of 2017]," *Yeditepe University Law Faculty Journal* 17, no. 1 (2020): 11, https://www.jurix.com.tr/article/20389; Abdullah Sezer, "Normlar Hiyerarşisi ve Cumhurbaşkanlığı Kararnameleri (Çok Boyutlu Normlar Piramidi Yaklaşımı) [Hierarchy of Norms and Presidential Decrees (Multidimensional Pyramid of Norms Approach)]," *Anayasa Yargısı* 36, no. 1 (2019): 372.

33 Yeniay and Yeniay, "Türk Hukukunda," 129; Sezer, "Normlar Hiyerarşisi," 371; Türker Ertaş, "Yürütme Organının Asli Düzenleyici İşlem Yapma Yetkisi Bağlamında Cumhurbaşkanlığı Kararnamelerinin Karşılaştırmalı Anayasal Düzenlerdeki Benzer İşlemlerle Kıyaslanması ve Türk Hükümet Sistemine Etkisi [Comparison of Presidential Decrees with Similar Acts in Comparative Constitutional Orders within the scope of the Power of Executive to Establish Primary Regulatory Act and Its Affect on the Turkish Governmental System]," in *Cumhurbaşkanının İşlemleri Hukuki Niteliği, Normlar Hiyerarşisindeki Yeri ve Denetimi*, ed. Oktay Uygun and Egemen Esen (İstanbul: On İki Levha, 2019), 10; Taylan Barın, "Cumhurbaşkanı Kararnamelerinin Normlar Hiyerarşisindeki Yeri Sorunu [The Issue of the Place of Presidential Decrees in the Hierarchy of Norms]," in *Cumhurbaşkanının İşlemleri Hukuki Niteliği, Normlar Hiyerarşisindeki Yeri ve Denetimi*, ed. Oktay Uygun and Egemen Esen (İstanbul: On İki Levha, 2019), 154; Artuk Ardıçoğlu, "Cumhurbaşkanlığı Kararnamesi [Presidential

regulate the matters regarding executive power without basing on a law. Within the scope of this primary regulatory power, the President may as well regulate administration in condition that it abides with the constitutional limits. In this way, it can be stated that PDs constitute an exception to the principle of legal administration.[34]

In the Constitution, while article 104/17 handles the general legal regime of the PDs, there are also some provisions that directly power the President to regulate some specific issues. Article 104/17 of the Constitution, which set limits to the regulative area of PDs, is as follows:

> The president of the Republic may issue presidential decrees on the matters regarding executive power. The fundamental rights, individual rights and duties included in the first and second chapters and the political rights and duties listed in the fourth chapter of the second part of the Constitution shall not be regulated by a presidential decree. No presidential decree shall be issued on the matters which are stipulated in the Constitution to be regulated exclusively by law. No presidential decree shall be issued on the matters explicitly regulated by law. In the case of a discrepancy between presidential decrees and the laws, the provisions of the laws shall prevail. A presidential decree shall become null and void if the Grand National Assembly of Turkey enacts a law on the same matter.

For the purposes of this study, we may detail the third sentence of the article, in which an "exclusive law area" is prescribed. Basing on this sentence, according to the Constitutional Court, in case that the constitution maker specifically indicates that an area shall be prescribed by law, this area shall be reserved to laws. In

---

Decree]," *Ankara Bar Journal*, no. 3 (2017): 25; Ali Ulusoy, "Cumhurbaşkanlığı Kararnameleri: Varoluşsal, Yapısal ve Hukuksal Bir Değerlendirme [Presidential Decrees: An Existential, Structural and Legal Consideration]," *Anayasa Yargısı* 37, no. 2 (2020): 43; Hasan Tahsin Fendoğlu, "Cumhurbaşkanlığı Kararnameleri Mahfuz Düzenleme Alanı Mıdır? [Are Presidential Decrees Exclusive Regulatory Area?]," *Ankara Bar Journal*, no. 3 (2019): 277; Esin Gürsel, "Cumhurbaşkanlığı Hükümet Sisteminde Yürütmenin Düzenleme Yetkisi ve Cumhurbaşkanlığı Kararnamelerinin Anayasal Sınırı [Power to Regulate of Executive Organ in Turkey and the Constitutional Limits of Presidential Decrees]," *Ankara Social Sciences University Journal*, no. 2 (2019): 402; Korkut Kanadoğlu, "Cumhurbaşkanlığı Kararnamesi [Presidential Decree]," *Galatasaray University Law Faculty Journal*, no. 2 (2018): 644; Gözler, *İdare Hukuku V. I*, 155. Constitutional Court also makes the same conclusion. For instance, see CC, M. 2019/71, D. 2020/82, 30.12.2020, OG 24.02.2021–31405, §4; CC, M. 2018/119, D. 2020/25, 11.06.2020, OG 09.11.2020–31299, §4; CC, M. 2018/124, D. 2020/56, 15.10.2020, OG 04.12.2020–31324, §4; CC, M. 2019/105, D. 2020/30, 12.06.2020, OG 20.08.2020–31219, §4; CC, M. 2018/126, D. 2020/32, 25.06.2020, OG 29.07.2020–31200, §4.

34 Gözler, *İdare Hukuku V. I*, 155.

other words, if the Constitution states that an area will be regulated by law, this area shall not be regulated by PDs.[35] To that end, there are many provisions in the Constitution that creates an "exclusive law area." For instance, according to the article 13 of the Constitution, fundamental rights and principles may be restricted only by a law. Or, article 127/1 states that principles of establishment and decision-making organs of local administrations are determined by law.

At this point, article 123/1 should be evaluated together with the third sentence of the article 104/17. As we already mentioned, article 123/1 stipulates that administration shall be regulated by laws. Therefore, the general rule on legality of administration continues its existence. Constitutional Court, too, has evaluated that article 123/1 is an "exclusive law area."[36] However, Constitutional Court ruled that limited to the issues that are specifically prescribed to be regulated by PDs in the Constitution, the President can issue PDs in the area of "administration" (which is an exclusive law area due to 123/1).[37] Therefore, in the presence of the principle of legality of administration, when the PD at hand concerns the establishment or functioning of administration, the High Court evaluates whether the PD before the Court is within the provisions that specifically authorizes the President to regulate.

For instance, in one of its decisions, a provision of the PD numbered 77 dated June 29, 2021, which authorized Economy Coordination Board with asking for any information and documents from the related public institutions, was evaluated by Constitutional Court.[38] In its decision, Constitutional Court mentioned article 123/1 of the Constitution and ruled that administration and duties and authorities of its organs should be regulated by law.[39] Afterward, the

---

35 For instance, see CC, M. 2020/94, D. 2022/61, 01.06.2022, OG 18.08.2002–31927, §17; CC, M. 2021/85, D. 2022/60, 01.06.2022, OG 18.08.2022–31927, §17; CC, M. 2021/88, D. 2021/105, 30.12.2021, OG 25.02.2022–31761, §11; CC, M. 2018/133, D. 2021/70, 13.10.2012, OG 27.12.2022–32056, §11; CC, M. 2020/58, D. 2021/19, 18.03.2021, OG 22.06.2021–31519, §11; CC, M. 2018/127, D. 2021/18, 18.03.2021, OG 17.06.2021–31514, §11; CC, M. 2020/71, D. 2021/33, 29.04.2021, OG 16.06.2021–31513, §11–19.

36 For instance, see CC, M. 2020/94, D. 2022/61, 01.06.2022, OG 18.08.2002–31927, §18; CC, M. 2021/85, D. 2022/60, 01.06.2022, OG 18.08.2022–31927, §22; CC, M. 2021/88, D. 2021/105, 30.12.2021, OG 25.02.2022–31761, §18.

37 For instance, see CC, M. 2018/133, D. 2021/70, 13.10.2012, OG 10.12.2021–31685, §21; CC, M. 2018/134, D. 2021/13, 03.03.2021, OG 16.06.2021–31513, §27; CC, M. 2020/8, D. 2021/25, 31.03.2021, OG 15.06.2021–31512, §22; CC, M. 2021/90, D. 2022/108, 28.09.2022, OG 03.01.2023–32062, §29.

38 CC, M. 2021/88, D. 2021/105, 30.12.2021, OG 25.02.2022–31761.

39 ibid. §18.

Constitutional Court noted that article 106/end of the Constitution allows PDs to regulate "the establishment, abolition, the duties and powers, the organizational structure of the ministries, and the establishment of their central and provincial organizations."[40] However, the Court indicated that while the Economy Coordination Board is situated in the central administration, it is not incorporated in the organization of any ministry[41] and therefore the provision of the PD is not within the scope of article 106/end. Due that the provision of the PD is contrary to article 104/17 in conjunction with article 123/1, the High Court annulled the provision.

Besides this general constitutional provision (104/17) regarding PDs, as we have mentioned, there are several more provisions in the Constitution that specifically addresses PDs. These provisions directly power the President to regulate some specific issues. Within this scope, there has been a wide discussion on whether these specific areas, which are indicated to be regulated by PDs in the Constitution, can be regulated by a law. That is to say, it has been discussed whether an "exclusive PD area" is valid.

While Constitutional Court has not answered whether there is an exclusive area reserved to the President, the High Court has evaluated whether the subject of the PD (which bases on the provisions that grant PDs with regulating specific areas) is "on the matters explicitly regulated by law" due to article 104/17.[42] In other words, while High Court evaluates the lawfulness of the PDs in the "alleged exclusive PD area," it searches if the subject of the PD is also regulated by a law.

For instance, in one of its decisions, the Constitutional Court evaluated that the provision of the PD at hand was within article 106/end of the Constitution (which specifically authorizes the President). Notwithstanding this evaluation, the Court also searched whether a law has a provision regarding the subject of the provision of the PD.[43] Therefore, we believe that the High Court rejects the existence of such an exclusive area and rules that the principle of generality of law is not changed.

---

40 ibid.

41 ibid. §20.

42 CC, M. 2018/134, D. 2021/13, 03.03.2021, OG 16.06.2021–31513, §62; CC, M. 2020/8, D. 2021/25, 31.03.2021, OG 15.06.2021–31512, §24; CC, M. 2019/71, D. 2020/82, 31.12.2020, OG 24.02.2021–31405, §32; CC, M. 2021/90, D. 2022/108, 28.09.2022, OG 03.01.2023–32062, §31.

43 CC, M. 2018/133, D. 2021/70, 13.10.2021, OG 27.12.2022–32056, §25.

In the Constitution, there are five areas which are stated to be specifically regulated by PDs. Firstly, in the subparagraph 9 of Article 104 stipulating duties and powers of the President, it is stated: "He/she shall appoint and dismiss the high ranking executives, and shall regulate the procedure and principles governing the appointment thereof by presidential decree." We believe that this provision should be interpreted in a narrow manner, since in the article 128/2 of the Constitution it is stipulated that "the qualifications, appointments, duties and powers, rights and responsibilities, salaries and allowances of public servants and other public officials, and other matters related to their status shall be regulated by law."

Secondly, according to the article 106/end of the Constitution "The establishment, abolition, the duties and powers, the organizational structure of the ministries, and the establishment of their central and provincial organizations shall be regulated by the presidential decree." Constitutional Court has interpreted this provision in a broad manner. The High Court states that since the President has the power of establishment, abolishment, duties and powers, the organizational structure and the establishment of central and provincial organization of ministries, it should be *a fortiori* accepted that the President may also regulate the institutions affiliated to the Presidency.[44] Therefore, the Court evaluated that institutions which do not possess a legal personality and which are affiliated to the Presidency are within the article 106/end of the Constitution and shall be regulated by a PD. Furthermore, even though "abroad organizations" of ministries are not counted in the article 106/end (only central and provincial organizations are counted), the Constitutional Court evaluated that "abroad organizations" are also within the "organizational structure," and therefore they can be regulated by PDs.[45]

Thirdly, according to the article 108/end, "The functioning of the State Supervisory Council, the term of office of its members, and other personnel matters relating to their status shall be regulated by presidential decree."

Fourthly, in the article 118/end, it is stated: "The organization and duties of the General Secretariat of the National Security Council shall be regulated by presidential decree."

---

44 CC, M. 2018/133, D. 2021/70, 13.10.2021, OG 27.12.2022–32056, §22; CC. M. 2018/127, D. 2021/18, 18.03.2021, OG 17.06.2021–31514, §41; CC, M. 2018/134, D. 2021/13, 03.03.2021, OG 16.06.2021–31513, §30; CC, M. 2019/71, D. 2020/82, 31.12.2020, OG 24.02.2021–31405, §27.

45 CC, M. 2018/133, D. 2021/70, 13.10.2021, OG 27.12.2022–32056, §24; CC, M. 2018/134, D. 2021/13, 03.03.2021, OG 16.06.2021–31513, §61.

And lastly, according to the article 123/3, "Public corporate bodies shall be established only by law, or by presidential decree." As seen, unlike the other four areas, the Constitution here both mentioned a law or a PD. Since we will handle this article regarding establishment of public corporate bodies under the subject of "Public Corporate Bodies," we will not detail this provision here. However, we may state that Constitutional Court has ruled that the power to establish a public corporate body also incorporates the power to regulate this public corporate body.[46]

As seen from these provisions, the areas which are specifically prescribed to be regulated by PDs mostly concerns "administration." Therefore, we may state that while legality of administration is still the rule (article 123/1), it may be stated that this rule has been subjected to serious exceptions.[47]

1.2. Public Corporate Bodies

In terms of law, when we say "person," "natural persons" and "legal persons" come into mind. Natural persons are humans who can possess rights and obligations. Legal persons are communities of persons and goods which the legal system gives authority to possess rights and obligations. The legal system accepts these communities of persons and goods as a separate entity from the persons and goods which create them. This legal entity has a will on its own and its authorized body can possess rights and get into obligations by using this will.

A particular segment of these legal persons is subject to private law. These persons may possess rights and obligations like natural persons in an equal manner, get into contracts and so forth. However, legal system entitles some legal persons a different qualification compared to natural persons and other legal persons. It entitles some legal persons with supremacy over other legal persons and natural persons. In the base of this supremacy, there is the function and power to be involved in activities for the public interest. In other words, these legal persons have the supremacy to act contrary to other person's will and to impose its own will by using force to involve in activities for the public interest. In brief, these persons have the power to use "public force." These legal persons, who have the

---

46 CC, M. 2021/95, D. 2022/118, 13.10.2022, OG 27.01.2023–32086, §29.

47 Melikşah Yasin, "Cumhurbaşkanlığı Kararnamelerinin Türk İdari Teşkilat Hukukuna Etkileri [Effects of Presidential Decrees on Turkish Administrative Organization Law]," *Anayasa Yargısı* 37, no. 2 (2020): 316; Halit Yılmaz, "Cumhurbaşkanlığı Kararnamelerinin Konu Bakımından Yetki Sınırları [Constitutional Limitations on the Subject of Presidential Decrees]," *İstanbul Law Review* 78, no. 1 (2020): 233.

mentioned superior rights and authorities, and at the same time more obligations compared to others are public corporate bodies.[48]

However, public corporate bodies are not obliged to use this "public force" all the time. Sometimes, they can act like private law legal persons. These persons can both benefit from the rights enjoyed by private law legal persons and use "public force." That is, a public corporate body may perform transactions in an equal manner with private law legal persons by acting like these as well as enjoying superior rights and powers compared to private law legal persons by using "public force."[49]

The subject of public corporate bodies is important in respect to Administrative Law since administration is a community of public corporate bodies. Below, we will detail the establishment and specification criteria of public corporate bodies.

1.2.1. Establishment of Public Corporate Bodies

Pursuant to the Constitution (article 123/3): "Public corporate bodies shall be established only by law, or by presidential decree." As seen, public corporate bodies are required to be established by law laid down by legislature. Or, these bodies may be established by PD laid down by executive—by the president.

At this point, it is possible to receive some remarks:

1. Since the Constitution itself is a law, a public corporate body may be established by the Constitution. In Turkey, some public corporate bodies are established by the Constitution: professional organizations having the characteristics of public institutions (article 135), local administrations (article 127), universities (article 130), The Atatürk High Institution of Culture, Language and History (article 134) and so forth…
2. A public corporate body may be established by a law.
3. A public corporate body may be established by a PD.
4. In case that law or PD authorizes an administration to decide on the establishment of public corporate bodies, then this administration too may establish public corporate body. In other words, provided that the framework is determined by a law or a PD, it may be concluded that public corporate

48 İl Han Özay, ed., *Günışığında Yönetim* [*Administration in the Sunshine*] (İstanbul: Filiz, 2017), 121.

49 Özay, *Günışığında*, 123.

bodies may be established via presidential decisions, presidential bylaws or bylaws of other administrations.[50]

However, the provisions of the Constitution related to PDs should also be considered within this regard. Firstly, it is a matter of wonder whether PDs can only establish a public corporate body or also regulate the organizational structure, duties and powers and such matters of this body. Constitutional Court has interpreted "the establishment of public corporate bodies" in a broad manner.

---

50 Before the amendment, article 123/3 of the Constitution laid down that public corporate bodies may be established "depending on the authorization as stated in the law." Pursuant to this, the establishment was seen to be possible by the administration if a law or a PD authorized administration on this regard by determining a framework. As a matter of fact, within the scope of Decree no. 233, state economic enterprises may have been established by the decision of minister of councils, in other words, with an administrative act. With the last constitutional amendment, the expression of "depending on the authorization as stated in the law" is excluded from the provision. In this case, it can be concluded that public corporate bodies are required to be established solely by law or PD. In other words, it can be interpreted that law or PD cannot authorize administration to establish public corporate bodies by determining the framework. The word "only" in the new clause of Constitution (123/3) seems to support this interpretation. On this regard, in doctrine some authors state that as a consequence of the constitutional amendment, establishment of a public corporate body via an administrative act is not possible. See Akyılmaz, Sezginer, and Kaya, *Türk İdare Hukuku*, 217; Gözler, *İdare Hukuku V. I*, 205–206. However, it is possible to approach to the subject from a different perspective when considering the purpose of the provision. Namely, the purpose of the establishment of public corporate bodies by law or PD is to provide judicial security on the establishment process of a legal person which can interfere with the area of fundamental rights and freedoms by using public force. The judicial review should be available on the establishment process. When a public corporate body is established by a law or a PD, the Constitutional Court may examine the constitutionality of the act in question. From this point of view, if adequate judicial security is provided, it can be argued that public corporate bodies may be established by administrative acts provided that the framework is determined. In this last case, a law or a PD will be in question which enables the establishment by an administrative act, and which determines the framework in this regard. At the same time, an administrative act which establishes a public corporate body will be in question. It is possible for the Constitutional Court to examine the PD or law as well as administrative judiciary to review the administrative act. From this point of view, it can be argued that depending on the authorization, a public corporate body may be established with an administrative act as stated in law by concluding that adequate judicial security is available in our legal system.

According to the High Court, the word "established" in the article 123/1 includes the regulation of public corporate bodies. The Court indicates that a contrary approach would render the provision which authorizes president to establish PDs meaningless.[51]

Secondly, as we have already mentioned, according to article 104/17, "No presidential decree shall be issued on the matters which are stipulated in the Constitution to be regulated exclusively by law. No presidential decree shall be issued on the matters explicitly regulated by law. In the case of a discrepancy between provisions of the presidential decrees and the laws, the provisions of the laws shall prevail. A presidential decree shall become null and void if the Grand National Assembly of Turkey enacts a law on the same matter."

In this case, a PD cannot provide an institution to be a public corporate body if the law explicitly lays down that this institution cannot be a public corporate body. Likewise, Grand National Assembly of Turkey (GNAT) may abolish a public corporate body with a law which was established by an earlier PD.

1.2.2. Specification Criteria of Public Corporate Bodies

In this section, we will detail how to sort out whether a legal person is a public corporate body. In this regard, several possibilities are available.

At first, the Constitution itself may explicitly rule that a legal person is a public corporate body.[52] In this case, the legal person in question is a public corporate body without doubt. In a variety of provisions of the Constitution (28, 82, 128, 161 and so forth), the expression of "state and the other public corporate bodies" draws attention. From the expression of "and the other," it is understood that the state is also a public corporate body.[53] Therefore, "the state" is a public corporate body specified by the Constitution.[54]

Other than the state, there are entities that have been prescribed as public corporate bodies by the Constitution. Radio and Television Institution (TRT) (article 133), provincial special administrations, municipals, villages (article 127), professional organizations having the characteristics of public institutions (for

51 CC, M. 2021/95, D. 2022/118, 13.10.2022, OG 27.01.2023–32086, §29.

52 Zabunoğlu, *İdare Hukuku*, 134.

53 Gözler, *İdare Hukuku V. I*, 195.

54 It should be paid attention that the state is a single public corporate body. The organs of the state, namely "legislature," "executive" and "judiciary," are not public corporate bodies on their own apart from the state. Some offices within these organs may only represent the state. See. Gözler, *İdare Hukuku V. I*, 196–197.

instance, bars) (article 135) are examples on this regard. When the Constitution clearly acknowledges the public personality of an institution, legislature cannot cease such personality of this institution by a law.[55]

Secondly, if a law or a PD explicitly states that a legal person is a public corporate body, the conclusion will be the same. In this case, that legal person is a public corporate body without doubt.[56] For instance, article 4 of Law no. 4628 is as follows: "An independent, administratively and financially autonomous public corporate body, namely the Energy Market Regulatory Authority, is hereby established to perform the duties assigned to it by this law." As seen, the law explicitly used the terms of "public corporate body." The law incorporates the term "public" before the term "corporate body." Therefore, Energy Market Regulatory Authority is a public corporate body without doubt.

Sometimes, the law or the PD does not involve the term "public" while stating that an institution is a legal person. To put it more simply, sometimes, a legal person may be established by the law, but the law may not state whether that legal person is a public corporate body. Likewise, sometimes a private law legal person is established by law; however, that legal person acts like a public corporate body. In other words, there is a possibility of that legal person to be a "veiled" public corporate body.

The first article of Law on The Establishment and Duties of Turkish Football Federation involves the two mentioned situations. Namely, the law lays down an expression as follows: "Turkish Football Federation which is subject to private law provisions and have a legal personality." As seen, the provision mentions Turkish Football Federation (TFF) as a legal person without mentioning its public characteristic as well as laying down that it is subject to the provisions of private law. In this case, it is not possible to conclude that TFF is most certainly a private law legal person. Likewise, it is not possible to allege that TFF is a public corporate body in a certain manner.[57] After an examination within the scope of the criteria mentioned below, we may reach to a conclusion.

---

55 Gözler, *İdare Hukuku V. I*, 201.

56 Turan Yıldırım "Genel Kuramlar ve Anayasal İlkeler [General Theories and Constitutional Principles]," in *İdare Hukuku*, ed. Turan Yıldırım (İstanbul: On İki Levha, 2022), 14.

57 Likewise, pursuant to article 1 of the Law on the Central Bank of the Republic of Turkey; "A bank, under the title of the 'Central Bank of Republic of Turkey,' is hereby established as a joint stock company having the exclusive privilege of issuing banknotes in Turkey and the powers and duties set forth in this Law. / The Bank shall be subject to the provisions of private law in cases where the Law is not explicit."

At this point we believe that two situations should be separated: a law or a PD stating that an institution is a private law legal person and a law or a PD stating that an institution is subject to the provisions of private law. If the law or the PD explicitly states that (X) is a private law legal person, then this institution should be accepted as such. However, if the law or the PD states that (Y) "is subject to the provisions of private law" or "acts pursuant to the provisions of private law," in this case, it cannot be concluded that (Y) is a private law legal person.[58] There are public corporate bodies which act pursuant to private law provisions. For instance, state economic enterprises act pursuant to private law provisions while these are established by administration with the authorization granted by the law.

Then, how can we understand if an institution is a public corporate body? Two cumulative conditions are necessary to conclude that an institution is a public corporate body:[59]

Central Bank of Republic of Turkey is established as a private law legal person (joint stock company) and subject to the provisions of private law. However, according to the State Council the Bank is a public corporate authority since it enjoys public force. See SCPSCAC, M. 2005/1846, D. 2006/746, 15.06.2006, www.kazanci.com. The related part of the decision is as follows: "... As will be understood from the stated legislation; Central Bank of the Republic of Turkey, whose primary object is to maintain price stability, which is the only authorized and liable institution regarding the determination and implementation of monetary policy, which has the exclusive privilege of issuing banknotes, is established as a joint stock company and is subject to the provisions of private law where the Law is not explicit; and considering that, in the sense of its establishment purpose, duties and powers, it is equipped with public duties and powers, it carries out public service, most of its shares belong to the Treasury, it is involved in the national budget, it entered into force with the Association of the Bank's Council of Ministries Decision, its governor is appointed with Council of Ministries Decision, vice governors are appointed with a joint decree, provisions of Law no 5434 on the Retirement Fund of the Republic of Turkey is implemented to the bank staffs except banknote printing works and the bank staff is public personnel, it is no doubt that the bank is a public institution and its personnel is public personnel and Fifth Circuit of State Council highlighted this situation in its decision. (...) It may be concluded that the Bank is an autonomous, sui generis public institution which is independent from the central administration."

58 Gözler, *İdare Hukuku V. I*, 213.

59 Gözler, *İdare Hukuku V. I*, 204; Zabunoğlu, *İdare Hukuku*, 136 ff.

- If this legal person is established by a law or a PD, then this person may be a public corporate body.
- If this legal person uses sovereignty (public force) and therefore has supremacy over other persons, it may be a public corporate body.[60]

Naturally, stating that a legal person may use sovereignty or this person have supremacy would not be sufficient by itself. This person should be able to reflect this supremacy in its acts and actions and should possess superior rights and powers compared to other persons. State Council highlights this basic difference between public corporate bodies and private law legal persons as follows: "Supremacy and privilege of the administration to act with the public force and power that it possesses in the relationships with persons."[61]

As seen, if a legal person is granted authorization to use supremacies and privileges, that person may be a public corporate body.[62] Within this scope, the regulation related to the legal person should be examined on whether this regulation granted it to use public force privileges and supremacies.

It should be highlighted that the first condition mentioned is not sufficient in itself. A private legal person may be established as well by a law or a PD. 13th Circuit of State Council ruled that Turkish Armed Forces Foundation is not a public corporate body despite the fact that it was established by a law. The related part of the decision is as follows: "(…) Despite the fact that the mentioned foundation is established by law, it is understood that the foundation is explicitly a private law legal person which carries out its activities according to the provisions of Turkish Civil Code, the foundation does not present a structure that is similar to public corporate bodies, nevertheless, the privileges granted to the foundation is not different than the other foundations which benefit from tax exemptions, the foundation does not use public funding and is not subject to a separate public scrutiny compared to other foundations operating according to Turkish Civil Act."[63]

60 Hasan Nuri Yaşar, *İdare Hukuku: Genel Esaslar* [*Administrative Law: General Principles*] (İstanbul: Der, 2016), 103.

61 SC 5th C., M. 2006/8525, D. 2007/2123, 04.05.2007, www.kazanci.com; SC 5th C., M. 2006/2586, D. 2006/5740, 28.11.2006, www.kazanci.com; SC 5th C., M. 2005/4897, D. 2006/666, 21.02.2006, www.kazanci.com.

62 Ramazan Çağlayan, *İdare Hukuku Dersleri* [*Administrative Law Lectures*] (Ankara: Adalet, 2022), 35.

63 SC 13th C., M. 2013/811, D. 2013/2659, 25.10.2013, www.kazanci.com.

On the other hand, if only the second condition is fulfilled, a legal person may be accepted as a public corporate body.[64] Below, we will detail the supremacies and privileges of the public force one by one.

64 In one of its decisions, The Court of Jurisdictional Disputes (CJD) (Court of Conflicts) ruled that the existence of the second condition is itself sufficient to accept a legal person as a public corporate body. According to the decision, Foundation for Strengthening the Organization of Justice (FSOJ) which is established pursuant to the provisions of Turkish Civil Code (which is not established by a law or an administrative act based on a law [as mentioned above, before the constitutional amendment of 2017, the Constitution laid down that a public corporate body shall be established by a law or an administrative act based on a law]) was ruled to be a public corporate body since it enjoys public force. The decision is open to criticism. The related part of the decision is as follows: "Accordingly, the action, carried out by the competent organ on its own motion and unilaterally, and as a conclusion of an examination pursuant to the objective rules prescribed priorly in Foundation Housing By-law related to the area of Administrative Law, has the characteristics of an administrative act with respect to all of its elements.
The fact that FSOJ is a private law legal person established pursuant to the provisions of Civil Code does not remove the administrative characteristic of the action which is carried out by Foundation Board of Management compromising of ranking public employees in the central administration pursuant to administrative procedure and principle.
Considering all of the issues mentioned above, administrative judiciary has jurisdiction on the resolution of the suit brought with the claim to annul the action regarding Foundation Board of Management's dismissal of the applicant's request regarding changing assignment model of the lodging building which the applicant accommodates, taken into consideration that Foundation for Strengthening the Organization of Justice's qualification spills over to public area from the perspective of its structure and functions since the founders and organs of the Organization all compromise of public employees notwithstanding that the Organization is a private law legal person, and it is established to provide the public service which is within the budget of general budget administration; also taken into consideration that the acts, instituted by competent commissions indicated in the Foundation Housing By-law on the assignment of lodging building before the contractual relationship with the beneficiaries of the foundation or as in the concrete case irrespective of the contract entered into, has administrative character which is carried out with justice service or which is adjacent to it." CJD Law Branch, M. 1999/1, D. 1999/11, 03.05.1999, www.kazanci.com.

1.2.2.1. Ability to Conduct Unilateral Actions[65]

In private law, principally mutual and consentaneous declarations of intention are required to make a legal transaction. For instance, in a contract of sale, the intentions of the buyer and the seller are obliged to be harmonious. The intentions are equal in the area of private law. On the other hand, public corporate bodies have the authority to act contrary to the wills of other legal or real persons. That is, the will of the opposing party is not decisive on the establishment of an administrative act.[66] What really matters is the will of the administration. This supremacy is a privilege of public force. For instance, administration may transfer public employees from one province to another. The will of the public employee is not decisive on this transfer. Public employee must accept the decision on transfer even though her will is not directed at moving to that province. Otherwise, she will bear the consequences.

Occasionally, an application is needed for the administration to establish an act. For instance, when a person desires to become a public servant, she applies to the administration. Principally, administration cannot assign a person to be public servant on its own, unless she applies for it. In this case, the image may seem as if a consentaneous intention is in question, rather than a unilateral one. However, this image is only on the surface. Even though the intention of the applicant is an intention which sets administration into motion or gives idea to administration on execution of an act, it is not the "main intention" regarding the administrative act.[67] When considering the prior example, administration is the only determiner on the assignment of the person who applies to be public servant. As seen, intention of administration is decisive.[68]

---

65 K. Begüm İşbir, *Kamu Tüzel Kişiliği* [*Public Corporate Body*] (Ankara: Turhan, 2017), 274–282.

66 Halil Kalabalık, *İdare Hukuku Dersleri* [*Lectures of Administrative Law*], Vol. 2 (Konya: Sayram, 2016), 42.

67 Bahtiyar Akyılmaz, *İdari Usul İlkeleri Işığında İdari İşlemin Yapılış Usulü* [*Establishing Procedure of Administrative Act Within the Scope of Administrative Procedure Principles*] (Ankara: Yetkin, 2000), 44.

68 The related part of one of the decision of the State Council is as follows: "It is clear that the provisions of the agreement is not designated within the limits of freedom of contract based on the parties' intentions, in other words, intention of the administration is decisive on the designation of the agreement's provisions, considering that the service agreement which is signed with contract teachers who are considered as public employees do not differ for each teacher, on the contrary these agreements are prescribed with all contract teachers in a general, objective and impersonal manner, the teachers that will be employed do not have an option other than to accept or refuse

Being unilateral does not only refer to the situations where the administrative act is a consequence of a single intention. In other words, the act of the administration may be a consequence of a variety of intentions (for instance, the decisions of municipal boards). However, these clusters of intentions constitute the act of administration and there are concerned persons in the opposing party. Even if there is more than one intention to establish the act, indeed the act in question is only the act of administration.[69] What is important is the direction of intentions. In light of the explanations, we may conclude that for the acts to bear legal consequences, the acceptance of the opposing party is not necessary in unilateral acts.[70]

1.2.2.2. Executability[71]

Executability refers to the power of administrative acts to be effectual when it is conducted.[72] In the doctrine, Özay defines it as "accepting that the aimed consequence of the administration is realized."[73] On the other hand, to accept that the act is executable, the act in question is not needed to be executed. Administration may drop to execute its act, or it may as well withdraw the act before executing it and so forth. Therefore, in the doctrine it is put forward that the change generated by the administrative act is "instant" and "general" in its legal existence, whereas in the real world the change is "delayed" and "exceptional."[74]

According to the State Council, the acts of the public force which generates legal consequences directly on the other party have executable characteristics.[75]

---

to sign the agreement." SC 12th C., M. 2006/3643, D. 2009/4943, 29.09.2009, www.kazanci.com.

69 Gözler, *İdare Hukuku V. I*, 768.

70 Gözler, *İdare Hukuku V. I*, 768.

71 Within the scope of the feature of executability, to explain the difference from the transactions in private law, such an example may be given: When a real person decides that another real person owes to him/her, this decision does not prove the existence of such debt and does not consequence in the collection of the debt. An office (like a court) needs to determine the real existence of the debt and if the debt is collectible. On the other hand, the contrary is valid when a public corporate body decides so. The decision of the public corporate body by itself is accepted to be sufficient to execute it.

72 Kalabalık, *İdare Hukuku Dersleri*, 42; Duran refers to the enforceable as "taking effectual decision." See Duran, *İdare Hukuku Ders*, 7.

73 Özay, *Günışığında*, 12; see, in the same direction, Kalabalık, *İdare Hukuku Dersleri*, 42.

74 Duran, *İdare Hukuku Ders*, 413.

75 "... The acts of public force or power, which shows its effects by directly generating various legal consequences on third persons without the need of existence of other

Executable acts arise from "the aim of public interest" which administrative acts should provide and "the public force" which administrative acts are based on.[76] The authority to conduct unilateral and executable acts is the most important privilege granted to the administration in order for it to carry out public services.

We should highlight that all unilateral acts are not entirely executable.[77] For instance, preparation acts, which are carried out before an executable act and which prepares such acts, are not executable. Some scholars mention a category of administrative acts called "administrative decisions" by leaving out the administrative acts which are not executable. Only for this category (for "executable administrative decisions"), executable and unilateral refer to the same situation.[78] We will explain this subject in advance in the section related to "administrative acts."

1.2.2.3. Ex Officio *Execution of Administration*

From the perspective of Administrative Law, "*ex officio* execution" means the ability of the administration to execute its own decision by itself. In private law, *ex officio* execution is not granted to persons: Vigilantism (to grant a right of a person by this person) is forbidden. In private law, persons must apply to courts or enforcement offices to be granted with the right. On the other hand, allegedly, administration has the authority of *ex officio* execution. In other words, the obligation to enforce the decision via court or enforcement offices (execution offices) are not valid for administration, unlike private law persons.

The difference between executability and *ex officio* execution is that while executability is related to the generation of a decision (act), *ex officio* execution is related to the enforcement of such decision (act). When an act is carried out by administration, this act is "executable," that is, the act is generated with the power to make a change in the legal existence. However, executing this act (transferring the act into the real world, realization of the act—which was realized in the legal existence—in the real world)[79] is a different subject.

---

acts, are executable acts." SC 5th C., M. 1995/4416, D. 1996/1911, 17.05.1996, www.kazanci.com.

76 Gözler, *İdare Hukuku V. I*, 777.

77 Metin Günday, *İdare Hukuku* [*Administrative Law*] (Ankara: İmaj, 2017), 124; Şeref Gözübüyük and Turgut Tan, *İdare Hukuku* [*Administrative Law*], Vol. I (Ankara: Turhan, 2001), 373.

78 Gözler, *İdare Hukuku V. I*, 776.

79 Günday, *İdare Hukuku*, 124–125.

Occasionally, administration does not need to make a further step to transfer the act into the real world.[80] This happens on its own. The act is transferred in the real world by being established. In such a case, establishment of the act and transferring this act in the real world interlace. "Permission" by administration is as such. The consequence of "permission" reflects to the real world by itself when it is established.

Pursuant to the principle of rule of law and—as an extension to this principle—principle of legal administration provisioned in the Constitution, administration principally does not have the authority to enforce its own decision by itself. For the administration to enforce its own decision, the law has to grant the administration with such an authority.[81] Doctrinal views differ on this subject. Gözler indicates that administration has the authority of *ex officio* execution in principle.[82] According to the author, the administration cannot execute its own act if and only if the law prescribed so (for instance, if the law prescribed that administration needs to apply to enforcement offices).[83] We are of the view that administration needs to be authorized by law in order to execute *ex officio* pursuant to the principle of rule of law.[84]

At this point, we should also mention "compulsory execution." Compulsory execution is the ability of the administration to use "coercive means" to enforce its decision.[85] 11. Circuit of the State Council has confirmed that the administration has the authority to execute *ex officio* in principle. However, the High Court ruled that administration does not have the authority of "compulsory enforcement" in principle and to use such authority, an explicit regulation is required in law. Related part of the decision is as follows: "As a natural consequence of administrative acts benefitting from presumption of legality, administration possess the authority to execute its decisions ex officio in principle. Administration is authorized to execute its own decisions, only by using the public force it possesses and without the need to obtain a decision by applying to a judicial authority. However, to execute some administrative acts ex officio, administration may need to invoke compulsive measures on the physical presence or assets of

80 Günday, *İdare Hukuku*, 125.

81 Günday, *İdare Hukuku*, 125; Kalabalık, *İdare Hukuku Dersleri*, 43.

82 It is understood that Çağlayan has the same view from the statements regarding the subject. See Çağlayan, *İdare Hukuku Dersleri*, 48.

83 Gözler, *İdare Hukuku V. I*, 779–780.

84 For the differing views, see Dilşat Yılmaz, *İdari İşlemin İcrailik Özelliği* [*The Feature of Executability of Administrative Act*] (Ankara: Astana, 2014), 150 ff.

85 Yaşar, *İdare Hukuku*, 294.

the related person, it may need to use force. In order to execute administrative acts, which generate such consequences, administration in principle does not possess the authority to compulsorily execute ex officio. This is because, usage of compulsory measures by administration amounts to restriction to the freedom of persons and right to property which are secured by the Constitution. The only condition which will provide such restriction to be consistent with law is the existence of a law which explicitly authorizes administration in this direction."[86]

It should be noted that *ex officio* execution does not necessarily require to use "compulsion." For instance, for administration to execute the act of disciplinary penalty, it does not need to use compulsion.[87] However, in the example of execution of demolishment, to bring people who oppose to this act compulsorily away is a "compulsion" directed to the aim of execution of the administrative act. As a conclusion, it is possible to separate "*ex officio* execution" into two as "*ex officio* compulsory execution" and "*ex officio* execution which is not compulsory."[88]

1.2.2.4. Benefitting from the Presumption of Legality

Administrative acts are accepted to be consistent with law.[89] However, since administrative acts do not constitute *res judicata*, inconsistency of administrative acts to law may be alleged.[90] Administrative acts are presumed to be legally correct, until these are annulled by a judiciary decision. Furthermore, bringing action cannot on its own suspend the execution of the act. Suspension of the act is only possible if administrative judiciary decides on "stay of execution." Granting this decision is also dependent on the conditions laid down in the law.

---

86 SC 11th C., M. 2008/6908, D. 2010/5831, 28.06.2010, www.kazanci.com.

87 Yılmaz, *İdari İşlemin İcrailik Özelliği*, 157.

88 It may be easier to understand the notions of executability, ex officio execution and compulsory enforcement with an example. Suppose that a person constructs an additional division to the real estate she owns contrary to construction legislation. Noticing this, administration decides on restitution by demolishing the part that is contrary to construction by the owner in a certain time, otherwise the demolishment to be realized by the administration. This decision is "executable." If the owner does not demolish the part contrary to construction timely, then administration takes action to demolish the part with heavy equipment. In this case, ex officio execution is in question. If the owner tries to stop administration from demolishment like by standing in front of the heavy equipment the administration brings the owner away by using force (with the help of police team which is also within administration), then it is a "compulsory execution."

89 Akyılmaz, Sezginer, and Kaya, *Türk İdare Hukuku*, 351; Gözler, *İdare Hukuku V. I*, 98.

90 Günday, *İdare Hukuku*, 126; Kalabalık, *İdare Hukuku Dersleri*, 44.

Article 27 of Procedure of Administrative Justice Act is as follows:

> 1) Filing an action in the Council of State or the administrative courts shall not prevent the execution of the administrative act which is the subject of the action.
> 2) State Council or the administrative courts can decide to stay the execution by showing justification after the plea of the defendant administration is taken or after the end of the time limit for the plea if the implementation of the administrative act both results in damage that are hard to recover or impossible to recover from and if the administrative act is expressly in contradiction to the law. The execution of the administrative acts whose effect will be exhausted through implementation can also be stayed without receiving the plea of the administration so that a decision can be made again after the plea is taken. However, the administrative acts regarding appointment, appointment by transfer, change of duty and title, temporary or permanent assignment established about the public officials shall not be deemed as an administrative act the effect of which will be exhausted through implementation. In the decisions for the stay of execution, it is mandatory to specify on which grounds the administrative act is expressly in contradiction to the law and what damages that are hard to recover or impossible to recover will arise if the act is applied. The decision for the stay of execution cannot be taken only on the grounds that an application has been made to the Constitutional Court requesting for the annulment of the relevant law or the provision of the decree law of the Presidency of the Republic.

While the rule is as such, exceptionally, law may prescribe situations where application against an act may stay the execution of that act. For instance, regarding the tax disputes, Procedure of Administrative Justice Act prescribes such an exception: "Filing actions arising from tax disputes at the tax courts shall stay the collection procedures of the part of the levied taxes, duties, charges and similar financial liabilities and the increases and penalties thereof which is the subject of the action" (article 27/4).

As seen, pursuant to Procedure of Administrative Justice Act, filing an action before tax courts by its own has the effect to suspend the act. In this case, a further "stay of execution" decision is not needed.

In brief, we may put forward that there are two exceptions to the presumption of legality:

1. Stay of execution decision by administrative judiciary.
2. A law granting to a certain application the effect to stay the execution of theact.

On the other hand, broadening of the presumption of legality is also possible. Pursuant to the article 125/6 of the Constitution, the law may restrict the issuing of an order on stay of execution of an administrative act in cases of state of emergency, mobilization and state of war, or on the grounds of national security, public order and public health. In other words, both in state of emergency times, mobilization and state of war and in ordinary times when national security or public order necessities in a certain way, stay of execution decisions of the administrative judiciary may be restricted by law.[91]

The presumption of legality grants administration an important supremacy over individuals. Furthermore, as mentioned, for removal of the presumption, certain conditions should be met. Thus, judiciary system enhanced a reflex to this supremacy of administration. In administrative judiciary, the judge does not depend only on the evidence provided by the parties like civil procedure. Administrative judiciary can come to a conclusion by examining on its own without confining itself with the evidence of the parties. This is called "principle of *ex officio* examination."

For instance, in a dispute, the court of first instance did neither apply to legal expert nor the reconnoiter due that the person who filed the action did not pay the expert and reconnoiter fee in a dispute regarding the establishment of hydroelectric power station. The court settled only with the present evidence and confirmed administration by highlighting that pursuant to presumption of legality, the acts of administration should be presumed to be consistent with law. Later on, 14. Circuit of State Council found the decision of the first instance unlawful, by stating that the court of first instance should have applied for legal expert and should have reconnoitered by charging the related fee to the party who lost the case.[92] In other words, court of first instance should have revealed the truth by applying to expert and reconnoitering and not settling with the evidence provided by the parties pursuant to principle of *ex officio* examination.

1.2.3. The Other Indicators

1.2.3.1. The Statute of Goods and Personnel of Public Corporate Bodies

1.2.3.1.1. Goods

Goods of public corporate bodies are secured more than goods of private law persons by the legal system.[93] For instance, the goods of public corporate bodies cannot be seized, expropriated or prescribed.[94] The reason behind this is that

---

91 The Constitution used the expression of "limitation." Therefore, abolishment or prohibition of "stay of execution" for an indefinite time shall be contrary to the Constitution.

92 SC 14th C., M. 2012/1672, D. 2014/7044, 25.06.2014, www.kazanci.com.

93 Günday, *İdare Hukuku*, 79; Çağlayan, *İdare Hukuku Dersleri*, 48.

94 İşbir, *Kamu Tüzel Kişiliği*, 303.

these goods are used for the aim of public interest, like a building belonging to a university or a health institution. In other words, these goods are used to carry out public services.

1.2.3.1.2. Personnel

Personnel of public corporate bodies are accepted to be public employees.[95] These personnel are secured more than other persons by the legal system.[96] For instance, in order to prosecute a public servant for the alleged offenses, the permission of the administrative authority is required in principal. Unless a permission is obtained, a public servant cannot be subject to trial. This rule is arisen due to the idea that public employees may not provide public services appropriately if they fear to be tried.

In return of the security granted, public employees get into more obligations compared to other persons. For instance, there are offenses which can only be committed by public employees.[97]

1.2.3.2. The Statute of Receivables and Debts of Public Corporate Bodies

1.2.3.2.1. Receivables

Regarding the receivables of public corporate bodies, Law on the Procedure for the Collection of Public Receivables is implemented.[98] Accordingly, administration can collect its own receivables without the need of another office.

1.2.3.2.2. Debts

Debts of public corporate bodies also differ from debts of other persons. Public corporate bodies cannot be exonerated for these debts and bankruptcy cannot be requested.[99]

---

95 İşbir, *Kamu Tüzel Kişiliği*, 314.

96 Günday, *İdare Hukuku*, 79; Çağlayan, *İdare Hukuku Dersleri*, 61.

97 Akyılmaz, Sezginer, and Kaya, *Türk İdare Hukuku*, 222.

98 Günday, *İdare Hukuku*, 79; Gözler, *İdare Hukuku V. I*, 98.

99 Sıddık Sami Onar, *İdare Hukukunun Umumi Esasları* [*General Principles of Administrative Law*], Vol. III (İstanbul: Hak Yayınevi İsmail Akgün Matbaası), 1999. The author indicates that public service may fail in case that exoneration is possible. Another issue that Onar highlights is that "exoneration" is a public force and exoneration against state may cause two public corporate bodies to confront.

1.2.3.3. Obligatory Membership and Contribution

A public corporate body can oblige other persons to be members of the body and receive contributions from them compulsorily. Most known examples on this regard are professional organizations having the characteristics of public institutions. For instance, a person who graduated from law school and accomplished her internship cannot become an attorney unless she is a member of the bar. At the same time, she is obliged to pay contributions.

1.2.3.4. Tax Exemptions

Some of the laws grant tax exemptions to public corporate bodies.[100] This feature may as well be considered when designating whether an institution is a public corporate body. However, some private law legal persons may as well benefit from tax exemptions to encourage investments and so forth. Therefore, tax exemptions or exceptions by themselves are not sufficient to conclude that the institution is a public corporate body.

1.2.3.5. Obligations of Public Force

Public corporate bodies are obliged to bear some obligations unlike private law persons in return of the privileges of public force.[101] On the root of this, the principle of acting for public interest lies. At the same time, money that is spent for the activities of public corporate bodies are supplied from the public cash box. In other words, public corporate bodies cannot spare the money collected from the taxes which is paid by the people. Therefore, they need to obey to some obligations. Even if these obligations cannot be counted wholly, we may give some examples on this regard:

(a) Public corporate bodies cannot carry out activities with a purpose other than public interest. In contrast with this, private law persons can carry out any activity that is not forbidden by laws.[102]
(b) Private law persons are free regarding the employment of personnel. They can employ any person they want. In contrast with this, public corporate bodies have to set an exam and employ the person who deserves the

---

100 Akyılmaz, Sezginer, and Kaya, *Türk İdare Hukuku*, 223
101 Özay, *Günışığında*, 123–124.
102 Gözler, *İdare Hukuku V. I*, 101.

position since that the person who will serve to the people needs to possess specific qualifications.

(c) Public corporate bodies do not have freedom of contract. Public corporate bodies cannot get into contracts as they want, these bodies need to initiate a tender in order for the determination of the other party of the contract.[103] By this way, the person who will carry out the duty in the best and cheapest way would be chosen. Carrying out the duty in the best way is for the public interest, while carrying out the duty in the cheapest way provides the money of the people to be spared.

As a conclusion, since that laws or PDs may sometimes grant private law legal persons with superior rights and obligations, if the law or the PD does not clearly prescribe the characteristic of being "public" of a legal person, then it cannot be concluded that a legal person is a public corporate body for sure. It can only be estimated. Regarding the issue, the exact decision will be made by judiciary.[104] When judiciary concludes that a person is a public corporate body than it will be accepted so within the perspective of positive law.[105]

In the doctrine, it is also stated that if the area of activity of a legal person pertains to monopolies, then this fact too can be an indicator of a legal person being a public corporate body.[106] We are of the opinion that this factor may also be paid attention to with the other factors.

State Council states that it is not bound with the characterization of a legal person as "private law person" which is established by administration.[107] As a matter of fact, according to the High Court, the acts of "interprovincial terminal operator" which is established by Ankara Metropolitan Municipality and Atatürk Forest Farm (two public corporate bodies) with the characterization of "ordinary partnership" shall be subject to administrative law.[108] State Council paid

103 Gözler, *İdare Hukuku V. I*, 100.

104 From the decision of the Constitutional Court regarding organized industrial zones (OIZ) which are private legal persons: "…Expropriation being only carried out by the state or public corporate bodies constitute a procedural safeguard regarding the restriction of right to property. Even though OIZ is granted with some public force privileges, this is not sufficient for OIZ to expropriate, since it needs to be a public corporate body pursuant to article 46 of the Constitution." CC, M. 2012/49, D. 2012/158, 18.10.2012, OG 12.05.2013–28645.

105 Zabunoğlu, *İdare Hukuku*, 135–136.

106 Günday, *İdare Hukuku*, 79; Gözler, *İdare Hukuku V. I*, 100.

107 Yayla, *İdare Hukuku*, 230.

108 SC 10th C., M. 1995/4326, D. 1996/2769, 21.05.1996, www.kazanci.com.

regard to the facts that terminal operator carries out public service, it is a monopoly, it uses public funding, its board of management is constituted by public employees when concluding that its acts are subject to administrative law.

1.3. The Principles of Centralization and Decentralization

According to the article 123/2 of the Constitution: "The organization and functions of the administration are based on the principles of centralization and decentralization." As seen, one of the basic features of Turkish administration is that both the principles of centralization and decentralization are implemented concurrently. Below, these principles are examined in detail.

1.3.1. Centralization (A Single Public Corporate Body: State)

Politically, centralization is the opposite of federation.[109] In other words, centralization refers to the situations in which a single legal system is implemented in a state and where law unity is provided.[110] In contrast with this, in federation, federate states may have different legal systems.

Article 126 of the Constitution lays down the below-mentioned provision regarding central administration: "In terms of central administrative structure, Turkey is divided into provinces on the basis of geographical situation, economic conditions, and public service requirements; provinces are further divided into lower levels of administrative districts."

As seen, the Constitution does not allow a wider administrative structure than provinces. This provision is a reflection of the "unitary" state understanding.[111]

---

109 The related part of the decision is as follows: "... In the constitution, which is designed with the fundamental of unitary state, federal state system is not adopted. For this reason, political parties cannot give space to the establishment of a federal state in their programs and cannot defend this structure. The principle of indivisible integrity in the structure of the state necessities sovereignty to integrate with a single state structure which is comprised of the integrity of the nation and territory. The principle of unitary state does not permit to the understanding of a multinational state and in such an organization, there is no space for a federative structure. In a federative system, sovereignty used by federated states are in question. In a unitary state structure, more than one sovereignty does not exist..." CC, M. 1993/3 (Political Party-Dissolving) D. 1994/2, 16.06.1994, OG 30.06.1994–21976 (Repeating).

110 Onar, *İdare Hukukunun Umumi Esasları V. II*, 589.

111 "... The principle in the article 123 of the Constitution, which states that administration is a whole with its formation and functions, does not mean that the administration should consist of a single institution and every unit of the administration has

Therefore, federation is not a possible structure from the viewpoint of the Constitution. On the other hand, "in condition that it is not nationwide and exceptional"[112] structures compromising several provinces may be established pursuant to article 126/3 of the Constitution. However, these cannot be situated over provinces and such regional structures cannot benefit from "devolution of powers."[113]

Administratively, "centralization" expresses that the function of administration is also centralized. According to the principle of centralization, public services[114] as well as public force which is performed to provide public services are gathered in the center.[115]

As a conclusion of this, central administration emerges as a "single structure"[116] (administration of state) compromising of institutions, public employees and offices that are bounded with hierarchy.[117] In other words, in central administration there is only one public corporate body which is the state.[118] The offices which are situated in the legal personality of the state (ministries, governorates,

---

the power and duty to conduct all of the missions of administration. This principle indicates that due to unitarity of the state, the word 'administration' shall refer to local administrations, decentral administration in service as well as general administration. In practice, it is seen that administration has duty and is authorized pursuant to the establishment purpose of a single unit and only serves within the scope of that purpose. Essentially, this situation is a consequence of principle of legal administration laid down in the article 8 of the Constitution. In the preamble of the article 123 of the Constitution, it is stated that "centralization and decentralization emerged as principles which are complementary to each other and has been implemented continuously as a consequence of the experiences in the historical development of the establishment of the administrative structure in Turkey. As a consequence of this, other than the public corporate body of state and with it, a variety of public corporate bodies have emerged. In other words, today, public service is carried out by local administrations and decentral administration in service, being general administration in the first place..." SC 1st C., M. 1984/291, D. 1984/294, 20.12.1984, www.kazanci.com.

112 Yayla, *İdare Hukuku*, 238.

113 Günday, *İdare Hukuku*, 414; Akyılmaz, Sezginer, and Kaya, *Türk İdare Hukuku*, 297.

114 Gözler, *İdare Hukuku V. I*, 170.

115 Onar, *İdare Hukukunun Umumi Esasları V. II*, 589; Yıldırım, "Genel Kuramlar," 37; Zehra Odyakmaz and Ümit Kaymak, *İdare Hukuku* [*Administrative Law*] (Ankara: Seçkin, 2022), 19.

116 Duran, *İdare Hukuku Ders*, 48.

117 Yayla, *İdare Hukuku*, 234.

118 Gözler, *İdare Hukuku V. I*, 170.

district governorates, State Planning Organization, Directorate of Religious Affairs, etc.) does not possess a separate public personality.

Since public services cannot be carried out countrywide only from the center, central administration also necessitates an organization that spreads all over the country. According to aforementioned article 126/1 of the Constitution, Turkey is divided into provinces, and provinces are further divided into lower levels of administrative districts. Such organizations that are situated out of the capital is called "the field service of the central administration" (country).[119] The organization of field service can be seen as the extension of the center. Today in Turkey, two kinds of field services of central administration are valid: provinces and districts (sub-provinces).[120]

Public employees that are in the field service are under the order and the instruction of the center and they do not possess separate powers.[121] However, the fact that central administration's purview is broad and all authority gathered in the center may bring its disadvantages with it. Specifically, consultation to central administration for every act in all over the country may cause public services to slow down and result in maladministration.[122] For this purpose, devolution of powers is adopted.[123] Likewise, according to the State Council, the purpose of devolution of powers is "to remove the disadvantages of central administration to an extent and to accelerate the functioning of the central administration within the bounds of possibility."[124]

Pursuant to the article 126/1 of the Constitution, "The administration of the provinces is based on the principle of devolution of powers." The meaning of this principle is that the governor of a province who is the head of provincial organization has the authority to decide on behalf of the central administration without consulting to the latter in case that the law lays down so or an authority of the

119 Gözler, *İdare Hukuku V. I*, 170.

120 Gözler, *İdare Hukuku V. I*, 328.

121 Gözler, *İdare Hukuku V. I*, 171.

122 Yayla, *İdare Hukuku*, 234–235; Yıldırım, "Genel Kuramlar," 37.

123 Akyılmaz, Sezginer and Kaya indicates that certain measures should be taken to avoid the disadvantages of central administration to a certain extent, to bring to the functioning of central administration contentment, speed and efficiency and to soften the central administration. Akyılmaz, Sezginer, and Kaya, *Türk İdare Hukuku*, 160–161.

124 SC 2nd C., M. 2004/1326, D. 2005/1786, 24.05.2005, www.kazanci.com.

center is transferred via delegation of competence.[125] Then, in case that devolution of power is implemented, the powers of the governors expand.[126]

Since the Constitution prescribed that only the governors are subject to devolution of powers, district governors cannot benefit from devolution of powers.[127] This conclusion has also been made by State Council in one of its decisions: "… Devolution of powers can only be implemented by province administrations pursuant to the Constitution, yielding the conclusion that central authority to make an act is to be used by governors in the provinces aiming to eliminate the harms of central administration to some part …"[128] Briefly, in Administrative Law, devolution of powers is only granted to the administration of province.[129]

---

125 "The purpose behind devolution of powers is to remove the disadvantages of central administration to an extent and to accelerate the functioning of the central administration within the brouds of possibility. To grant the authorities which arise from the public force such as deciding and implementing from the center to a public service who is at the head of a region or service is defined as devolution of powers..."; SC 2nd C., M. 2004/1326, D. 2005/1786, 24.05.2005, www.kazanci.com.

126 Özay, *Günışığında*, 159.

127 Akyılmaz, Sezginer, and Kaya, *Türk İdare Hukuku*, 268; Gözler, *İdare Hukuku V. I*, 173.

128 SC 5th C., M. 2007/168, D. 2009/2800, 20.05.2009, www.hukukturk.com.

129 Related part of a Constitutional Court's decision is as follows: "… Pursuant to a preconceived fundamental, devolution procedure which also aims to relieve the burden of central administration can be realized in two ways. First of these is the method of granting public powers such as making decisions and implementing these decisions in order to carry out certain duties to a public servant who is the head of a region or public service by a law. This is called 'devolution of powers.' Governors of provinces and ambassadors who are representatives of the state and government … separately every unit of ministries in provincial areas are examples of this system. In the devolution of powers, public corporate bodies, in other words autonomy, is not in question. The person who has the authority to decide and implement is within the central administration. She acts as a representative or on behalf of the central administration. She is subject to hierarchy. Hierarchy is the bound and power which secures the unity and integrity of the authorities and responsibilities of the central administration. Within this perspective and pursuant to article 126 of Constitution, provinces established 'in terms of central administrative structure … on the basis of geographical situation, economic conditions, and public service requirements' are based on the principle of devolution of powers." CC, M. 1987/18, D. 1988/23, 22.06.1988, OG 26.11.1988–20001. The decision may be criticized since it involves ambassadors and the other institutions of central administration to the devolution of power which is only granted to governors of provinces in the constitution. Constitutional Court seems to mention delegation of power rather than devolution of power.

1.3.2. Decentralization (Public Corporate Bodies Other Than the State)

The principle of decentralization allows organizations to adopt enforceable decisions.[130] These organizations each have separate public legal personalities, and thus are situated out of the legal personality of the state. Therefore, decentral administrations are not subject to the hierarchy of central administration. In this sense, decentralization necessitates administrative and financial "autonomy."[131] Administrative autonomy refers to the freedom of action of decentral administrations to the extent that the laws grant them.[132] On the other hand, to secure financial autonomy, decentral administrations are provided with separate budgets.

In Turkish administrative law, decentral administration is examined in two main categories, namely, local administrations and decentral administrations in service.[133]

1.3.2.1. Local Administrations

Decentralization originally refers to the institutions which are established to provide the common needs in a specific "place" and which possess a separate legal personality outside the hierarchy of the central administration. These institutions which focus on the common needs in a specific place are called local administrations.

The constitutional basis for the local administrations is found in the article 127 of the Constitution. According to the first paragraph of the article, "Local administrations are public corporate bodies established to meet the common local needs of the inhabitants of provinces, municipal districts and villages, whose principles of constitution and decision-making organs elected by the electorate are determined by law."

As seen, according to this article, "special provincial administrations (which are different than provinces under the hierarchy of central administration), municipal districts and villages" are decentral administrations and they are established to provide "common local needs" in a specific region.

130 Onar, *İdare Hukukunun Umumi Esasları V. II*, 610.

131 Gözler, *İdare Hukuku V. I*, 178.

132 Akyılmaz, Sezginer, and Kaya, *Türk İdare Hukuku*, 276.

133 Gözler, *İdare Hukuku V. I*, 176.

In the Constitution, the notion of "common local needs" is not explained. Constitutional Court ruled that this notion refers to "the common expectations of those living within the borders of any local administration unit, which are created, intensified and constantly updated by the concrete situations arising from living together in the same region, which do not exceed local borders in terms of effectiveness scale and benefits, which can be divided and competitive, and where the character of being local and public predominates."[134] The Court ruled that the mentioned "common expectations" shall not mean "the private benefits of a person, family, clan or class that live within the borders of any local administration unit."[135] Within this scope, "common local needs" constitutes the limits of local administration's duties and powers. In one of its decisions, Constitutional Court ruled that since preschool education is national, it cannot be seen in a local nature.[136]

Furthermore, Constitutional Court has indicated that the Constitution itself did not designate which needs are within common local needs. According to the High Court, the law may designate the borders of the duty between central administration and local administrations pursuant to Constitution and public interest.[137] The Court in one of its decisions ruled that the provision of a law was unlawful, which granted Council of Ministers with the authority to designate "the scope and the limits of the local and common needs which are within the duties of special provincial administrations." The Court indicated that the authority that is granted to the Council of Ministers may as well be used for political direction, favor or deterrence and subjective discretion and choices may result

134 CC, M. 2014/72, D. 2014/141, 11.09.2014, OG 10.01.2015–29232.

135 CC, M. 2015/34, D. 2015/48, 13.5.2015, OG 23.05.2015–29364.

136 CC, M. 2005/95, D. 2007/5, 24.01.2007, OG 29.12.2007–26741; Likewise, in another decision of the Constitutional Court, the Court evaluated whether the exclusion of airports which are open to civil air transportation and facilities in these airports from the Municipal Law no. 5393 is in conformity with the Constitution. The Court ruled that since civil air transportation by its nature and mandatorily concerns more than one city or state. Furthermore, the Court evaluated that it is mandatorily related to national and international security. In conclusion, the Court stated that civil air transportation is not within the field of "common local needs" and the provision of the law in question is in conformity with the Constitution. CC, M. 2006/131, D. 2007/4, 24.01.2007, OG 26.01.2008–26768.

137 CC, M. 2015/34, D. 2015/48, 13.5.2015, OG 23.05.2015–29364; CC, M. 2014/72, D. 2014/141, 11.09.2014, OG 10.01.2015–29232.

in imbalance between regions.[138] Likewise, we believe that duties and powers of local administration cannot be designated by a PD since abovementioned article 127 of the Constitution explicitly indicates that principle of constitution of such institutions shall be designated by law.

1.3.2.2. Decentral Administrations in Service

In addition to local administrations, some public services which were previously situated in the central administration has gained legal personality over time and separated from the central administration due that the central administration does not suffice to provide public services which require technical specialties.[139] These institutions are also a part of decentral administration.

In line with its purpose of establishment, decentral administrations in service refer to public corporate bodies which are separated from the legal personality of the state, and which carry out technical public services that require special information and expertise.[140] Decentral administrations in service are also referenced as "public institutions."[141]

Unlike local administrations, public institutions can provide public services countrywide. Therefore, these institutions do not necessarily carry out its activities in a restricted area.[142] For instance, General Directorate for Highways carries out duties regarding the public service of transportation all over the country. While these institutions carry out its services all over the country, they can only perform the service that they are assigned to. This situation is referred as "specialty principle."[143]

As a conclusion, organically administration compromises of central administration (public corporate body of the state, a single legal personality), local

---

138 CC, M. 1987/16, D. 1988/23, 22.06.1988, OG 26.11.1988–20001; Akyılmaz, Sezginer, and Kaya also states that common local needs should be designated by a law, and it would be contrary to the Constitution in case that a law allows these needs to be determined by the administration. Akyılmaz, Sezginer, and Kaya, *Türk İdare Hukuku*, 279.

139 Onar, *İdare Hukukunun Umumi Esasları V. II*, 615; Yayla, *İdare Hukuku*, 237; Gözler, *İdare Hukuku V. I*, 184.

140 Akyılmaz, Sezginer, and Kaya, *Türk İdare Hukuku*, 321–322.

141 Akyılmaz, Sezginer, and Kaya, *Türk İdare Hukuku*, 163; Gözler, *İdare Hukuku V. I*, 184.

142 Due that a word with a close meaning to "local" ("yerinden" in Turkish) is in the foreground in the Turkish expression of decentral administration, reference to these institutions interpretable in a local sense has gathered critiques. See Duran, *İdare Hukuku Ders*, 54; Gözler, *İdare Hukuku V. I*, 176.

143 Gözler, *İdare Hukuku V. I*, 186.

administrations each having public legal personality[144] (special provincial administrations, municipal districts[145] and villages) and decentral administration in service (public institutions). Below, there is a chart explaining the fundamentals of Turkish administration and benefits and harms (pros and cons) associated to it.

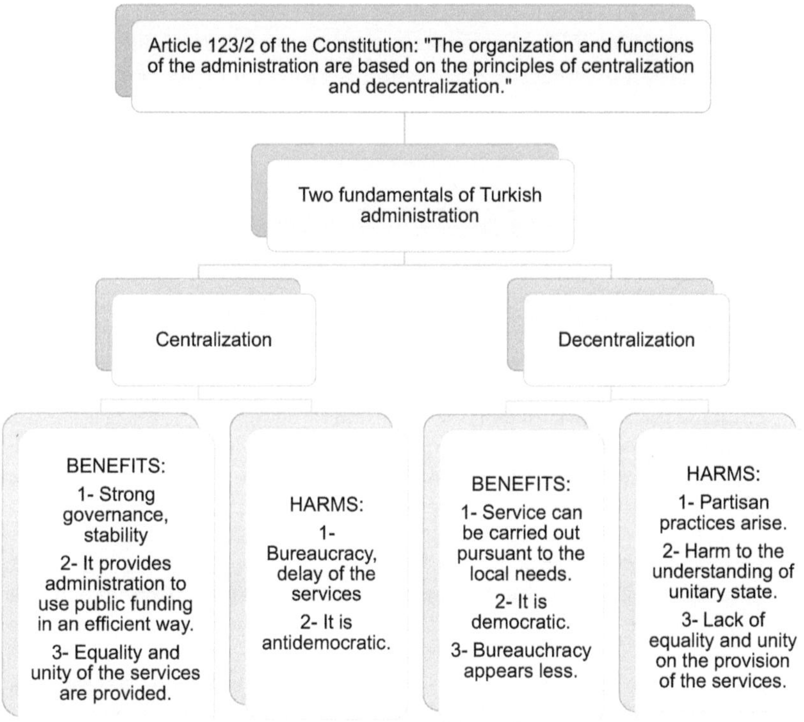

Figure 2: Principles of Centralization and Decentralization

144 Odyakmaz and Kaymak, *İdare Hukuku*, 16.

145 State Council highlighted that municipalities have separate personalities from the public corporate body of the state: "The municipalities should not be evaluated within the notion of state since they have separate personality other than the state and autonomous budget which is not within central administration budget, pursuant to the provisions laid down above …." SC 8th C., M. 2009/4695, D. 2010/2033, 21.04.2010, www.kazanci.com.

1.4. The Principle of Integrity of Administration

As a consequence of unitary state principle, the principle of integrity of administration has been foreseen.[146] Administrative organization of the Turkish Republic has a structure compromising of the state and other public corporate bodies. Due to the unitary state understanding, to conjoin public corporate bodies situated in this fragmented structure is obligatory.[147]

Another reason for this obligation is to prevent the failure of public services. As a point of fact, if the integrity of the administration cannot be provided, services cannot be carried out as it should be.

---

146 "... Integrity of administration is a fundamental principle of unitary state model in the area of governance. This principle suggests that institutions which are administrative functions and are based on different legal statutes compromise an integrity. Integrity of administration is actualized by the scrutinization and observance of the central and three main legal tools such as hierarchy, administrative tutelage and devolution of powers are used in order to provide the integrity in the governance. Among these, administrative tutelage ensures the integrity between the central governance and decentral administrations and prevents resolution, differentiation and dissociation ..." CC, M. 2008/28, D. 2010/30, 04.02.2010, OG 21.06.2010–27619.

147 In the annulment decision of the Constitutional Court regarding Law on Ombudsman Institution no. 5548, it is stated: "Pursuant to article 123 of the Constitution, even though it is possible to establish a public corporate body by a law or explicit authorization granted with a law, an administrative institution which is established as a public corporate body needs to be within the body of administration and within the administrative organization structure due to the principle of administrative integrity ..." CC, M. 2006/140, D. 2008/185, 25.12.2008, OG 04.04.2009–27190. High Court found that establishment of Ombudsman Institution by binding it to Grand National Assembly of Turkey is contrary to the Constitution. According to the High Court, binding an institution, which should have been situated among central administration or decentral administration, to legislature and therefore situating it out of administration is not possible pursuant to the Constitution. High Court adopted an organic approach in this decision.
"... Integrity of the administration is the fundamental principle in the unitary state model in the area of governance and with this principle, the integrity between the various duties carried out by administration and institutions which carry out these duties is envisaged and it is aimed that the institutions situated in administrative structure work in an integrity." CC, M. 2011/149, D. 2012/187, 22.11.2012, OG 04.12.2013–28841.

According to the article 123/1 of the Constitution, "the administration is a whole with its formation and functions …." Then, how should be the mechanism to provide the integrity of the administration?

- First, the integrity within the public corporate bodies should be ensured. By this way, units and servants in this public corporate body shall not act independently.
- Secondly, a bond is necessary between different public corporate bodies and it should be ensured that these do not act self-ordained.

In the first situation, the mechanism of "hierarchy"[148] and in the second situation, "administrative tutelage" are in question. Briefly, we may state that there are two mechanisms comprising of "inner integrity" (hierarchy) and "outer integrity"[149] (administrative tutelage).[150]

1.4.1. Hierarchy

Hierarchy refers to the inferior and superior relationship within[151] a public corporate body.[152] In other words, hierarchy means that the servants in the organization are bounded to their superior in succession and at the end to the top superior. In this way, the inner integrity of the public corporate body would be ensured.

---

148 State Council indicated: "It is necessary for the claimant which is liable to the minister who is superior to obtain permission from the minister while leaving the city … when executing its duties and services, in order to carry out public service within integrity and without delay…" SC 8. C., M. 1995/3706, D. 1995/3622, 14.11.1995, www.kazanci.com.

149 Onar, *İdare Hukukunun Umumi Esasları V. II*, 617. The author described administrative tutelage with the words of "a high and outer supervision."

150 "… Integrity of administration is a fundamental principle of unitary state model in the area of governance. This principle suggests that institutions which are administrative functions and are based on different legal statutes compromise an integrity. Integrity of administration is actualized by the supervision and observance of the central and three main legal tools such as hierarchy, administrative tutelage and devolution of powers are used in order to provide the integrity in the governance." CC, M. 2005/32, D. 2007/3, 18.01.2007, OG 29.12.2007–26741.

151 "… hierarchical authority is an authority which is granted to ensure the integrity within a public corporate body." SC 8th C., M. 2003/3309, D. 2004/1912, 21.04.2004, www.kazanci.com.

152 Yayla, *İdare Hukuku*, 385; Gözler, *İdare Hukuku V. I*, 248.

Due that hierarchy refers to the relationship "within" a public corporate body, within the state or other public corporate bodies, hierarchy is valid. Hierarchy is also valid within the decentral administration (the local administrations and decentral administration in service). For instance, hierarchy is also intrinsic within the universities or municipalities.

Each public corporate body has "the top superior" hierarchical governor within itself. For instance, the mayor in a municipality or the rector in a university is in the most superior position.

Then, who is the top superior governor in the central administration? After the constitutional amendment, the president has become the top superior hierarchical governor in the central administration.[153] Ministers and deputies of the president are in a position inferior to the president hierarchically. They are obliged to obey the orders and instructions of the president.

An important issue is that the hierarchical authority does not have to be prescribed by a law.[154] Every public corporate authority has hierarchy in it. Hierarchy is accepted as a general principle of law.

Hierarchical authority may be separated as the hierarchical authorities over "persons" and "acts."[155] We will elaborate these notions in the titles below.

1.4.1.1. Over Persons

Hierarchical authority over persons includes three powers:

1. To make acts regarding status: Superior may make acts regarding inferior's record, his/her assignment and promotion. Superior may inflict disciplinary penalties to the inferior.[156] However, the powers to implement disciplinary measures and to make assignments should be prescribed by a law unlike the other hierarchical authorities.[157]

---

153 Gözler, *İdare Hukuku V. I*, 249.

154 Duran, *İdare Hukuku Ders*, 56; Yayla, *İdare Hukuku*, 385–386; Yıldırım, "Genel Kuramlar," 25; Gözler, *İdare Hukuku V. I*, 256; Akyılmaz, Sezginer, and Kaya, *Türk İdare Hukuku*, 189.

155 Gustave Peiser, *Droit Administratif* (Paris: Dalloz, 2014), 105.

156 Peiser, *Droit Administratif*, 105; Gözler, *İdare Hukuku V. I*, 253; Duran, *İdare Hukuku Ders*, 57; Çağlayan, *İdare Hukuku Dersleri*, 134.

157 Akyılmaz, Sezginer, and Kaya, *Türk İdare Hukuku*, 194.

2. To make decisions and take measures regarding the organization within the institution:[158] Superior may take measures, share tasks[159] and instruct (and so forth) to organize the institution.
3. To give orders:[160] Superior may give orders to her inferiors. Inferior is obliged to obey the order given by the superior. In principle, the inferior does not have the right to bring an action before judicial organs or to complain or object before the superior office against this order.[161] The reason behind this is the need to provide the integrity within the administration.

As an exception, State Council has accepted the right to bring a lawsuit relating to the acts regarding personnel rights. In other words, the servant in the inferior position may bring a lawsuit against the acts taken by her superior regarding personnel rights. However, according to the High Court, inferior cannot bring a suit against acts related to the "organization and operation of public services."[162]

The boundary to give orders is laid down in the article 137 of the Constitution. Accordingly,

> If a person employed in any position or status in public services finds an order given by her superior to be contrary to the provisions of by-laws, presidential decrees, laws, or the Constitution, she shall not carry it out, and shall inform the person giving the order of this inconsistency. However, if her superior insists on the order and renews it in a written statement, her order shall be executed; in this case the person executing the order shall not be held responsible.
>
> An order which in itself constitutes a criminal offence shall under no circumstances be executed; the person who executes such an order shall not evade responsibility.

As seen in the event that the inferior objects an order regarding its inconsistency to legislation and the superior insists with a written statement, the inferior shall obey the order without bearing responsibility. However, in case that the order is a criminal offense, and the inferior obeys to such an order, her responsibility does not evade regardless of the insists of her superior on the execution of the order.

Then, how should we interpret the article 137 in conjunction with the article 129/6? The article 129/6 of the Constitution is as follows: "Prosecution of public

158 Duran, *İdare Hukuku Ders*, 57.

159 Gözler, *İdare Hukuku V. I*, 253.

160 Duran, *İdare Hukuku Ders*, 57; Gözler, *İdare Hukuku V. I*, 253; Çağlayan, *İdare Hukuku Dersleri*, 134; Akyılmaz, Sezginer, and Kaya, *Türk İdare Hukuku*, 189.

161 Akyılmaz, Sezginer, and Kaya, *Türk İdare Hukuku*, 190; Gözler, *İdare Hukuku V. I*, 257.

162 SC 10th C., M. 1994/5335, D. 1997/227, 04.02.1997, www.kazanci.com.

servants and other public officials for alleged offences shall be subject, except in cases prescribed by law, to the permission of the administrative authority designated by law."

It may be argued that the latter article (article 129/6) diminishes the safeguard which the provision regarding unlawful order (article 137) provides for the governed. This is because, to prosecute the servant—who executed the order constituting a criminal offense—a permission will be needed in principle.

It should be noted that according to the judiciary, an order "not to implement the judicial decisions" is within the scope of "unlawful order." For instance, First Circuit of the State Council found that the order by the ministries to a governor (of a province) not to obey the judicial decision preventing the foundation of a factory in that province constitutes an unlawful order.[163]

On the other hand, according to the last subparagraph of the article 137, "Exceptions designated by law relating to the execution of military duties and the protection of public order or public security in urgent situations are reserved." In other words, during military duties and in "urgent situations," if prescribed by law, the rules regarding the boundaries on the authority to give order shall not be implemented.

1.4.1.2. Over Acts

The superior has the authority to "withdraw," "abolish,"[164] "alter," "correct"[165], "postpone the execution or cease," "confirm subsequently" the acts of the inferior.[166] The superior may exercise these authorities due that she finds the act "inconsistent with law" or she decides that the act is not "expedient."[167]

However, it is important to note that the superior cannot take inferior's place and use her power instead.[168] This is called "prohibition of replacement." The superior can only give an order to her inferior to act in a certain way.[169] If

163 SC 10th C., M. 2005/1377, D. 2006/83, 24.01.2006, www.kazanci.com.

164 As we will explain below, the authorities of withdrawal and abolishment may be used when the act is contrary to law. Gözler, *İdare Hukuku V. I*, 257. The reason of this is that sometimes the act may bear prescribed rights for the interested persons.

165 Antoine Louvaris, *Droit Administratif* (Paris: PUF, 2011), 241.

166 Duran, *İdare Hukuku Ders*, 57; Günday, *İdare Hukuku*, 83–84.

167 Çağlayan, *İdare Hukuku Dersleri*, 134; Akyılmaz, Sezginer, and Kaya, *Türk İdare Hukuku*, 193; Gözler, *İdare Hukuku V. I*, 255.

168 Çağlayan, *İdare Hukuku Dersleri*, 135; Akyılmaz, Sezginer, and Kaya, *Türk İdare Hukuku*, 193.

169 Duran, *İdare Hukuku Ders*, 57.

prescribed by law, the superior can as well compel her inferior by using her disciplinary authority. In case that the superior replaces the inferior and decides on her behalf, the act shall be unlawful and shall be annulled by the administrative judiciary.[170]

Provided that the same authority is granted to the superior, "replacement" will not be in question and the act will be consistent with law.[171] For instance, suppose that Provincial Directorate for National Education implemented a disciplinary measure to a teacher. In a suit in which it was alleged that this measure should have been applied by the principal of the school which the teacher works at, State Council indicated that prohibition of replacement is not in question since Provincial Directorate for National Education is also authorized to implement disciplinary measures.[172] In other words, the superior did not replace the inferior and decide on her behalf in the concrete case due that the law authorized the superior to decide on the same subject.

It is also important to note that some persons are not subject to hierarchy. First, judges[173] are independent when executing their duties pursuant to article 138 of the Constitution:

> Judges shall be independent in the discharge of their duties; they shall give judgment in accordance with the Constitution, laws (legal codes), and their personal conviction in accordance with the law.
>
> No organ, authority, office or individual may give orders or instructions to courts or judges relating to the exercise of judicial power, send them circulars, or make recommendations or suggestions.

Secondly, it is not possible to use the hierarchical authority over technical specialists in the central administrations regarding the acts and actions on their specialties.[174] For instance, a superior cannot command to a technical specialist

---

170 "… Hierarchy refers to the inferiority and superiority relationship between employees within the same administration and accordingly the superior may annul, withdraw, correct the acts of inferior regarding the expediency and legality, however she cannot replace inferior and decide on her behalf and the inferior does not have the right to bring an action." SC 8th C., M. 2003/3309, D. 2004/1912, 21.04.2004, www.kazanci.com.

171 Yayla, *İdare Hukuku*, 264; Gözler, *İdare Hukuku V. I*, 255.

172 SC 12th C., M. 1999/3488, D. 2001/392, 08.02.2001, www.kazanci.com.

173 Gözler, *İdare Hukuku V. I*, 258.

174 Gözler, *İdare Hukuku V. I*, 258.

working in a public institution to make a report on a certain way. Lastly, faculty members cannot be given order about their academical and scholarly studies.[175]

1.4.2. Administrative Tutelage

Another necessity of the unitary structure of the state is to prevent public corporate bodies to conduct self-ordained actions, so it is a must to conjoin public corporate bodies with each other and with the central administration (state) and to supervise these bodies. The mechanism serving to this purpose is administrative tutelage.[176]

This authority originates from the article 127/5 of the Constitution: "The central administration has the power of administrative tutelage over the local administrations in the framework of principles and procedures set forth by law with the objective of ensuring the functioning of local services in conformity with the principle of the integrity of the administration, securing uniform public duties, safeguarding the public interest and meeting local needs properly."

The first remark from this article is that two public corporate bodies are in question when implementing administrative tutelage: public corporate body that possesses the authority of administrative tutelage (supervisor) and public corporate body that is subject to administrative tutelage (supervisee). Surely, according to article 127/5, while central administration is supervisor, local administrations are supervisee in this relationship.

However, as seen, this article only refers to administrative tutelage authority of central administration over local administrations (special provincial administrations, municipal districts and villages). So, can we say that there is administrative tutelage over public institutions (decentral public service-oriented public corporate bodies)? At this point, the provision of the Constitution regarding the principle of integrity of administration is considered. To provide the integrity, it should be accepted that decentral administrations in service should also be subjected to administrative tutelage.[177]

175 Gözler, *İdare Hukuku V. I*, 258.

176 It is highlighted that in French administrative law administrative tutelage may also be in question between private law persons who carry out public services and public corporate bodies. See Louvaris, *Droit Administratif*, 241.

177 Constitutional Court also states that since local administrations may be subject to administrative tutelage, the same power of central administration should also be used over public institutions. The Court also highlights that the principle of integrity of administration (laid down in the article 123 of the Constitution) also necessitates this

It should also be questioned whether the relationship of administrative tutelage may be between two public corporate bodies other than the central administration. In doctrine, Gözler states that local administrations also possess the authority of tutelage over local public institutions (local decentral administrations in service). According to the author, for instance, metropolitan municipality of İstanbul has the authority of tutelage over İSKİ (Istanbul Water and Drainage Authority). However, the author believes that administrative tutelage between other institutions cannot be settled other than the relationship between central administration and decentral administrations.[178]

Unlike Gözler, in the doctrine, by giving the relationship between bars and Turkish Bars Union or metropolitan municipalities and district municipalities or universities and Higher Education Council as examples, the relationship between these administrations are named as "external administrative supervision" as a subdivision of administrative tutelage.[179] We are of the view that these views are accurate due to article 123/1 of the Constitution. While article 123/1 indicates that administration is a whole, it does not state that the link to provide this wholeness should be solely between central administration and decentral administrations. Therefore, we think that administrative tutelage between two public corporate bodies other than the state may be established. However, we believe that since the content of administrative tutelage may differ according to the relevant law, attempt to create subdivisions to tutelage (as external administrative tutelage) may cause a variety of subdivisions to emerge; however, this attempt would not be sufficient to designate the scope of such relationship. Therefore, we think that handling the relationship between two public corporate bodies under the title of "administrative tutelage" is more accurate. However, it should be accepted that sometimes administrative tutelage gets closer to hierarchy.[180]

---

conclusion. See CC, M. 2011/142, D. 2013/52, 03.04.2013, OG 29.05.2014–29014; Gözler, *İdare Hukuku V. I*, 265.

178 Gözler, *İdare Hukuku V. I*, 268.

179 Ali Ulusoy, "Regülasyon Kurumları Hakkında Genel Bir Değerlendirme [A General Evaluation on Regulation Institutions]," in *Günışığında Yönetim*, ed. İl Han Özay (İstanbul: Filiz, 2017), 173 ff; Oğuz Sancakdar, Lale Burcu Önüt, Eser Us Doğan, Mine Kasapoğlu Turhan, and Serkan Seyhan. *İdare Hukuku Teorik Çalışma Kitabı* [*Administrative Law Theorical Study Book*] (Ankara: Seçkin, 2022), 139–140; Yayla indicates that the relationship between universities and Higher Education Council cannot be characterized as administrative tutelage (by pointing out that the president of Higher Education Council is disciplinary chief of rectors and Higher Education Council has general authorities over universities). Yayla, *İdare Hukuku*, 380.

180 Yayla, *İdare Hukuku*, 380, footnote 893.

At this point, it should be noted that in principle there is no administrative tutelage over regulatory and supervisory institutions (independent regulatory agencies). Relevant laws usually do not grant the authority of tutelage over these institutions (Energy Market Regulatory Authority, Capital Market Boards of Turkey and so forth). This situation arises from the idea that these institutions are required to be independent from the state. However, the fact that relevant laws do not grant the authority of tutelage at the moment should not mean that a law will never grant such an authority. Unless the Constitution lays down a safeguard on this regard, legislature can always grant the authority of administrative tutelage to state or to another public corporate body over regulatory and supervisory institutions.

Second remark to be drawn from article 127/5 of the Constitution, administrative tutelage can only be prescribed by law, since that the Constitution has an expression such as "in the framework of principles and procedures set forth by law" (article 127/5). The Constitutional Court has answered why a law is needed on this regard: "... The reason why the Constitution oblige the principles and procedures of the authority of administrative tutelage to be prescribed by law clearly is the thought to prevent the administration from violating the autonomy of the local administrations by arbitrary interventions..."[181]

At this point, it may be argued that article 127/5 only covers administrative tutelage authority over local administrations. Other than article 127/5, there are several more articles in the Constitution which state that scrutinization of the State over some institutions will be established by law. For instance, in the article 130/9 regarding universities, it is stated that "the establishment of institution of higher education, ... the procedures to be followed by the state in the exercise of the right to supervise and inspect universities ... shall be regulated by law." Likewise, according to the article 135/5 regarding professional organizations having the characteristics of public institutions, "the rules concerning the administrative and functional supervision of these professional organizations by the state shall be prescribed by law." Other than these specific articles, the general article of Constitution on the establishment of administration (123/1) should be considered: "The administration ... shall be regulated by law."[182]

181 CC, M. 2013/19, D. 2013/100, 12.09.2013, OG 18.09.2014–29123.

182 As we have mentioned, article 123/1 constitutes an "exclusive law area" and PDs can only regulate the areas which the Constitution specifically address to be regulated by the President when administration is regulated. According to the article 106/end of the Constitution, "the ... duties and powers ... of the ministries shall be regulated by the presidential decree." Well, from this article, the question emerges whether

Within this scope, two main conclusions can be reached:

1. Administrative tutelage is an exceptional authority. If the law (code) does not prescribe administrative tutelage by the state or a public corporate body over another public corporate body, then this authority is not valid.[183]
2. Authority of administrative tutelage only includes the situations where the law explicitly grants such an authority. This authority cannot be broadened by way of interpretation.[184] For instance, if the law only states that the public corporate body possessing the authority of administrative tutelage shall "send back the act for reevaluation" of the public corporate body which is subject to administrative tutelage, the body (possessing the authority) may only send back the act, it cannot annul or correct it.[185] Briefly, administrative tutelage only exists if laid down by law and to the degree that the law lays down.

---

administrative tutelage authorities of ministries can be regulated by PDs. Since article 130/9 regarding universities, 127/5 regarding local administrations and 135/5 regarding professional organizations are more specific than article 106/end, the answer should be negative. We also believe that administrative tutelage over public corporate bodies established by laws cannot be prescribed by PDs since this would result in the alteration of the scope of the laws. See in the same direction: Yasin, "Cumhurbaşkanlığı Kararnamelerinin," 331; Çiğdem Sever, "Cumhurbaşkanının Teşkilatlanma Konusundaki Yetkileri ya da 'Panthenogenesis' Olmak [The Powers of the President on Organization or Being 'Panthenogenesis']," in *Cumhurbaşkanının İşlemleri Hukuki Niteliği, Normlar Hiyerarşisindeki Yeri ve Denetimi*, ed. Oktay Uygun and Egemen Esen (İstanbul: On İki Levha, 2019), 372; Metin Günday and Çiğdem Sever, "2017 Anayasa Değişiklikleri ve Uyumlaştırma Sürecinin İdare Hukukunda Yarattığı Etki Üzerine Bir Değerlendirme [An Evaluation Concerning the Effects of Constitutional Amendments of 2017 and Process of Harmonization on Administrative Law]," in *Prof. Dr. Nami Çağan Anısına Armağan* (Atılım Üniversitesi Yayınları no. 63, 2020), 642. Then, can PDs regulate administrative tutelage authority of ministries over public corporate bodies established by PDs? Within this scope, in doctrine Yasin states that the relationship between ministries and public corporate bodies established by PDs can be regulated by PDs. Yasin, "Cumhurbaşkanlığı Kararnamelerinin," 331.

183 See Louvaris, *Droit Administratif*, 241; Gözler, *İdare Hukuku V. I*, 274; Yıldırım, "Genel Kuramlar," 36.

184 "... It is not legally possible to broaden the limits of administrative tutelage envisaged in law by interpretation..." SC 8th C., M. 2008/4976, D. 2010/1108, 05.03.2010, www.kazanci.com.

185 "... In the paragraph (b) of the article 6/A of the Law no 3030, the duty to confirm the praxis construction plan which district municipality will prepare in accordance with master plan and to supervise the implementation is granted to metropolitan municipalities, in the article 14 of the same Act it is laid down that the decisions

Administrative tutelage can be separated into two categories as "over the persons" and "over the acts."[186] These will be examined in detail below.[187]

1.4.2.1. Over Persons

Administrative tutelage over persons may be in question in case of "provisionally removal from office."[188] The Constitution prescribed two different situations in this regard.

1.4.2.1.1. Provisionally Removal of Organs of Local Administrations from Office

In the Constitution and some laws, central administration is granted with the power of provisionally removal of the organs of the local administrations and to ask judiciary to remove those organs of the local administration from office.[189]

Within this regard, article 127/4 of the Constitution states: "Loss of status and objections regarding the acquisition of the status of elected organs of local administrations shall be decided by judiciary. However, as a provisional measure until the final court judgment, the Minister of Internal Affairs may remove from Office those organs of local administration or their members against whom an

---

taken by metropolitan and district municipality assembly will be sent to metropolitan municipality mayor, metropolitan municipality mayor can request the subject to be reevaluated in the assemblies, assemblies can only insist on their decisions with 2/3 majority, in these situations their decisions will be final.

Evaluating abovementioned provisions, it may be concluded that the construction plans consistent with master construction plan will be prepared by district municipality and will be enforced after metropolitan municipality mayor approves or if not approved, will be resent to municipality assembly to be reevaluated, these subjects are within the authority of metropolitan municipality mayor, however, she does not have the authority to approve with modification the decisions of district municipality assembly regarding the implementary development plan..." SC 6th C., M. 1998/6235, D. 1999/5470, 10.11.1999, www.kazanci.com.

186 Gözler, *İdare Hukuku V. I*, 279.

187 "... Since that the authority of administrative tutelage arise from law and is restricted with law, the power of tutelage offices are limited to what is granted to them by law with that purpose. The authority of tutelage may be over persons as well as over acts as is in sport federations..." CC, M. 2011/63, D. 2013/28, 14.02.2013, OG 31.12.2013–28868.

188 Peiser, *Droit Administratif*, 106.

189 Akyılmaz, Sezginer, and Kaya, *Türk İdare Hukuku*, 212.

investigation or prosecution has been initiated on grounds of criminal offences related to their duties."

As seen, Minister of Internal Affairs is only authorized with the provisionally removal of the organs of local administration. In addition, this authority is narrowed to the situations in which a criminal proceeding is initiated against the members of the organs of local administration in relation with their duties. Therefore, the notions of "investigation or prosecution" shall not include "administrative investigations or prosecutions."[190] In other words, provisional removable is only possible in case of a criminal investigation or prosecution is initiated.

Other than this exceptional authority, the loss of status of elected organs of local administrations shall be decided by judiciary. Therefore, it may be concluded that central administration does not possess the administrative tutelage authority in which it can directly cause the loss of status of elected organs. Central administration can only initiate judicial proceedings on this regard.[191]

1.4.2.1.2. Provisionally Removal from the Office of Responsible Organs of Professional Organizations Having the Characteristics of Public Institutions

Responsible organs of professional organizations having the characteristics of public institutions can only be removed from office with a court decision. According to the article 135/6 of the Constitution, "The responsible organs of professional organizations which engage in activities beyond their objectives shall be dissolved by court decision at the request of the authority designated by law or the public prosecutor, and new organs shall be elected in their place."

Notwithstanding that a court's decision is compulsory, article 135/end article of the Constitution provides an exception: "However, where it is required for and delay constitutes a prejudice to national security, public order, prevention of commission or continuation of a crime, or an arrest, an authority may be vested with power by law to suspend the professional organizations and their higher bodies from activity. The decision of this authority shall be submitted for the approval of the judge having jurisdiction within twenty-four hours. The judge shall announce her decision within forty-eight hours; otherwise, this administrative decision shall be void automatically."

---

190 Onur Karahanoğulları, *İdare Hukuku* [*Administrative Law*] (Ankara: Turhan, 2022), 271.

191 Akyılmaz, Sezginer, and Kaya, *Türk İdare Hukuku*, 213.

1.4.2.2. Over Acts

As we have mentioned, prescription by law is fundamental for the authority of administrative tutelage. A public corporate body—possessing the authority of administrative tutelage—may have the authority over acts of a public corporate body—that is the subject of tutelage—provided that the law explicitly grants so. The discretionary power to prescribe administrative tutelage and the degree of such authority is within the discretionary power of legislature. Therefore, the authorities within the scope of administrative tutelage cannot be counted one by one.

However, principally, tutelage office cannot give "orders and directives" to the office that is subject to tutelage.[192] Likewise, tutelage office cannot replace and give decisions on behalf of the latter.[193] However, exceptionally (for instance, when the service would be hindered) a provision that is contradictory to this may be prescribed by law.[194] If prescribed by law, prohibition of replacement will not be valid in case of administrative tutelage unlike hierarchy. For instance, Construction Law grants the ministry with the authority to replace and give a decision on municipality's behalf.[195]

The laws may prescribe administrative tutelage authority such as authority to approve, to annul, to postpone, to request reevaluation and to bring action before administrative courts.

1.4.2.2.1. Authority to Approve

Approval may be about the acts which are taken, but have not been enforced yet.[196] Therefore, if law explicitly lays down that tutelage office can approve the act of office that is subject to tutelage, the act shall not be enforced and implemented

---

192 Gözler, *İdare Hukuku V. I*, 294.

193 Gözler, *İdare Hukuku V. I*, 296.

194 Onar, *İdare Hukukunun Umumi Esasları V. II*, 628; Ender Ethem Atay, *İdare Hukuku* [*Administrative Law*] (Ankara: Turhan, 2022), 162.

195 Yayla, *İdare Hukuku*, 379. Article 9/3 of Construction Law is as follows: "Where it is necessary to reserve space for public buildings and facilities or make amendments for this purpose in the construction plans for the purpose of a public service to be carried out, the Ministry may instruct the relevant municipality accordingly through the governorship or shall make and approve ex officio the part of the construction plan relating to public buildings and facilities."

196 Gözler, *İdare Hukuku V. I*, 283.

unless tutelage office approves. In other words, the act shall not be executable unless it is approved.

1.4.2.2.2. Authority to Annul

If law grants the authority to annul explicitly, tutelage office may annul the act of office that is subject to tutelage.

1.4.2.2.3. Authority to Postpone

When authority to postpone is in case, the decision of tutelage office to postpone the act removes the executability of the act of the office that is subject to tutelage.

1.4.2.2.4. Authority to Request for Reevaluation

Within the scope of the authority to request for reevaluation, tutelage office may resend the act of office that is subject to tutelage for it to be reevaluated. However, if the office that is subject to tutelage insists on its act, then the act will be enforceable.

1.4.2.2.5. Authority to Bring Action Before Administrative Courts

The tutelage office may bring an action against the act in administrative courts. This authority may also be considered within the authority of administrative tutelage.

However, in several decisions, Constitutional Court ruled that bringing an action against the decision of a public corporate body by state or another public corporate body does not amount to usage of authority of administrative tutelage.[197] In these decisions, the Constitutional Court seemed to be of the view that such an authority is too weak to be within the authority of tutelage. As a consequence of these decisions, the central administration could bring an action against the acts of decentral administration only if the general condition of interest (to file a suit before administrative courts) envisaged in Procedure of Administrative Justice Act was satisfied.

---

197 "…the rule laid down … as 'local authority can apply to administrative judiciary against the decisions which she evaluates as inconsistent with law.' does not involve the authority of tutelage which should be used by central administration within the framework of the article 127 of the Constitution." CC, M. 2008/28, D. 2010/30, 04.02.2010, OG 21.06.2010–26719. See in the same direction: CC, M. 2008/27, D. 2010/29, 04.02.2010, OG 21.06.2010–27619; CC, M. 2005/32, D. 2007/3, 18.01.2007, OG 29.12.2007–26741.

After these decisions, Constitutional Court abandoned its case law. In its decision dated 2011, the Court noted that since administrative tutelage is not a "duty" but an "authority," it does not include an absolute obligation to use such an authority. Basing on this reasoning, the Court evaluated that "...to designate the method and intensity of administrative tutelage is within the discretion of the legislature. While this authority may be used by tutelage offices in the way of annulment, approval, postponing, allowance, asking for reevaluation, correction, it may also use it by bringing an action before administrative courts."[198]

As a conclusion, it is understood that Turkish Republic Administration consists of public corporate bodies which are interconnected. Below, there is a chart explaining the Turkish Republic Administration from the perspective of "community-" and "service-"oriented public corporate bodies.

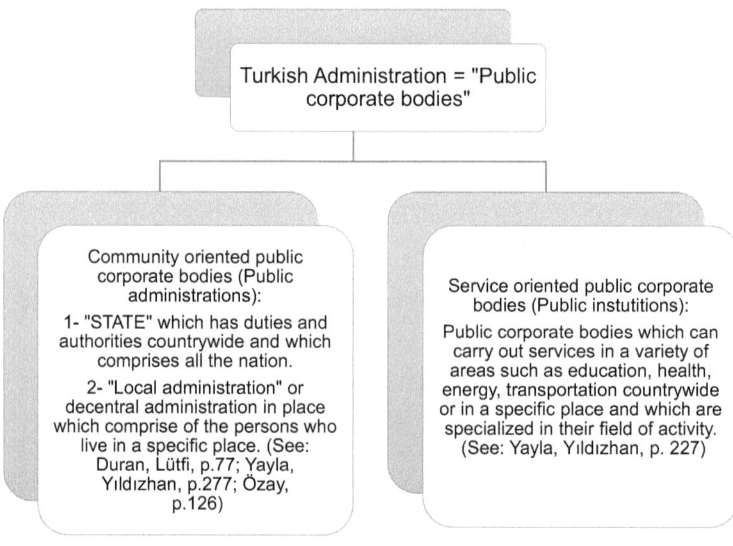

Figure 3: Types of Public Corporate Bodies

198 CC, M. 2011/11, D. 2011/151, 03.11.2011, OG 07.02.2012-28197.

1.4.3. A Different Organization from the Perspective of Integrity of Administration: Regulatory and Supervisory Institutions (Independent Regulatory Authorities)

Regulatory and supervisory institutions are public corporate bodies which carry out the activity of regulation and supervision of the services rather than carrying out the services itself in important areas such as banking, capital markets, energy and so forth.[199] We think that these institutions are better to be named as "regulatory and supervisory institutions" which are also mentioned as "independent regulatory authorities"[200] in the doctrine[201] for the reasons that

- These institutions are referred as "regulatory authority," "authority" or "board" in the relevant laws and decisions of the judiciary and their activities are ruled as regulation and supervision.[202]
- It is hard to allege that these institutions are completely "independent."

One of the primary reasons of the emergence of these institutions is "insecurities toward politicians."[203] The need to keep political interventions out in some of the sensitive and technical areas has emerged in history.[204] For instance, at the end of allegations and concerns regarding politicians siphoning off bank accounts, the need for "Banking Regulation and Supervision Agency" has emerged.

---

199 Ali Ulusoy, "Regülasyon Kurumları Hakkında," 139. The author has preferred the expression of "sensitive sectors." In the base of being important or sensitive, the close relationship between fundamental rights and freedoms and institutions carrying out activities in this area lies as also indicated by Ulusoy.

200 See Louvaris, *Droit Administratif*, 41 ff.

201 Main regulatory and supervisory institutions in Turkey are as follows:
1. Competition Authority
2. Energy Market Regulatory Authority
3. Capital Markets Board
4. Radio and Television Supreme Council
5. Public Procurement Authority
6. Banking Regulation and Supervision Agency
7. Information and Communication Technologies Authority

202 Ender Ethem Atay, "Bağımsız Idarî Otorîteler ve Türkîye Uygulaması [Independent Regulatory Authorities and Turkish Practice]," *Gazi University Law Faculty Journal* 10, no. 1, 2 (2006): 272, https://dergipark.org.tr/tr/download/article-file/789830.

203 Ulusoy, "Regülasyon Kurumları Hakkında," 139.

204 Ulusoy, "Regülasyon Kurumları Hakkında," 139; Atay, *Bağımsız Idarî Otoriteler*, 261.

Secondly, judiciary has not been able to carry out the expected functions. Within this scope, it should be noted that judiciary's examinations are *a posteriori* and are limited with concrete cases, the decisions may retard, and judges do not possess the technical information and specialization.

Lastly, specialization is needed[205] in new and important services in which technical expertise and specialization outweigh, also in the fields such as energy and economy, which traditional administrative structure may have difficulties in controlling.

It would also not be wrong to state that economic crisis has also played a part on the emergence of these institutions. These institutions emerged in the USA after the economic crisis of 1930. Likewise, in Europe, economic collapse after the Second World War has created these institutions.

1.4.3.1. Organic Features of Regulatory and Supervisory Institutions

Regulatory and supervisory institutions are laid down to be "administratively and financially autonomous" in their laws. For instance, article 20 of Act on the Protection of Competition is as follows: "The Competition Authority having a public legal personality, and an administrative and financial autonomy is established in order to ensure the formation and development of markets for goods and services in a free and sound competitive environment, to observe the implementation of this Act, and to fulfill the duties assigned to it by the Act."

Regulatory and supervisory institutions are administratively autonomous since they have separate legal personality, in other words they are not within the state public corporate body. In addition, they are also autonomous financially, meaning that they have separate budgets and assets.[206] The reason why these institutions are required to be autonomous is because the independency of these institutions is required from the functional perspective.

What is autonomy? This notion refers "to be governed by its own decision-making body" and "not to be dependent when making decisions." According to Constitutional Court, autonomy means "the freedom and authority of a social community or legal personality to designate the rules governing themselves in whole or in part or to act within the boundaries set by constitution or law."[207]

As seen, the mechanism which provides specific sectors to be out of political pressure (which also constitutes the emergence of these institutions) is

---

205 Ulusoy, "Regülasyon Kurumları Hakkında," 140.
206 Akyılmaz, Sezginer, and Kaya, *Türk İdare Hukuku*, 327.
207 CC, M. 1987/19, D. 1987/31, 24.11.1987, OG 29.03.1988–19769.

autonomy. Autonomy is also the most important factor sought by foreign investors to invest in a country.

Within the scope of "autonomy," an important issue is the relationship between ministries and regulatory and supervisory institutions. In the related laws of regulatory and supervisory institutions, the expression of "related ministry" is used. In other words, these institutions are being related to a ministry.[208] At the first sight, this term may be seen contrary to the feature of "independency."

The meaning of the term "related" has been a subject of discussion and following questions have emerged: Is administrative tutelage envisaged? Or is this term used to designate the ministries whose area of duty is related? In relevant laws, ministries are not authorized regarding the acts of regulatory and supervisory institutions. Pursuant to the principle of legal administration, the authority should be granted by law. Since administrative tutelage is only possible where law designates, it is not possible to accept that there is an authority of tutelage. Since regulatory and supervisory institutions have distinct personalities than the state, hierarchy is also not possible.

Then, does the term "related" reference a cooperation between regulatory and supervisory institutions and ministries? An affirmative answer to this question also seems not to be possible since the members of some regulatory and supervisory institutions are assigned by central administration and central administration have authority on their salaries.

As a conclusion, the term "related" clearly does not reference to administrative tutelage or hierarchy. However, it is also hard to allege that the term references to coordination rather than a supervisory relationship.

Maybe, to extinguish the contradiction between the principle of integrity of administration[209] and independent features of regulatory and supervisory institutions, a formula is tried to be invented by using the term "related" rather than a term "attached." In other words, it may be concluded that to sustain the understanding of "impossibility of independency" which is required by the principle of integrity of administration, a substantially limited supervision authority is envisaged.[210]

208 Gözler, *İdare Hukuku V. I*, 380.

209 Akyılmaz, Sezginer and Kaya state that since these authorities are established as being "related" to a ministry and since judicial review is possible on their acts, the principle of integrity of administration is not distorted. Akyılmaz, Sezginer, and Kaya, *Türk İdare Hukuku*, 327.

210 Yayla, *İdare Hukuku*, 268; Ulusoy, "Regülasyon Kurumları Hakkında," 143; Atay, "Bağımsız İdari Otoriteler," 282.

Constitutional Court has ruled that Radio and Television Supreme Council which is a regulatory and supervisory authority cannot be considered wholly separate from administration even though it possesses an autonomous and impartial personality, on the basis of principle of administrative integrity.

Therefore, it may be concluded that regulatory and supervisory institutions cannot be considered as wholly independent. Secondly, regulatory and supervisory institutions may also be affected from private law persons operating in the sectors which are regulated by these institutions. Maybe, to avoid this situation, a supervision authority is granted to some extent. Also, ministries have duties to designate the policy and strategies regarding the sectors. This fact requires a relationship and an authority to supervise between ministries and regulatory and supervisory institutions.

The fact that administrative tutelage is not envisaged over regulatory and supervisory institutions should not mean that these institutions will never be subject to such relationship. It is always possible to grant an authority of tutelage by law.

Lastly, there is no guarantee that powers of these institutions will remain. For instance, after the "banker" incidents, the old Capital Markets Board was closed by a law and its powers were delegated to finance ministry. Therefore, an autonomy granted by law is not adequately secure. In order for it to be secured, autonomy should be granted by the Constitution.

1.4.3.2. Supervision of Regulatory and Supervisory Institutions

We have indicated that hierarchy and administrative tutelage is not valid over regulatory and supervisory institutions. The fact that central administration does not possess such an authority does not mean that regulatory and supervisory institutions are exempt from any audit. These institutions are subject to the audit of legislature and judiciary.

1.4.3.2.1. Administrative and Financial Supervision

Pursuant to article 160 of Constitution, "revenues, expenditures and assets of public administrations financed by central government budget" are subject to the Supervision of Turkish Court of Accounts on behalf of TBMM. The budget of the regulatory and supervisory institutions are within central government budget pursuant to Law no. 5018, therefore these institutions are subject to audit of the Turkish Court of Accounts.

In history, a law was in force which disabled audit by the Court of Accounts over regulatory and supervisory institutions. However, Constitutional Court annulled this law. High Court has indicated that principally all the public institutions should be audited by legislature. According to the High Court, regulatory and supervisory institutions cannot be exempted from such an audit.

1.4.3.2.2. Supervision of Judiciary

Acts of regulatory and supervisory institutions are subject to judicial review since these acts are administrative in nature. It is important to note that since hierarchy and tutelage are not envisaged for these institutions, the fundamental supervision is achieved through judicial review of the acts of these institutions.

1.4.3.3. Functional Features of Regulatory and Supervisory Institutions

The feature of regulatory and supervisory institutions differentiating them from other administrative institutions are their functional features. Regulatory and supervisory institutions carry out an activity called "regulation."[211] Within this activity, the authorities similar to the functions of legislature, executive and judiciary are eminent.

Regulation refers to the authorities of laying down rules, monitoring and supervision, implementing sanctions, consultancy and dispute resolution.[212]

1.4.3.3.1. Laying Down Rules

Regulatory and supervisory institutions may lay down abstract rules basing on a law in condition that these are not contrary to laws and the Constitution. This authority of regulatory and supervisory institutions stand out within the scope of *ex ante* supervision such as designating the qualifications of the undertakings which will enter the market, other conditions of entering into the market, designating the principles regarding the activities in the market and so forth.

Pursuant to article 124 of the Constitution, public corporate bodies are authorized to issue bylaws. From this point of view, it is hard to allege that regulatory and supervisory institutions are privileged or different.

---

211 See Louvaris, *Droit Administratif*, 173–175; Ulusoy, "Regülasyon Kurumları Hakkında," 140. Ulusoy states that regulation may be defined as "laying down the rules of the game" (regulation) and "securing that these rules are obeyed" (supervision).

212 We have used the word regulation throughout the book to refer "laying down rules." Here, we use this term to refer the functional features of regulatory and supervisory institutions.

1.4.3.3.2. Monitoring and Supervision

Regulatory and supervisory institutions are authorized to request information and documentation, to conduct on the spot inspection, to investigate or to initiate judiciary examination (and so forth) in order to fulfill their duty. The authority of monitoring and supervision are carried out on an ongoing basis.

1.4.3.3.3. Implementing Sanctions

Regulatory and supervisory institutions are authorized to impose penalties on related persons when they detect inconsistency with the law after they monitor and supervise. Sanctions imposed are mostly administrative fines. However, other sanctions such as suspension of the activities or cancellation of license may also be in question.

European Court of Human Rights examines the fines of regulatory and supervisory institutions within the scope of right to a fair trial. For instance, the Court has ruled that right to a fair trial is violated since a person is both a member of the board of a regulatory and supervisory institution which imposed the sanction and had duties during the investigation procedure. State Council too has ruled that the member of Competition Board (which is a regulatory and supervisory institution) being investigator at the same time is contrary to the principle of impartiality.[213]

1.4.3.3.4. Consultancy, Guidance and Delivering Opinion

(a) *Guidance:* Regulatory and supervisory institutions may guide undertakings in a market to act in a specific way rather than imposing fines.
(b) *Consultancy:* Regulatory and supervisory institutions have the duty and authority to give information regarding the market at the request of state organs.
(c) *Delivering Opinion:* Regulatory and supervisory institutions may deliver opinion *ex officio* on the activities in the market as well as at request.

1.4.3.3.5. Dispute Resolution

Since that the sectors which regulatory and supervisory institutions carry out their activities require technical information and specialization and resolving disputes take a long time in courts, regulatory and supervisory institutions are authorized to resolve some disputes. However, it not possible to indicate that this

---

213 SC 13th C., M. 2006/3783, D. 2007/1439, 19.03.2007, www.rekabet.gov.tr.

authority involves resolving disputes like a "final" decision within the scope of our legal system. Even though related laws of regulatory and supervisory institutions involve expressions such as "it resolves disputes," the authority to resolve disputes wholly and finally cannot be in question, since that the same laws involve provisions indicating that recourse to judicial review is available for all acts of such institutions. A contrary approach would be inconsistent with the Constitution since judicial power can only be exercised by independent courts.

1.4.3.4. Constitutional Position of Regulatory and Supervisory Institutions

It is clear that regulatory and supervisory institutions are public corporate bodies with specific features. Then, how can we locate them in Turkish administrative structure?

First, accounting these institutions as the fourth power is not possible. The Constitution only accepts three powers: Legislature, executive and judiciary.

Since these institutions possess separate public personality, we cannot locate them in central administration.

Then, can we accept them to be one of decentral administrations? As mentioned before, decentral administrations are separated into "local administrations" and "decentral administrations in service" (public institutions). Local administrations are designated in the Constitution in a limited manner. These are special provincial administrations, municipal districts and villages. The Constitution did not allow for other local administrations to be established. Therefore, regulatory and supervisory institutions cannot be located within local administrations. In this situation, regulatory and supervisory institutions are needed to be located in decentral administration (public institution) in service.[214]

On the other hand, as Atay indicates, since that regulatory and supervisory institutions do not perform a deed or provide a good or service, it may be thought that these institutions may be distinct from public institutions.[215]

---

214 For a similar approach see, Günday, *İdare Hukuku*, 575.
215 Atay, *İdare Hukuku*, 382–383.

2. Public Employees

Administration is in need of organization, personnel and assets in order to carry out the activities of public service and policing. Then, what does personnel mean from the perspective of administrative law?

There is not any direct definition of public servant or administrative personnel in the Constitution. However, article 128/1 of the Constitution provides that persons carrying out certain activities are public employees: "The fundamental and permanent functions required by the public services that the State, state economic enterprises and other public corporate bodies assigned to perform in accordance with principles of general administration, shall be carried out by public servants and other public employees."

Considering this article, the following conclusions may be reached: First, since the sentence includes the expression of "other public corporate bodies," the state is also a public corporate body. Therefore, this part of the sentence may be shortened by indicating solely "public corporate bodies." Likewise, from the expression of "public servants and other public employees," it may be concluded that public servants are also public employees. Therefore, indication of "public employees" may be sufficient.

In brief, it may be interpreted from the Constitutional provision that public employees are persons who carry out activities of a public corporate body. That is to say, public employees work under[216] public corporate bodies.

In the Constitution, it is also indicated that public employees carry out public services "in accordance with the principles of general administration." "The principles of general administration" are not defined in the Constitution or in the laws. Furthermore, there is no consensus regarding the definition. However, the same expression was also included in the Constitution dated 1961. In the Constitutional Draft designed back then, the expression of "private administrative procedures" which was the opposite of the principles of general administration

216 "… Fundamental and permanent functions are functions which are carried out by using public force in accordance with principles of general administration. Public employees are public servants and other public employees who work under administration with a public law relationship on the fundamental and permanent functions required by public service, who are assigned post, who are paid from the budget and on whom private rules designated by laws are implemented…" SC 1st C., M. 2000/29, D. 2000/59, 14.7.2000 (advisory opinion), www.kazanci.com.

was included.[217] Later on, this expression was removed from the draft and only "the principles of general administration" remained. Special administration procedure refers to the situations where administration acts pursuant to private business procedure (which means administration acts according to private law). Therefore, the principle of general administration refers to the situations where administration uses public force and where it does not act like a private law person.[218]

Constitutional Court also has highlighted that the principle of general administration is "usage of public force and authority to dictate which the state possesses."[219]

Briefly, the principle of general administration is the contrary business model or governance in the field (which is subject to private law) where the state's authority to dictate is not used in the communal living. In other words, the principle refers to the service carried out by using "public force" and by "public procedures."

In addition to the principle of general administration, in the Constitution, it is indicated that "fundamental and permanent" functions are needed to be carried out by public employees. Then, what are "fundamental and permanent" functions that are required by public service?

Being fundamental refers to the functions which are indispensable in order to conclude that public service is carried out properly.[220]

Permanency should be understood as the functions which are to be carried out in a minimal way for the beneficiaries as long as the need arises in order for the existence of that service. In other words, persons making temporal activities which are not essential for the service, and which are subsidiary to that service are not public employees.

---

217 Yayla, *İdare Hukuku*, 271–272; Mehmet Ruaf Karslı, *İdare Hukukunda Kamu Görevlisi Kavramı* [*The Notion of Public Employee in Administrative Law*] (İstanbul: On İki Levha, 2016), 21.

218 Nur Kaman, "Kamu Görevlileri [Public Employees]," in *İdare Hukuku*, ed. Turan Yıldırım (İstanbul: On İki Levha, 2022), 262–263. Akyılmaz, Sezginer and Kaya state that the principles of general administration should be understood as "public law regime" and "public management procedures." The authors add that public law regime and public management procedures necessitate the usage of public force and the notion of "principles of general administration" is the contrary of the notion of "private business principles." Akyılmaz, Sezginer, and Kaya, *Türk İdare Hukuku*, 682.

219 CC, M. 2015/72, D. 2016/44, 26.05.2016, OG 21.09.2016–29834.

220 Mehmet Rauf Karslı, *İdare Hukukunda Kamu Görevlisi*, 39.

In brief, these functions are essential functions for the existence of a public service. For instance, fundamental and permanent functions of education as a public service are lecturing, conducting exams and so forth. If those functions do not exist, we cannot state that education as a public service is valid. According to the Constitution, such functions should be carried out by public employees. Subsidiary functions to education service (cleaning the class, delivering lunch, building a new library and so forth) are not needed to be carried out by public employees.

On the other hand, elected persons and persons who carry out activities as a right and obligation are also public employees. Mayor, municipality councilor, village leader (headman) may be given as examples for persons who are elected for the duty. Soldiers that are called to arms obligatorily and temporarily for the national service may be given as an example for the latter.[221]

In a decision the Constitutional Court applied fundamentality and permanency criteria as follows: "… The function of the contract employee who is envisaged to be employed by the rules that is subject to this case is preparation, realization and implementation of the important projects which are included in the strategical plan and performance programs of Revenue Administration. The term of service of the contract employee is restricted to the term of the project and she is envisaged to be employed temporarily. Accordingly, since that the duty of the contract employee is not required to be carried out pursuant to the principles of general administration and is not in a permanent characteristic, although the duty mentioned is a public service, it cannot be counted as a fundamental and permanent function provisioned in the Article 128 of the Constitution."[222]

The term "working under" in the Constitution (article 128/1) refers to working permanently in a particular duration which would not be seen as temporal. The bound between this person and administration may be constructed by a contract or an administrative act (such as assignment). What is important here is that the bound should be subject to public law.

If this bound is constructed by assignment (an administrative act), there is no need for further investigation on whether this bound is subject to public law. However, if the bound between employee and administration is a contract, it is compulsory to assess the contract to reach a conclusion. If this contract grants administration with superior rights and authorities—if the parties are not equal compared to a private law contract—then an administrative contract is in

---

221 Yayla, *İdare Hukuku*, 275.

222 CC, M. 2010/93, D. 2012/20, 09.02.2012, OG 26.07.2013–28719.

question.[223] In this case, the person who is employed by a contract is a public employee. If this contract constitutes a private law contract—if the administration is not superior and has acted like a private law person—then the contract employee is not a public employee. At this point, note that public corporate bodies can both enforce an act by using public force and make private law acts.[224] A public corporate body may as well get into a labor law contract (private law contract) just like a joint stock company. In this case, the employee will be a laborer and will not be counted as public employee.

For instance, if a lawyer works independently, she is not a public employee. If a lawyer has an attorney contract with a public corporate body and represents it in a single suit, she is not a public employee. This is because the function is not fundamental and permanent and attorney contract is a private law contract. If a lawyer is employed in the office of legal affairs of a public corporate body which is envisaged in a law (in other words she is employed via assignment) and represents the body in all the lawsuits or an administrative contract is valid between her and administration (fundamental and permanent), she may be counted as a public employee.[225]

In this title, we will firstly detail fundamental principles regarding the subject of public employees. Secondly, we will explain the disciplinary regime of public employees, more specifically dealing with the principles, procedures and penalties. Lastly, we will touch upon the safeguards provided to public employees in case of criminal and legal actions.

---

223 In some of the decisions of the administrative judiciary, it is also mentioned where a person is put into a status. If the person possesses a status which has been priorly designated by a law or other administrative regulations via a contract and if the rules regarding the status will be implemented to that person beginning from the execution of the contract, then an administrative contract is in question. For instance, MHAC has qualified "specialized sergeant agreement" as follows: "… The "specialized sergeant agreement" between the claimant and defendant administration is an administrative agreement which is entered into pursuant to the provisions of Law on Specialized Sergeant dated 18.03.1986 and numbered 3269 and By-Law on Specialized Sergeant which has been issued based on this Law. The claimant has entered into a status which has been priorly designated with this law and by-law by signing this agreement…" MHAC, 1st C., M. 2005/319, D. 2005/1064, 18.10.2005, www.kazanci.com.

224 Sarıca, *İdari Kaza*, 5.

225 Yayla, *İdare Hukuku*, 275.

2.1. Fundamental Principles Regarding Public Employees

There are several principles governing the subject of public employees. Under this title, we will examine "principle of freeness," "principle of equality" and "principles of career and qualification" which govern public employees.

2.1.1. Principle of Freeness

Pursuant to article 70/1 of the Constitution, "Every Turk has the right to enter public service." The Constitution has defined "Türk" as "everyone bound to the Turkish State through the bond of citizenship" (article 66/1). Within this scope, fundamental principle arises as "principle of freeness"[226] since "having right to enter" means that being a public employee is based on demand.

Since it is laid down as a right, not entering into or quitting from public service is also possible. In other words, "forced labor" is not possible. Pursuant to article 18/1 of the Constitution forced labor is prohibited. At this point, "forced labor" and "compulsory labor" should be distinguished. According to the Constitution and laws regarding state of emergency, compulsory labor is envisaged in times of war, natural disaster, epidemic and such state of emergency times. However, in this case, compensation to labor will be provided. In such emergency times, rules such as differentiation on labor conditions compared to regular times or prohibition on resignation for a specific term are laid down.

2.1.2. Principle of Equality

Principle of equality refers to equality when entering public service. However, "everyone" is not equal. Equality is between citizens who are qualified for the service. Therefore, persons who are citizens and qualified for the service cannot be discriminated when they desire to be a part of public service.

It should be noted that being a citizen is not an absolute condition to be a public employee. It may be possible for noncitizens to enter into public service if prescribed by a law. In the past, a law permitting immigrants coming from Bulgaria to be public employees was enforced.[227]

Regarding the second condition, the important issue is that required qualifications may vary depending on the type of public service.[228] For instance, some physical requirements may be sought for police personnel.

---

226 Yayla, *İdare Hukuku*, 275.

227 Yayla, *İdare Hukuku*, 278.

228 Yayla, *İdare Hukuku*, 278–279.

2.1.3. Principle of Career and Qualification

Principle of career refers to carrying out a duty as an "occupation" and proceeding in this occupation. In other words, public employees shall carry out their duties as an "occupation" and furthermore some of these employees shall not carry out another activity which brings revenue. At the same time, regulations regarding public employee to carry out its occupation in a better way (inner service education, sending abroad) and advancement in the duty shall be laid down.[229]

According to State Council, at the base of principle of qualification, "giving duty to its expert within the framework of objective rules and the notion of deserving" lies.[230] Truly, entering public service and advancing should only be possible for the expert of this service. Otherwise, public service will not be carried out as it should be and sometimes the service will be carried out defectively. For instance, if the person who will be employed as a driver is not chosen between experts of this duty, accidents arising from the deficiencies of the driver would be inevitable. In this case, "fault" regarding the public service of transportation will be in question.

2.2. Disciplinary Regime of Public Employees

Another important issue regarding public employees is their disciplinary regime. Faulty acts or actions of public employees regarding their duties compromise disciplinary sanctions. Counting some acts or actions of public employees as disciplinary sanctions and penalizing these employees provide public services to be carried out as they should be.[231]

It should be indicated that administration cannot restrict liberty and security of persons via disciplinary measures. As a matter of fact, pursuant to article 38/11 of the Constitution, administration cannot restrict liberty and security of persons in general. A contrary approach will be inconsistent with the principle of constitutional state. On the other hand, in the same provision, it is laid down that

---

229 Yayla, *İdare Hukuku*, 282; Kaman, "Kamu Görevlileri," 278.

230 Kaman, "Kamu Görevlileri," 279. Also see SC 2nd C., M. 2014/1289, D. SE 17.06.2014, www.kazanci.com.

231 Ender Ethem Atay, "Müfettişlerin Hazırladıkları Disiplin Soruşturma Raporlarından Dolayı Sorumlu Tutulabilirliği Sorunu [The Issue of Holding The Inspectors Accountable For Disciplinary Proceedings Reports Prepared By Them]," *Court of Jurisdictional Disputes Journal*, no. 7 (2016): 168. https://dergipark.org.tr/tr/pub/mdergi/issue/24952/263382.

"Exceptions to this provision may be introduced by law regarding the internal order of the armed forces."[232]

Regarding the principles governing disciplinary regime of public employees, similar principles are valid between disciplinary law and criminal law. However, some features of disciplinary law differ from criminal law:

1. In disciplinary law, principle of legality is valid on "penalties": It is obligatory to prescribe disciplinary penalties which will be imposed to public employees priorly by law. In our legal system, disciplinary penalties are laid down in laws regarding the disciplinary regime of public employees.
2. The principle of "non bis in idem" is valid in disciplinary law[233]: More than one disciplinary penalty cannot be imposed to public employees for one wrongful action.
3. "Principle of individual criminal responsibility" is valid in disciplinary law.[234]
4. Principle of legality is not valid on crimes in disciplinary law: In disciplinary law, principle of legality is not valid on crimes unlike criminal law.[235] Usually, in the statutes, expressions like "and similar actions" are laid down after several disciplinary crimes are defined.[236] In other words,

---

232 Constitutional Court has annulled a related provision within the scope of the principle of constitutional state: "… Even though with the rule that is subject to the claim, sui generis controlling mechanism is laid down in order to safeguard discipline, the fact that there is not any provision which lays down on how long the superior and chief may detain the person who violated discipline emerges the danger of persons being deprived of their liberties in an unlimited period of time. Even though with the article 38/11 of the Constitution, the possibility to introduce provisions which may restrict liberty of persons by law regarding the internal order of armed forces where necessary, it is obvious that the rule which is subject to the claim and which grants broad authority to administration is not predictable in terms of period and does not safeguard persons against the arbitrary practices and interpretations of administration. Within this scope, the rule is contrary to the principle of legal certainty which is a sub-element of the principle of rule of law. For the reasons explained above, the rule that is subject to claim is contrary to article 2 of the Constitution…" CC, M. 2012/1, D. 2012/147, 11.10.2012, OG 22.11.2013–28829.

233 Atay, *İdare Hukuku*, 874.

234 Atay, *İdare Hukuku*, 870.

235 Atay, *İdare Hukuku*, 868.

236 Article 125 of Law on Public Servants may be given as an example: "Persons who take actions similar to the actions and situations mentioned above which requires disciplinary penalties to be imposed on the basis of qualification and severity shall be subject

prohibition on comparison is not valid in disciplinary law unlike criminal law.[237]

State Council Plenary Session of Administrative Law Chambers is of the view that "in case that a subsequent law laying down a more favorable provision compared to prior law which was in effect when the action is taken, the favorable provision should be implemented."[238] As seen, the principle of implementation of favorable law is valid in disciplinary law.

The procedure of imposing disciplinary measures is also important to satisfy the needs of a constitutional state. Below, there is a simple chart regarding the procedures of imposing disciplinary penalties:

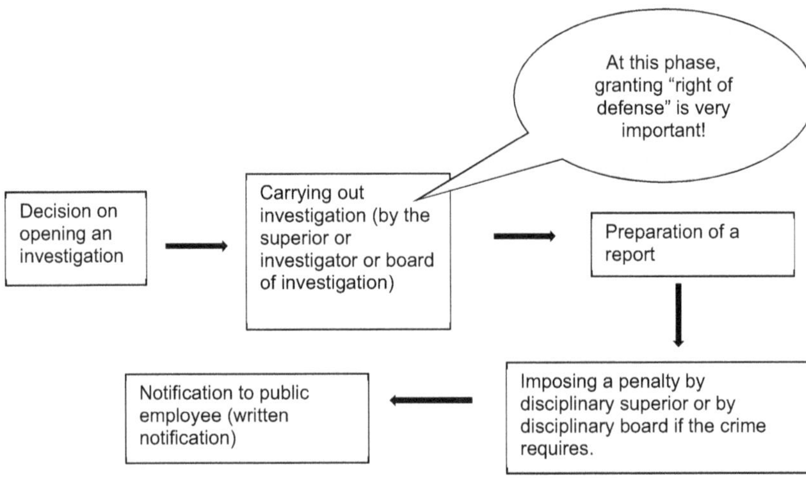

Figure 4: Procedures of Disciplinary Penalties

It is important that unless right of defense is granted to public employees, disciplinary penalty cannot be imposed according to the Constitution (article 129/2). Otherwise, administrative judiciary will annul the decision regarding the

to similar penalty." As seen, administration shall impose penalties envisaged in law to public employees who take similar actions to those laid down in the law.

237 Atay, *İdare Hukuku*, 868.

238 SCPSCAC, M. 2015/4973, D. 2017/1715, 20.04.2017, www.kazanci.com.

disciplinary penalty. This is because, nonobedience to right to defense constitutes inconsistency with law regarding the procedure element of administrative act.[239]

What are disciplinary penalties? An absolute answer which compromises all the public employees is not possible to give since there is a variety of laws regarding public employees in our legal system. For instance, "judges and prosecutors," "personnel of armed forces," "university lecturers" and so forth are subject to different laws and different penalties are envisaged in such laws.

However, examples may be given from Law on Public Servants numbered 657 which has the broadest implementation area. The penalties envisaged in this Law are as follows from the lightest to the heaviest: warning, denouncement, salary cut, halt of promotional course and expulsion from public service. It should be once again indicated that in other laws different penalties may have been envisaged.

Two remedies are possible against disciplinary penalties:

- Administrative remedy: Public employees may apply to related administrative offices or boards within the period which the law prescribes against the penalty imposed to her and demand the penalty to be reduced or extinguished. In this case, public employee applies to administration, not to judiciary. At the end of this application, if conditions are fulfilled, the penalty may be extinguished or reduced; however, a heavier penalty cannot be imposed.
- Judicial remedy: According to the article 129/3 of the Constitution, "Disciplinary decisions shall not be exempt from judicial review." Accordingly, the public employee who is imposed with a disciplinary penalty may apply to administrative judiciary and demand the annulment of the penalty and/or demand for compensation if she is damaged because of the penalty. In this case, it is accepted that at the end of this examination judiciary cannot decide on imposing a heavier penalty.[240]

It is important to note that disciplinary investigation and criminal prosecution are not connected to each other: According to this rule, if the action taken requires both criminal prosecution and disciplinary investigation at the same time, these two procedures do not affect each other and should be carried out independently.[241] Principally, results of these investigations are independent from

239 Atay, *İdare Hukuku*, 874.
240 Atay, *İdare Hukuku*, 874–875.
241 Akyılmaz, Sezginer, and Kaya, *Türk İdare Hukuku*, 723.

each other. That is to say, a public employee may be imposed disciplinary penalty even though she is acquitted of the crime at the end of the criminal proceedings because of lack of evidence.

For instance, both criminal prosecution and administrative investigation may be initiated against a public employee who is employed in a girl's dormitory as a suspect of indecent assault. Even though this public employee acquits due to lack of evidence in the criminal procedure, administration may expel this employee as a consequence of an administrative penalty.

As a second example, in a case that was subject to a dispute, criminal suit was initiated against a public employee with the reasoning that this person peculated. At the end of a disciplinary investigation, penalty of removal from office was imposed for the same action against this public employee. However, at the end of criminal prosecution, acquittal was granted due to lack of evidence. Thereupon, the person applied to administration to return to duty; however, administration rejected this application. The dispute was brought before the State Council. The High Court reached the conclusion that the act of rejection by the administration was lawful.[242]

Likewise, in case that the public employee who is sentenced at the end of a criminal prosecution and is pardoned or general amnesty is issued, disciplinary penalty is not affected from this. For instance, suppose that a public employee is both sentenced in criminal judiciary and is imposed an administrative penalty of expulsion from public office. If the criminal sentence is ceased due to general pardon, this situation does not affect the disciplinary penalty of expulsion.[243]

The only exception to this rule arises in case that a material fact is reached regarding the public employee not committing the crime (like reaching to a conclusion that the crime is committed by another person) at the end of criminal proceedings.[244] In this case, disciplinary penalty will also be ceased which was imposed for the same action. The practical consequence of this rule should be as follows: When a suit is brought before administrative judiciary against a disciplinary penalty, administrative judiciary should wait for the decision which will be issued at the end of the criminal procedure, if criminal suit is brought forward for the same action too. This is because, it may be proved that the public employee did not commit such a crime at the end of criminal procedure. A Decision of State Council is also in the same direction.[245]

---

242 SC, 12th C., M. 1995/7836, D. 1997/846, 08.04.1997, www.kazanci.com.

243 Atay, *İdare Hukuku*, 869.

244 Atay, *İdare Hukuku*, 871; Akyılmaz, Sezginer, and Kaya, *Türk İdare Hukuku*, 724.

245 SC 8th C., M. 2009/6676, D. 2010/3100, 31.05.2010, www.kazanci.com.

2.3. Legal and criminal liability of public employees: "criminal and legal protection"

Public employees are secured during their duties. This security involves "criminal prosecution" and "civil proceedings." Pursuant to the article 129 of the Constitution: "(1) Compensation suits concerning damages arising from faults committed by public servants and other public officials in the exercise of their duties shall be filed only against the administration in accordance with the procedure and conditions prescribed by law, as long as the compensation is recoursed to them. (2) Prosecution of public servants and other public officials for alleged offences shall be subject, except in cases prescribed by law, to the permission of the administrative authority designated by law."

Within this scope, we will examine the safeguard provided to public employees against criminal prosecution and compensatory safeguard before administrative courts.

2.3.1. Safeguard Regarding Criminal Prosecution

Safeguard regarding criminal prosecution has emerged from the idea that if public employees are under the pressure of being subject to trial during the course of their duties, the duty may be affected negatively from this threat.[246] Truly, it may be thought that it is hard for a public employee to carry out duty thinking all the time that an action may be brought against her.

Pursuant to the Constitution, to prosecute a public employee, permission must be obtained from administration. In addition to this rule, in the Law on Public Servants, the condition of crime being related to the duty or committed during fulfillment of the duty is sought. In other words, in case that the public servant commits an offense unrelated to her capacity as a public servant, a permission for prosecution is not sought.[247] Therefore, if the crime is not related to the duty or is not committed during fulfillment of the duty, a criminal (public action) public suit may be brought directly. For instance, permission would not be necessary to bring action against a public employee who stabs someone at the end of an argument during a private evening party.

---

246 Atay, *İdare Hukuku*, 882; Nur Kaman, "Disiplin Soruşturması, Ceza Soruşturması, Görevden Uzaklaştırma [Disciplinary Investigation, Criminal Investigation, Removal from Duty]," in *İdare Hukuku*, ed. Turan Yıldırım (İstanbul: On İki Levha, 2022), 332–333.

247 Akyılmaz, Sezginer, and Kaya, *Türk İdare Hukuku*, 745.

Secondly, since the Constitution lays down that permission would be necessary "except in cases prescribed by law," if a law lays down that criminal prosecution is not subject to permission, public suit may be initiated directly without obtaining a permission. For instance, pursuant to Law no. 3628 (law regarding fight against bribery and corruption), permission is not needed to bring criminal action. Pursuant to Code of Criminal Procedure, criminal action may be brought against police officer who did not fulfill her judicial duties. Or for crimes regarding torture, permission is also not needed.[248]

An important exception is when public employee is caught red-handed on a crime which requires severe penalty. In this case again a permission is not needed.[249]

In case that permission is required, Public Prosecutor will request for permission from the related office upon a denunciation, a complaint or another way of gathering information regarding a public employee committing a crime. Related office differs according to the characteristics of public employees. For instance, TBMM should permit for the prosecution of head ombudsperson and ombudsperson according to the Law.[250] Permission of Minister of Internal Affairs for prosecution of metropolitan municipality mayors, permission of district governor for prosecution of district municipality mayors are required. At the end of an inspection of related office, permission is given or not given. If not, public action will not be brought. In this case, the party (if permitted public employee or if not public prosecutor) may apply to administrative judiciary. This application will be toward District Administrative Courts or State Council depending on the situation. The decision upon application is final. In this case, District Administrative Court or State Council do not function as judiciary. In other words, it acts like an impartial administrative unit.[251]

2.3.2. Safeguard Regarding Tort Liability

Public employees may harm persons who are administered. In this case, the Constitution forbids administered persons to file suits concerning damages directly to that public employee. Pursuant to Constitution, this suit may only

---

248 Kaman, "Disiplin Soruşturması," 337–338.

249 Kaman, "Disiplin Soruşturması," 337.

250 Atay, *İdare Hukuku*, 888.

251 State Council has ruled that "… Inspection and conclusion of the objections pursuant to Law no 4483 of district administrative courts and State Council are not judiciary in function." SC 1st C., M. 2014/49 D. 2014/22, 15.01.2014, www.lexpera.com.

be filed against administration. Administration will recourse to the public employee afterward.[252]

Two reasons are valid for this: First of these reasons is, likewise in criminal prosecutions, to safeguard public employee to fulfill her duty as it should be by preventing her to be under pressure of suits being filed. Secondly and more importantly, there is a possibility that public employee may not be able to afford the compensation ruled by the court.[253] Truly, it may not be possible for a public employee to pay the compensation at once. As an alternative, cutting from the salary would take a long time. For this reason, administration whose financial power is strong should pay the compensation and afterward recourse to the public employee.

It is important that damage needs to be arisen during the usage of authority. Otherwise, suits regarding compensation will be filed directly against the public employee.[254] For instance, when public employee harms someone with an action that is separable from the duty, the actions should be brought against the employee directly.

---

252 According to high courts, recourse (taking compensation which administration have paid back from the public employee who is at fault) is obligatory: "The mentioned provision of the Constitution (as long as the compensation is recoursed to them) refers to the obligation of the administration to collect compensation which administration had to pay by applying to legal remedies … and because of this constitutional obligation claimants do not have to demand recourse separately in their petitions in such cases." SC 10th C., M. 2004/13990, D. 2007/739, 27.02.2007, www.kazanci.com.
Since that administration pays compensation from the public budget, which is comprised of taxes which folk pays, folk does not have the responsibility to finance the public employee who acts faulty.

253 Atay, *İdare Hukuku*, 841.

254 Atay, *İdare Hukuku*, 845–846.

3. Public Property

Besides organization and personnel, administration needs movable and immovable property to carry out public services. Thus, the notion of "public property" has emerged.

Then, what is public property? While the Constitution mentions public property,[255] there is no definition of the notion in the Constitution and laws. Furthermore, there is not a general law governing public property in our legal system. The fact that different laws have several provisions which are dispersed and sometimes contradictory makes the subject more difficult and controversial.[256]

What is meant by "publicly owned property" or "property in the possession of public"? These phrases have two different meanings according to the doctrine, legislation and judicial decisions:

- Firstly, these terms refer to the property that belongs to administration subject to public law.
- Secondly, these terms refer to the property that belongs to administration which are subject to private law. (It should be noted that administration can purchase a property just like a private person since administration is a legal person. In this case the property is in "private property" status until the property is allocated to public service.)

In this section, public property with its first meaning will be explained. As the occasion arises, goods of administration that are subject to private law will also be mentioned.

Public property may be defined as property of a public corporate body allocated (dedicated) to a public service. Only being owned by a public corporate body, does not suffice to make the property subject to public law, "allocation to a public service" is needed. In other words, while the property owned by a public corporate body may be "public's property," it will not be counted as "public

---

255 For instance, in article 23 of the Constitution it is stated that "Freedom of residence may be restricted by law for the purpose of … protecting public property."

256 Aydın Gülan, "Kamu Mallarına İlişkin Sorunlara Uyuşmazlık Mahkemesinin Yaklaşımı [Approach of Court of Jurisdictional Disputes to the Issues Concerning Public Property]," *Journal of Administrative Law and Administrative Sciences* 11, no. 1, 3 (1990): 19.

property in the strict sense."[257] Briefly, "public's property" and "public property" are not the same.

Within this scope, three conditions should be fulfilled to conclude that a property is a public property. Firstly, a public corporate body should be in question. Secondly, the property should belong to this public corporate body. Thirdly, this property should be allocated to public service.

As to the first condition, a property belonging to a private law person principally cannot be a public property. On the other hand, property owned by public corporate bodies may be public property even though these public corporate bodies act like a private law person. In fact, although government business enterprises act like private law persons in several markets, some laws regulate that their property are public property.[258]

Then, what will be the status of a property that is rented by a public corporate body from a private person in order to be used for public service? Designation of the status of this property as public property may violate the right to property. On the other hand, since the service carried out is in favor of public interest, there is a need to secure these properties with provisions securing public property. For instance, it may be alleged that the authorities of the owner should be limited on this property to provide the service to be continuous. Thus, even though these goods are not counted as public property, laws may lay down provisions to secure these properties for the sake of public service to be performed properly.[259]

Likewise, suppose that a public service is carried out by a private person via concession. There is no doubt that the property provided by administration to this private person to be used for public service is public property if the property is in possession of administration.[260] However, the status of the property that are obtained afterward by this private person is controversial. Property that are in the characteristic of inseparable parts to the property (which was made available

257 See Aydın Gülan, *Kamu Mallarından Yararlanma Usullerinin Tabi Olduğu Hukuki Rejim* [*Legal Regime of the Procedures to Benefit from Public Properties*] (İstanbul: Alfa, 1999), 23–24; Akyılmaz, Sezginer, and Kaya, *Türk İdare Hukuku*, 626.

258 See article 57 of Statutory Decree no. 233. According to this provision, crimes committed against the properties of government business enterprises will be counted as if they are committed against public properties.

259 Nur Kaman, "Kamu Malları [Public Properties]," in *İdare Hukuku*, ed. Turan Yıldırım (İstanbul: On İki Levha, 2022), 370.

260 Gözler, *İdare Hukuku V. II*, 848.

by administration to private person) may be counted as public property.[261] But, what should be the status of property obtained afterward that are not inseparable from the main property? It may be concluded that such property should also benefit from a protection regime like public property, while it should not be counted as public property.

Second condition is that the property should be owned by a public corporate body.[262] It is not necessary that the property should be in the possession of the same public corporate body which uses it in public service, it may as well be in possession of another public corporate body.

It is controversial whether public corporate bodies have property rights on public property. There are two different views on the issue.[263] According to the view that there is no property right, there is a "protection and supervision" in question rather than a property. This view highlights the principle governing public goods which is non-transferability of public goods. That is to say, alienation authority of administration on public goods is limited. In contrast with the non-transferability principle, property right covers the authorities of *usus, fructus* and *abusus* (using, deriving profit and disposing [alienating]). Indeed, there are public law-related limitations regarding the authorities of using and deriving profit.[264] Accordingly, since public corporate bodies cannot use all the authorities provided by property right, public corporate bodies do not possess such a right.

On the other hand, according to the dissenting view, public corporate bodies have the right to use public property. In other words, the authority to use the property that are allocated to public service are granted to public corporate bodies.

261 In this dispute, the High Court upheld the decision of the 13th Circuit of State Council which found that the termination of the concession agreement between Çukurova Elektrik A.Ş. and administration, and transfer of property to the administration, including "the inseparable parts" of the property, was in accordance with the law. SCP-SCAC, M. 2008/906, D. 2010/175, 11.02.2010, www.kazanci.com.

262 Exceptionally, the property obtained by private persons may be counted as state good. For instance, Law no. 2860 on Gathering Charity provides that the money gathered by private persons with permit are state property. See Gülan, *Kamu Mallarından Yararlanma*, 24.

263 For a detailed explanation, see Gözler, *İdare Hukuku V. II*, 861–862.

264 According to Gülan, non-transferability principle shows that the property is inseparably connected to its owner, rather than being a limitation on the authority to alienate. Thus, the author is of the view that non-transferability does not mean that there is no property right. See Gülan, *Kamu Mallarından Yararlanma*, 74.

Besides, public corporate bodies can derive profit from these goods. Lastly, public corporate bodies can also alienate property by removing their allocation to public service.

Then, if it is accepted that property right is valid, would this right have the same context as in private law? Considering provisions regarding public property, it is seen that the regime prescribed for public property is different than private law property regime. Administration cannot use authority on public property arbitrarily due to the features of public service and public interest. For instance, administration does not have total discretion on the alienation of these assets.

Meanwhile, public property is under a status which has more protection than private law. For instance, public property cannot be seized, expropriated and their acquisitive prescription is not possible. Thus, it can only be possible to indicate that public corporate bodies have property rights on "public property" that is essentially different than private law regime.[265] Constitutional Court also uses the expression of "public property (ownership)"[266] in a sense that this ownership differs than private ownership. Court of Cassation, in one of its decisions, also ruled that there is no property in public law as in the meaning of private law.[267] State Council preferred the expressions of "administrative law property"[268] and "a kind of administrative law property." State Council's view on not accepting a property right in terms of civil law may be seen reasonable, since "in civil law the owner, in public law the property is being protected."[269]

Third condition is that this property should be allocated to public service. Allocation may be possible *de facto* or via an administrative act. However, it should

265 Akyılmaz, Sezginer, and Kaya, *Türk İdare Hukuku*, 633.

266 CC, M. 2015/2, D. 2016/19, 16.3.2016, OG 15.04.2016–29685.

267 Court of Cassation 4th C., M. 2002/11801, D. 2003/1731, 24.02.2003, www.kazanci.com.

268 SC 3rd C., M. 1980/157, D. 1980/181, 13.10.1980, www.kazanci.com.

269 Yayla, *İdare Hukuku*, 334. The author's expression may be explained as such: even though some limits are also available in private property to protect public order, the owner has more authorities than administration has on public good. For instance, she/he can alienate her/his property and even destroy it. However, administration does not possess such great powers on the property that are protected by Constitution and property that are allocated to public services. It can be said that it is especially aimed to protect the property which are legally under the rule and disposal of the state such as coasts, forests and mines, by restraining their alienation by the state and private persons.

be indicated here that, as we will touch upon in the following title, the characteristics of public property emerge for some property by their own nature, without the need to be allocated to public service. That is to say, these do not necessitate an allocation to be qualified as public property.

Allocation to public interest may appear in property

- that are left to direct use of the public and
- that are used in public service.

Since these two criteria broadens the notion of public property, an additional criterion is sought. Accordingly, the property that is used in public service "should be subject to a special arrangement that is suitable to the service provided," in other words, it "should be adapted to that service."[270] For instance, in a building which will be used for educational activity, classes that are suitable for education or rooms for lecturers should be provided.

Lastly, it should be indicated that in case a law or the Constitution designates a property as public property, abovementioned conditions do not have to be met. In other words, the related property's "public property" character is unquestionable.

3.1. Emergence of Public Property Quality

The characteristics of a property as public property may emerge in several ways. First, some properties are public property by their nature. Secondly, there are traditional public property. Thirdly, as mentioned above, a property may be qualified as public property by an act of allocation.

3.1.1. Public Property by Their Nature

Some immovables are public property by their nature.[271] Immovables which have never been subject to property by their nature or immovables that are incapable of being subject to property are public property.[272] Coastal waters, seas, mountains, lakes and rivers (natural public goods) are as such.

---

270 Gülan, *Kamu Mallarından Yararlanma*, 38; Akyılmaz, Sezginer, and Kaya, *Türk İdare Hukuku*, 626.

271 Akyılmaz, Sezginer, and Kaya, *Türk İdare Hukuku*, 631.

272 On the other hand, in doctrine, Gözler indicates that some things are incapable of being under possession of either private persons or administration, such as sea, wind or air. Therefore, the fact that the public uses these things directly does not amount these things to be public property. Gözler, *V. II*, 854.

These immovables (natural public property) are inherently public property. A distinct allocation act is not necessary for these properties. In other words, there is no need for administration to declare implicitly or explicitly that it will use these properties for public service.

A property may also turn into a public property even though it is in possession of a private person. For instance, when a real estate belonging to a private person is swallowed by the sea because of a landslide or when a river changes its bed and a private property is swept away, these immovables will become public property.[273]

In Constitution, there are several properties counted that are designated to be public property. In the article 43, it is ruled: "The coasts are under the authority and disposal of the state. (2) In the utilization of sea coasts, lake shores or river banks, and of the coastal strip along the sea and lakes, public interest shall be taken into consideration with priority." In addition, according to the article 168, "Natural wealth and resources shall be under the authority and at the disposal of the state. The right to explore and exploit these belongs to the state. The state may delegate this right to real or legal persons for a certain period. Which natural wealth and resources, are to be explored and exploited by the state in partnership with real or legal persons, and those to be directly explored and exploited by real or legal persons shall be subject to the explicit permission of the law. The conditions to be met in such cases by real or legal persons, the procedure and principles governing supervision and control by the state, and the sanctions to be applied shall be prescribed by law." Pursuant to this article of Constitution, "mines" are also within property that are under the authority and disposal of the state. However, by being taken out from the underground, mines become movable property. In this case, they may be subject to private law.[274]

As well as Constitution, Turkish Civil Code[275] also provides a similar provision. According to the article 715, "Unowned places and property that their benefits belong to the public shall be under the authority and disposal of the state. (2) Unless the contrary is proved, waters that benefits belong to the public and places which are not suitable for agriculture such as rocks, hills, mountains,

---

273 Court of Cassation 18th Civil C., M. 2014/2357, D. 2014/8570, 08.05.2014, www.kazanci.com.

274 Aydın Gülan, *Maden İdare Hukukumuzun Ana İlkeleri ve Temel Müesseseleri* [*The Essential Principles and Foundations of Our Mine Administrative Law*] (İstanbul: Lamure, 2008), 59–60.

275 No. 4721, 22.11.2001, OG 08.12.2001–24607.

glaciers and resources extracted from them are under no one's property and shall not be subject to private property in any way." The notion of "unowned place" does not imply places that are unowned in reality, since state has authorities similar to property right on these places. Civil Code has this expression to highlight that these places cannot be subject to private property.[276]

Two questions arise from above-mentioned provisions: What does "under the authority and disposal" mean? Why is this notion preferred instead of "property right" in the Constitution and Civil Code? The reason of this may be to highlight that there is no property right in the sense of civil law when public goods are in question.[277]

3.1.2. Traditional Public Property

Places which are left to the use of public from the past to present, such as grasslands, summer pastures, winter quarters and old marketplaces, are public property.[278] These properties have been used by public directly for a long time. In addition, there is a "belief" that these immovables are public property in both administration and people.

Allocation is not always required for them to be qualified as public property. However, loss of the characteristic of being a public property or being allocated to another service is only possible with a removal of allocation act.

3.1.3. Allocation Act

A property in possession of administration gains the characteristics of a public property when it is allocated to public service. For instance, when administration purchases an immovable, this becomes initially its private property. However, in

276 Akyılmaz, Sezginer, and Kaya, *Türk İdare Hukuku*, 630; Gözler, *İdare Hukuku V. II*, 853.

277 Gözler, *İdare Hukuku V. II*, 864; Akyılmaz, Sezginer, and Kaya think that the expression of "under the authority and disposal of the state" covers all public property that belong to public corporate bodies. Akyılmaz, Sezginer, and Kaya, *Türk İdare Hukuku*, 633; In one of the decisions of Court of Jurisdictional Disputes, it was stressed that "The State's property right on places, which are under the authority and disposal of the State and in the characteristics of 'State property' ('public property'...) that cannot be subject to private ownership, is not a property right in the sense of civil law, but is a kind of "right to property according to administrative law." CJD, Civil Chamber, M. 2001/70; www.kazanci.com.

278 Nur Kaman, "Kamu Malları," 368.

case this property is allocated to public service either *de facto* or via an administrative act, it becomes a public property.[279] When the act on allocation is withdrawn, this property will again turn into a private law property.

In doctrine, Onar defined allocation as "an administrative act that puts a state property for public use or connects it to a public service, in other words, an administrative act that puts private real estate in the category of common *property* or service *property* or makes it a means of public service."[280]

From the definition, it is understood that allocation is an act which

1. dedicates the private property belonging to administration to public service or
2. leaves it to the direct use of public.

As it is mentioned, it is possible for administration to allocate a property to public service via an explicit "allocation act." While allocation act is most of the time an individual administrative act, allocation is also possible via regulatory acts or administrative agreements.[281] For instance, in a dispute before State Council, it was ruled that "… Administrative act in the nature of allocation may arise with the agreement between administrations regarding public service."[282] In addition, allocation may as well emerge with an attribution referred in the Constitution or the laws. For instance, the articles 43 (regarding coasts) and 168 (regarding natural wealth and resources) which were quoted in the title above may be given examples on this regard.

Allocation may also emerge actually (*de facto*). Actual allocation is defined in the Law on "Real Estates *De Facto* Allocated to Public Services by Public Legal Persons or Institutions"[283] as "establishment of facilities or construction in accordance with the nature and purpose of public service on the real estate."[284]

In case of actual allocation, there is no allocation act made by administration. Administration erects a building or makes a facility and opens it to the direct use of public or begins to carry out a public service in them. When this is the case,

---

279 Akyılmaz, Sezginer, and Kaya, *Türk İdare Hukuku*, 627.

280 Onar, *İdare Hukukunun Umumi Esasları V. II*, 1340.

281 Gülan Aydın, "Kamu Malları [Public Property]," in *Günışığında Yönetim*, ed. İl Han Özay (İstanbul: Filiz, 2017), 681–682; Akyılmaz, Sezginer, and Kaya, *Türk İdare Hukuku*, 631.

282 SC 8th C., M. 1986/46, D. 1986/159, 31.03.1986, www.kazanci.com.

283 No. 221, 05.01.1961, OG 12.01.1961–10075.

284 This definition is made only to show how *de facto* allocation is understood within the terms of this law.

the buildings or the facility turn into public property. For instance, when administration builds a museum building and puts historical artifacts in it and opens it to the public, there is an allocation even though there is no allocation act.

It should be mentioned here that a formal administrative act may not be sufficient on its own for the allocation. In doctrine, it is alleged that a formal allocation will not bear consequences when there is no *de facto* allocation.[285] We are also of the view that formal allocation without an actual allocation is not sufficient to conclude that the related property is a public property.

Administration may as well make changes on the allocation. First, when administration decides that it no longer needs the property allocated to the public service, it may use the property in another public service by changing the allocation. Administration may as well remove the allocation on the property, so that the property turns into a private property of administration.

Secondly, a public corporate body may allocate its public property to the needs of another public corporate body. However, to this end, there should be a provision on this regard or administrations should come to an agreement for this purpose. Transference of the property by mutual will may only be possible for the private property of the administration. According to the principle of non-transferability of public property, a property which is qualified as a public property cannot be transferred via an agreement between administrations. In doctrine, Gözler puts forward that, since public property will become a private property with the removal of the allocation, its transfer will be possible afterward.[286] Yet, as Gülan also draws attention, in this case, the principle of non-transferability will lose its meaning. According to the author, the principle of non-transferability only makes sense when the office which removes the allocation act is different than the one which establishes the allocation. At the same time, the principle of non-transferability rules in case that the Constitution or a law qualifies a property as public property.[287] For instance, natural wealth and resources are under the disposal of the state according to the article 168 of the Constitution. Thus, this kind of property cannot be transferred or sold as long as the Constitution is not amended.

285 Aydın Gülan, *Kamu Mallarından Yararlanma Usullerinin Tabi Olduğu Hukuki Rejim* [*Legal Regime of the Procedures to Benefit from Public Properties*] (İstanbul: Alfa, 1999), 100.

286 Gözler, *İdare Hukuku V. II*, 895.

287 Gülan, *Kamu Mallarından Yararlanma*, 123.

3.2. Distinction of Public Property According to The Aim of Allocation

Public property may be classified in three categories based on the aim of the allocation. In this title, we will mention these categories, namely, unowned things, common property and service property.

3.2.1. Unowned Things

As we have mentioned above, unowned things are under the authority and disposal of the state. These things cannot be subject to private property.[288]

3.2.2. Common Property

Common properties are properties such as roads, bridges, squares and tunnels. Administration constructs and leaves them to the public use, or these properties have for a long time been open to the use of the public. Administration cannot interfere with these properties unless the conditions require so.[289]

---

288 Nur Kaman, "Kamu Malları," 370–371. "Provisions for private property do not apply to properties that are unowned or publicly owned. Such *property* cannot be bought and sold, cannot be prescribed, and cannot be registered in the land registry. Since the territorial waters of seas are under the sovereignty of the state, it is the public's right to benefit from them. The coasts are the continuation of the seas, whether they are sandy, pebbly, stony or rocky. It is impossible to be separated from the sea. In this respect, the land registrations do not possess legal value for these places." Court of Cassation Plenary Session, M. 1980/1-967, D. 1980/1365, 27.02.1980, www.kazanci.com.

289 "As for the village common *property*, which are public property, such places are reserved for the use of all villagers." SC 8th C., M. 1989/675, D. 1990/1153, 18.10.1990, www.kazanci.com; "In our law system, roads are qualified as common *property* which are allocated to public interest and subject to the legal regime of public *property*. Roads cannot be prescribed, seized, and land registry for them is not necessary. It is enough only to be measured and shown on their maps." SC 6th C., M. 2012/1904, D. 2013/6299, 05.11.2013, www.kazanci.com; "While some of the immovables owned by the village legal personality are the common *property* such as grasslands, pastures, squares, roads, which are left for the use of village people, some of the immovables owned by the village legal personality are places subject to private property such as lands and fields, which the village legal personality owns according to the rules of private law. Villages use their immovables that are subject to private property in accordance with the decisions of their authorized boards, and civil jurisdiction handles the settlement and resolution of disputes regarding these immovables. As for the village common goods, which are public goods; such places are reserved for the use of all villagers.

3.2.3. Public Service Property

Service properties are allocated to a specific public service by administration.[290] These are either used by administration alone or with the public commonly.

3.3. Legal Regime of Public Property

Public property is protected by the legal system more than private properties. Under this title, we will explain the legal protection provided for public property.

3.3.1. Public Property Cannot Be Transferred and Alienated (Abalienated)

Public property cannot be sold and transferred. As long as the allocation continues, private law transactions such as exchange or sale are invalid in terms of law. On the other hand, if allocation is removed or the property has not yet allocated to a public service, the property of administration is subject to private law and the prohibition on transfer and alienation does not apply. In a case before the Constitutional Court, it was ruled that the places, which become unnecessary due to the change in construction plan, have become private property of administration, and may be transferred and sold as long as it is not allocated to public interest.[291]

Behind the prohibition on transfer and alienation, the aim to which the property is dedicated lies rather than the qualification of the property. Allocation and prohibition on transfer and alienation relate to each other since allocation means a property being dedicated to a public service. As mentioned, when the allocation is removed, the prohibition ends. Of course, this prohibition is absolute

---

They can be used by other individuals with the decision of authorized board. Their sale may be in question if the public *property* are excessive to the needs of the village people..." SC 8th C., M. 1989/675, D. 1990/1153, 18.10.1990, www.kazanci.com.

290 Nur Kaman, "Kamu Malları," 369.

291 "Roads can be closed by making changes in the construction plans depending on the developing needs over time and it is possible that some road parts can become unnecessary. Since the road or road parts that are closed or become unnecessary will lose their public property character and become private property of the administration, the protection regarding public property is also removed. … If they are not re-allocated to public interest, the administration will dispose of these properties within the framework of the private law regime and can sell them if necessary." CC, M. 2011/23, D. 2012/3, 12.01.2012, www.kazanci.com.

for some properties which are specially protected by the Constitution, such as coasts, mountains,[292] natural wealth and resources.[293]

Limitations may be brought to the prohibition on transfer and alienation by a law. For instance, according to the Law on Swamp (Marshland) Drying and Land Acquired Through Drying Process,[294] in case that swamps (marshlands), that are under the disposal and authority of the State, are dried the land generated shall be registered to the person that dried the swamp (marshland). Privatization is also an exception envisaged by law to this principle. In the Law on Implementation of Privatization,[295] sale of public property is also envisaged as a privatization method.

The below-mentioned prohibitions also are consequences of the prohibition on transfer and alienation.

3.3.2. Public Property Cannot Be Prescribed

No one can acquire the ownership of a public property or any other real right over it (unless the law provides for a clear provision to the contrary) via acquisitive prescription.[296] Accordingly, public corporate bodies may retrieve public property from the person who become the possessor in any way.[297] In addition, the person who becomes the possessor of the public property in any way cannot benefit from the provisions protecting possession.

The Constitution has a specific provision regarding forests. According to the article 169/2, ownership of state forests shall not be acquired by prescription. Another related provision may be found in article 18/2 of the Cadastral Law. Accordingly, common properties, service properties, forests, places which are under the disposal and authority of the State, and which are allocated to a public

---

292 According to the article 169/2 of the Constitution, the ownership of state forests shall not be transferred. The provision contains the implication that artificial forests can be transferred. On the other hand, according to the first paragraph of article 169, all forests shall be under the care and supervision of the State. Therefore, even though the ownership of a forest which is created by a private person may be transferred, the regime of them will be under the supervision of the State.

293 Akyılmaz, Sezginer, and Kaya, *Türk İdare Hukuku*, 633.

294 No. 5516, 18.01.1950, OG 23.01.1950–7413.

295 No. 4046, 24.11.1994, OG 27.11.1994–22124.

296 Akyılmaz, Sezginer, and Kaya, *Türk İdare Hukuku*, 634.

297 SC 6th C., M. 1990/2427, D. 1991/1340, 03.06.1991, www.kazanci.com.

service, and immovables left to the State pursuant to their laws, cannot be acquired with acquisitive prescription either registered or not.

In a dispute regarding immovables left to the State, State Council ruled that "The ownership of the immovables left in Turkey by the Exchanged Greeks is transferred to the State of the Republic of Turkey, and since the ownership of the immovables left to the State in accordance with the laws, whether registered in the land registry or not, will not be acquired through acquisitive prescription, it is clear that in case of occupation, compensation may be claimed."[298]

As for movable public property, even if these are stolen and then sold and passed into the hands of a *bona fide* third party, they can be taken back by public corporate bodies. For instance, cultural and natural assets can be protected this way.

3.3.3. Limited Real Rights Cannot Be Established on Public Property

Principally, real rights cannot be established over public properties in favor of private persons.[299] It is accepted that this rule has two exceptions. First, the laws may have a provision to the contrary.[300] Secondly, the real rights that were established before the property became a public property, protect its validity to the extent that it complies with the allocation. In case that it does not comply, the real right expires, and a compensation is given in return.

It should be indicated that even though easement is possible in exceptional situations on public property, the meaning and scope of easement over public property do not correspond with the easement right in the civil law.[301] Administration may terminate an easement that prevents or dangers the allocation. Also, if the allocation on the property changes, administration may cease the easement which is not compatible with the new allocation.[302]

---

298 SC 10th C., M. 2008/7202, D. 2009/44, 21.01.2009, www.danistay.gov.tr.

299 Kaman, "Kamu Malları," 385.

300 For the examples of limited rights that are established by laws see Kaman, "Kamu Malları," 387–389.

301 Kaman, "Kamu Malları," 386.

302 Kaman, "Kamu Malları," 386.

3.3.4. Public Property Cannot Be Subject to Private Law Agreements

Principally, it is accepted that private law agreements cannot be made over public properties. It should be stressed that with the enforcement of Law no. 4706 on Evaluation of Immovable Properties of Treasury and Amendment of the Value Added Tax Law, application of this principle is very limited.[303]

The principle is also not applied if a private property of administration is in question.[304] For instance, administration can rent its private property which is not allocated to public service.

3.3.5. Public Property Cannot Be Confiscated

Public property cannot be confiscated due to the aim for which it is allocated. Otherwise, there may be disturbances on the public service provided. In other words, the principle of continuity may be violated.

Private property of administration, on the other hand, may be confiscated. The basic problem with this matter is that there is not a sufficient assessment method on how to designate whether a property is a public or private property. This problem makes it difficult to confiscate the private property of administration.

There is also an exception to the rule that private property may be confiscated. Accordingly, private property of the "State" cannot be confiscated.[305] Pursuant to the article 70 of Procedure Law on Collection of Public Claims no. 6183, "State property and property that are prescribed not to be confiscated in their special laws shall not be confiscated excluding the property of state economic organisations, state economic enterprises, their institutions, subsidiaries, affiliates subject to the provisions of the Decree no 233 on State Economic Entities and property of local administrations."

For instance, income of a local administration from a rent agreement of a property may be confiscated.

---

303 Kaman, "Kamu Malları," 390.

304 Akyılmaz, Sezginer, and Kaya, *Türk İdare Hukuku*, 634.

305 For the evaluation and critique of a decision of Constitutional Court which affirms this rule, see Gülan, Aydın, "Borcunu Ödemeyen Devlete Karşı Ne Yapılabilir? [What Can Be Done Against the State Which Does Not Pay its Debt]," *Journal of Administrative Law and Administrative Sciences* 13, no. 1, 11 (1995): 11–29, https://dergipark.org.tr/tr/pub/iuihid/issue/57855/14642.

3.3.6. Public Property Cannot Be Expropriated

Expropriation Law[306] explicitly provides that public property cannot be expropriated (article 30). Accordingly, a property which belongs to a public corporate body cannot be expropriated by another public corporate body. However, "transfer" of public property between public corporate bodies are possible.[307] A public corporate body may take over a property of another public corporate body by following the procedure in the law. We will explain this subject under the title of "Procedure of Transfer."

Since Expropriation Law does not make a distinction between private property or public property, it should be accepted that private immovable property of administration can also not be expropriated.

3.4. Usage of Public Property

As we have already mentioned, public property may be used for a public service or may be left to the direct use of public.

3.4.1. Public Property Allocated to Public Service

Public properties which are allocated to public service are to be used by administration. Solely administration may use some of these properties. Military posts, buildings belonging to the law enforcement agency or National Intelligence Organization are as such. Persons other than the ones that have right to use these buildings need to have a permission to enter them.[308]

On the other hand, some service properties may be used by individuals as well. Schools, hospitals are examples to these service properties. These are also subject to provisions which regulate their usage. There may be sanctions prescribed by laws for acting contrary to these provisions.

---

306 No. 2942, 04.11.1983, OG 08.11.1993–18215.

307 Akyılmaz, Sezginer, and Kaya, *Türk İdare Hukuku*, 624.

308 When administration unlawfully imposes restrictive rules on entrance to these places, administrative judiciary may annul such rules. For instance, in a dispute before State Council, the Council annulled a regulation that restricted the contact visit in prisons by concluding that this provision is contrary to law. SC 10th C., M. 2006/5393, D. 2009/10123, 02.12.2009, www.kazanci.com.

3.4.2. Places That Are Left to the Direct Use of the Public

Places left to the direct use of public are primarily used by public rather than the administration. Roads, squares, coasts, seas and lakes are within this category. The usage of these goods may be in two ways. While there are places that are open to common usages, there are also places which are allocated to private usage.

3.4.2.1. Common Usage

Some places which are open to direct use of public are used in a "general," "common" and "anonymous" way. For instance, coasts, roads, lakes or squares are places for common usage.[309] Within common usage, the principles of "freeness," "equality" and "gratuitousness"[310] are valid.[311]

3.4.2.2. Private Usage

In private usage, only persons who are designated beforehand can use the public property. In this case, there is a usage in the form of occupation. Private law persons partially occupy the public property. For instance, bookstalls that we see on the roads, tables and chairs that are placed in the street in front of the cafes are such occupancies. It should be stressed that the word "occupation" may be misleading giving the impression that this type of usage is unlawful and without permission. However, this method of usage is only possible in case of a prior permission granted by the administration.[312] Additionally, administration can only

---

309 "It is everybody's, in other words public's, right to freely use public waters and lakes and the sandy, stony and rocky places around them. The public's use of the general waters and the sandy, stony and rocky places that are their integral parts can be possible by keeping the coastlines of the general waters open to everyone and by preserving these qualities." Court of Cassation, 1st C., M. 2004/2741, D. 2004/3236, 22.03.2004, www.kazanci.com.

310 According to the High Court, it is unlawful to condition the usage of coasts in return for a payment. SC 13th C., M. 2007/1238, D. 2009/7169, 26.06.2009; www.kazanci.com.

311 Akyılmaz, Sezginer, and Kaya, *Türk İdare Hukuku*, 639–640; Kaman, "Kamu Malları," 399.

312 "... Permission to the temporary occupation of areas on public *property* such as roads, parks, squares, which do not prevent people from passing by and which are not inconvenient in other ways, is a an act of allocation. After the allocation, in case of any inconveniences after the rental of the kiosk installed in the area, the allocation for the public interest can be withdrawn and the space may be requested to be evacuated. For this reason, even though the presence of the kiosk is based on a rent agreement, the cancellation of the allocation based on the public power and the evacuation is basically

permit such usages when the occupation is in line with the aim of the allocation of the property.

The usage of such places is subject to this basic rule: The persons who use these places cannot restrict or prevent the public to use them freely and equally. For instance, in one of its decisions, State Council dealt with a tender act through which a buffet place to be rented was located on the coast. In this dispute, State Council concluded that the tender act should have been annulled by the court of first instance with the following reasoning: "… it is not possible to make a disposal that will eliminate or limit the right of everyone to benefit from the coasts equally and freely, in accordance with the provisions of the Constitution and Coastal Law…, in other words, it is not possible to rent the places within the coast edge line and the first 50 meters of the coastline..."[313]

Private usage of public property is subject to the principles of "being subject to permission," "temporariness" and "being priced."[314] That is, this type of usage is only possible with a permission of administration, which is granted in return of a price and this permission can be withdrawn when necessary.

3.5. Procedures of Property Acquisition By Administration

As we have mentioned, administration needs property when providing public service. Therefore, it is also a matter of interest how administration acquires these properties. Undoubtedly, administration may purchase property in accordance with the civil law. But sometimes public interest requires property to be unilaterally acquisitioned by administration. In this section, we will explain the methods of "expropriation," "transfer," "requisition" and "nationalization" through which administration acquires the needed property by using public force.

3.5.1. Expropriation

According to the first two paragraphs of article 46 of the Constitution,

the act of withdrawal of the allocation. In the incident, since the rent agreement was invalidated when the allocation of the kiosk left to the plaintiff's use was withdrawn, there is no lawfulness in the court decision which ruled that an eviction lawsuit should have been initially filed in the civil jurisdiction." SC 8th C., M. 1996/1127, D. 1996/2737, 21.10.1996, www.kazanci.com.

313 SC 13th C., M. 2007/1238, D. 2009/7169, 26.06.2009, www.kazanci.com.

314 Akyılmaz, Sezginer, and Kaya, *Türk İdare Hukuku*, 640–641; Kaman, "Kamu Malları," 400–402.

> The State and public corporations shall be entitled, in case the public interest requires, to expropriate private immovable property wholly or in part and impose administrative easement on it, in accordance with the principles and procedures prescribed by law, provided that the actual equivalence is paid in advance.
>
> The payment for expropriation and the amount regarding its increase rendered by a final judgement shall be paid in cash and in advance. However, payment method for expropriated land for the purposes of carrying out agriculture reform, major energy and irrigation projects, housing and settlement schemes, afforestation, preservation of the coasts, and tourism shall be regulated by law. In the cases where the law may allow payment in instalments, the payment period shall not exceed five years and payments shall be made in equal instalments.

As seen, administration may acquire immovables belonging to private law persons with a unilateral will by using public force. Expropriation is an act established by the State or other public corporate bodies, which provides for the transition of the property or real right of an immovable property belonging to a "private law person"[315] to administration, with the unilateral will of administration to fulfill public interest in condition that principally the price is paid in cash and in advance.

However, instead of payment of an equivalent payment, administration may also barter (swap) to expropriate an immovable. In this case, if there is a difference in values of the two properties, the difference is paid in cash.[316]

As the above quoted article of the Constitution prescribes, expropriation may either concern the whole immovable or a part of an immovable. The second situation is mentioned as "partial expropriation."[317]

It should be highlighted that private law persons cannot expropriate. Constitutional Court annulled a provision of law which granted Organized Industry Regions (OIZ) which are private law persons, with the power of expropriation.[318]

---

315 Meltem Kutlu Gürsel, *Kamulaştırma Hukuku* [*Expropriation Law*] (Ankara: Seçkin, 2009), 88.

316 H. Eyüp Özdemir, "Kamulaştırma [Expropriation]," in *İdare Hukuku*, ed. Turan Yıldırım (İstanbul: On İki Levha, 2022),744.

317 René Chapus, *Droit Administratif Général Tome II* (Paris: Montchrestien, 2001), 695.

318 "The fact that expropriation can only be carried out by the State and public corporate bodies constitutes one of the procedural guarantees for the limitation of property rights. Although the OIZ is equipped with some public power privileges, this is not sufficient for the OIZ to expropriate, and it must also be a public corporate body pursuant to the article 46 of the Constitution. Since the first paragraph of article 5 of the Law no 4562 clearly stipulates that the OIZ is a private law legal person, granting the OIZ with the authority to expropriate will be contrary to the guarantees provided

On the other hand, administration may expropriate an immovable "in favor" of private law persons.[319] In this case, the payment for expropriation shall be paid by the related private person and administration holds property rights of the expropriated immovable while the property is used by the private law person.[320] The reason for property rights not transferring to the private person is that the latter will collect the amount of payment for expropriation from the users of the public service. However, in practice, sometimes making necessary acts regarding expropriation (besides the final expropriation act) are left to private law persons even though administration is authorized. Therefore, practically, "implicit" expropriation acts which are established by private law persons but accepted by administration emerge. In these cases, administrative judiciary evaluates the lawfulness of the act by presuming that there is an implicit expropriation act at hand.[321]

---

in the Constitution regarding expropriation of a privately owned immovable. With the reasons explained, the contested rule is contrary to the articles 35 and 46 of the Constitution. It must be annulled." CC, M. 2013/49, D. 2013/125, 31.10.2013, OG 28.12.2013–28865.

319 In fact, second paragraph of article 1 of the Expropriation Law is as follows: "The rules of this Law is applicable in the expropriations made in favor of real and private law legal persons based on their special laws." As seen, Expropriation Law explicitly lays down that expropriation can be made in favor of private law persons.

320 Akyılmaz, Sezginer, and Kaya, *Türk İdare Hukuku*, 650.

321 In a dispute, a private law person filed a suit before civil court for the court to designate the expropriation equivalence. After the decision of the civil court, the private person applied to administration to obtain public interest decision for expropriation process, since the private person could not come to an agreement with the owner of the property. When the owner of the property filed a suit before administrative court, the first instance court rejected the case since an expropriation act established by "administration" was not present. State Council reserved the decision with the following reasoning: "As a result of the fact that all these works and transactions made by private law legal person are first implicitly and then explicitly depend on the acceptance of the defendant administration, it is obligatory to accept that administration makes an implicit act regarding expropriation, in other words, it should be accepted that there is an 'implicit (expropriation) act' at hand… A contrary assessment would contradict with the 'positive duty' of the State in terms of the property right to ensure that this right is protected 'concretely and effectively,' and it will not be possible to establish a fair balance that should prevail between the requirements of the public interest and the protection of personal rights and to implement the principle of proportionality within this framework." SC 6th C., M. 2011/8290, D. 2012/1937, 24.04.2012, www.hukukturk.com.

Another important point is that all public corporate bodies do not possess the authority of expropriation. Current legislation prohibits some public corporate bodies to expropriate. When the law lays down that a certain public corporate body is not granted with such an authority, this public corporate body will not be able to expropriate.[322]

For instance, according to the additional article 7 of Law no. 2547 on Higher Education, higher education institutions which are established by foundations (foundation universities) cannot acquire immovables through expropriation. Therefore, foundation universities do not have the authority to expropriate.

Lastly, the property which can be expropriated may be explained. Firstly, only immovables can be subject to expropriation. Movable goods cannot be expropriated.[323] If other conditions are met, requisition may be possible for movable property. Likewise, public property cannot be expropriated. Contrary acts to this rule will be null and void. An immovable can only be subject to "transfer" between two public corporate bodies, as will be mentioned below under the title of "procedure of transfer."

3.5.1.1. Expropriation Process

The act of expropriation is established pursuant to Expropriation Law. In this title, we will mention the stages of expropriation prescribed in this Law.

3.5.1.1.1. Acts Before Expropriation

There are some stages before the final expropriation act. Accordingly, the administration should obtain sufficient allowance (subsidy), take a decision of public interest and determine the property that will be expropriated.

First, according to the last paragraph of article 3 of Expropriation Law, expropriation acts cannot be made without obtaining sufficient allowance beforehand. Since administration pays the equivalent in return of the expropriation, it is accepted that essence of the property right is not touched.[324]

---

322 It is questionable that these laws are in compliance with the Constitution, since Constitution grants "public corporate bodies" with the authority to expropriate without making a distinction or providing for an exception. In doctrine, several authors indicate that the provision, which prohibits higher education institutions that is established by a foundation to expropriate, is contrary to the Constitution. Akyılmaz, Sezginer, and Kaya, *Türk İdare Hukuku*, 649; Gözler, *İdare Hukuku V. I*, 226.

323 Chapus, *Droit Administratif*, 695.

324 Kutlu Gürsel, *Kamulaştırma*, 88.

As prescribed by the Constitution, principally the equivalent payment for expropriation is made in advance. Therefore, it can be stated that the amount of equivalent should be paid to the owner of the property beforehand and in total. If exceptional situations that the payment can be made with installments according to the Constitution are valid than their amounts shall be shown in the budget.

According to the Expropriation Law, after the phase of obtaining the allowance, administration should make a public interest decision before expropriation act. A public interest decision comprises a declaration that accomplishment of a work is in favor of public interest.[325]

Expropriation Law envisages the offices which shall make the public interest decision. This decision consists of a determination that the administration is in need of an immovable property owned by a private person in order to carry out a public service.[326] The public interest decisions of these offices sometimes may be subject to an approval. For instance, it is laid down by the Law that public interest decisions held by village council and municipal commission are required to be approved by district governors and governors. If the approval is not obtained, administrative judiciary will annul the expropriation act.[327]

Additionally, since public interest decision is in the characteristics of a preparatory act, this decision cannot be solely brought before the court.[328] But its conformity with the law may be examined during an annulment case against the final expropriation act.

As for the last preparatory act before expropriation, administration makes a scaled plan showing the border, surface area and type of the relevant immovable or resource. Owners of the immovable property or in case that there is no

---

325 "Both in the article 46 of the Constitution and article 1 of the Expropriation Law no 2942 … it is envisaged that immovables in the characteristic of a private property can be expropriated … in case that public interest requires. According to these rules, the first condition of expropriation is the existence of public interest, and public interest decision constitutes the essence and basis of the expropriation act." SC 6th C., M. 1986/310, D. 1986/559, 28.05.1986, www.kazanci.com.

326 Atay, *İdare Hukuku*, 754.

327 "Since it is evident that the expropriation amount subject to the lawsuit has been blocked to the bank to be paid with a second instruction, and the public interest decision taken by the municipal commissioner has not been approved by the approval authority, there is no lawfulness in the expropriation act …" SC 6th C., M. 1997/3697, D. 1998/2219, 24.04.1998, www.kazanci.com.

328 SC 6th C., M. 2004/718, D. 2007/454, 30.01.2007, www.kazanci.com.

registry the possessors and their addresses are determined from land registry, civil registration, tax population records or with external research.

After the expropriation decision is taken, the administration notifies the land registry administration for the annotation (reservation) of the expropriation.

If a document, to be obtained from the court regarding the determination of the expropriation amount and that a registration request on behalf of administration has been made, is not shown within six months from the date of this annotation, the annotation will be deleted from the registry.

3.5.1.1.2. Phase of Expropriation

Initially, the administration should implement the method of purchasing when expropriating. In case this method is bypassed, administrative judiciary rules on the unlawfulness of the expropriation act.

Through this method, firstly, administration assigns a value appraisal commission as well as a reconciliation commission. Value appraisal commission determines the price of the immovable. Administration notifies the owner, without indicating the price, that it intends to purchase the immovable or acquire it through barter (swap) (or acquire a limited real right) with an officially registered letter.

If the owner agrees, negotiation process begins. In case that the parties come to an agreement without exceeding the determined price, the immovable is transferred to the ownership of the administration (or a limited real right is acquired by the administration) by owners waiver at the registry with the realization of the payment. It is accepted that an immovable that is purchased or bartered (swapped) by this way is expropriated, and such an expropriation and the related payment cannot be subject to an action of objection.[329]

When expropriation cannot be executed through purchasing method, administration applies to the Civil Court of first instance for the determination of the expropriation price and annotation (reservation) of the immovable for the administration.

The judge determines the hearing day and invites the parties to agree on the price of the property on this day. If an agreement is reached, the provisions of the law regarding "the purchasing method" are applied. (Expropriation Law, article 10/5)

If there is no agreement on the price, the court makes an on-site discovery to determine the value of the immovable property by means of experts. The experts

329 Kutlu Gürsel, *Kamulaştırma*, 198.

determine the price of the immovable property in accordance with the principles specified in the Expropriation Law and submit their reports to the court (article 10/6).

The Court determines a fair and equitable expropriation price by making use of expert reports. However, the Court is not bound with these reports. The Court sets a time limit for the administration to deposit the expropriation amount to the bank and block it on behalf of the owner. If the bank receipt is submitted to the court by the administration within this period, the court decides to register the immovable property in the name of the administration and to pay the expropriation price to the owner.

The decision is notified to the land registry office and the bank. The registration decision is final. However, the parties have the right to appeal against the determined price.

3.5.1.2. Renouncement of Expropriation

Administration may renounce expropriation partially or wholly in any phase of the expropriation. Disputes arising from unilaterally renouncement of administration are resolved before civil courts.[330] After all the phases of expropriation are finalized, administration cannot renounce expropriation unilaterally.[331] Expropriation is finalized when the "report of the agreement is signed" in case that the expropriation is realized through purchasing method. If not, expropriation is finalized with the "annotation decision of the civil court."[332]

After the expropriation is finalized, parties may only "agree" on renouncement and transfer. Administration makes a notification to the prior owners of the property in case that the need for expropriation and related public interest is no longer valid after the expropriation and the related payment has become final and exclusive.[333] The prior owners may take the property back by returning the

330 "Since it was evident that the defendant administration unilaterally renounced the expropriation process in accordance with the article 21 of the Law no 2942, with the decision of the municipal commissioner which is the subject of the case, it was not appropriate for the [administrative] court [of first instance] to make a decision by examining the merits of the case, regardless of considering that the civil jurisdiction should have reviewed and resolved the dispute." SC 6th C., M. 1998/4999, D. 1999/4461, 06.10.1999, www.kazanci.com.

331 Akyılmaz, Sezginer, and Kaya, *Türk İdare Hukuku*, 663.

332 Akyılmaz, Sezginer, and Kaya, *Türk İdare Hukuku*, 663.

333 In case that administration does not use the expropriated immovable for the purposes of public interest and transfer it to third persons without proposing to agree on

payment. Renouncement of expropriation through agreement is only possible for a certain time. After five years have passed from the finalization of the expropriation, parties cannot agree on renunciation.

It should also be noted that in case the need for expropriation is no longer valid, and if another administration needs the immovable subject to the expropriation, the immovable shall be allocated to the public service provided by the other administration free of charge. The disputes arising from these situations are also resolved before civil courts.

3.5.1.3. Annulment Case Before Administrative Courts Against Expropriation

As we have mentioned, in case that purchasing method cannot be executed within the expropriation phase, administration applies to the civil court of first instance for the determination of the price and annotation of the immovable. Within 30 days after the first notification of the civil court of first instance or proclamation (where notification could not be possible) date, an annulment case concerning the expropriation act may be brought before the administrative courts (Expropriation Law article 14). Since expropriation is an administrative act, annulment of this act is within the jurisdiction of administrative courts.

With the annulment case filed, stay of execution of the expropriation act may be demanded. If the conditions are valid (if the act is both clearly unlawful and damages hardly reparable or irreparable may be caused by the implementation of the act), administrative court may issue stay of execution.

---

renouncement with the prior owner, property right of the owner may be breached. In an individual application decision of the Constitutional Court, it was ruled that "In the dispute subject to the application, the immovable of the applicant is expropriated by metropolitan municipality on 24.04.1998 for the aim of building sports ground, however on 20.07.1998, construction situation is changed as trading area, and the immovable is sold to third persons on 2.11.1998. Accordingly, it is seen that the immovable has never been used for the purposes of public interest. … The applicant has a legitimate expectation on remand of the expropriated immovable since it is not used for public interest. Therefore, the immovable property of the applicant expropriated on the basis of public interest falls within the guarantee provided by article 35 of the Constitution … By interfering the property right regarding the share of the applicant on the immovable without the purpose of public interest, the applicant is bereft of property contrary to article 35 of the Constitution." CC, IA, AN 2013/6151, 21.04.2016, OG 24.06.2016–29752.

In this case, the civil court of first instance (which has authority to determine the amount of expropriation payment and annotation of the immovable, but which does not hold the authority to annul the expropriation act) makes the annulment case before the administrative court a "preliminary issue." However, in practice, while administrative courts annul the expropriation act, there are instances where civil courts rule on annotation of the immovable on behalf of the administration, giving rise to legal uncertainty.[334]

3.5.1.4. Right of the Owner to Reclaim the Property

It is possible that administration does not commence any operation on the property after the expropriation. In such situations, the prior owner of the immovable property or her heirs may recover the immovable property by firstly paying back the expropriation payment[335] with its legal interest.

The owner has the right to reclaim, when five years pass after the expropriation price is determined, and in case that

- No act or facility, which complies with the aim of expropriation or transfer, is made or built by the administration or
- The property is left as is and is not allocated to any public interest.

The right to reclamation should be used within one year after the right is born (after the expiration of five-year period). Within this scope, the owner should request the reclamation from the related administration within one year. In case of rejection, the owner may file a suit before civil court of first instance. Otherwise, reclamation right shall be forfeited.

3.5.1.5. Urgent Expropriation

In some situations, it may be necessary for administration to acquire an immovable property within a short period of time. In these situations, if the conditions

334 For a legal evaluation for these situations, see Ramazan Çağlayan, "Kamulaştırma İşleminin İptali ve Mülkiyetin Akibeti [Annulment of Expropriation Act and Aftermath of the Property]," *Journal of İstanbul University Law Faculty* 69, no. 1, 2 (2011): 453–466.

335 Eren Solmaz, *Kamulaştırma Hukukunda Malikin Geri Alma Hakkı* [*Right of the Owner to Reclaim in Expropriation Law*] (İstanbul: On İki Levha, 2016), 105.

are fulfilled, administration may implement an exceptional procedure, namely, urgent expropriation.[336]

According to the article titled "Urgent Expropriation" (article 27) of the Expropriation Law, three situations are laid down for urgent expropriation to be implemented:

- In situations where need for homeland defense emerges in implementation of Law no. 3634 on National Defense Obligation,
- In situations where the president decides on its urgency,
- In expropriation of the property required in extraordinary situations, which are prescribed in their special laws.

From the provision, it may be understood that it is sufficient for the president to declare the urgency of a situation for urgent expropriation. In one of its decisions, State Council indicated that "... When article 27 of Law no 2942 is examined, since urgent expropriation of the immovable is prescribed as an exceptional method through which some expropriation procedures are not applied, the existence of special conditions compared to ordinary expropriation was sought in urgent expropriation with this provision and it is possible to expropriate the immovable by means of urgent expropriation in three cases. It has been stated that urgent expropriation can be executed in order to realize the superior public interest and protection of public order, by clearly counting two of these conditions, as the need for homeland defense in the implementation of Law on National Defense Obligation or the cases where they are necessary in extraordinary situations stipulated in special laws. In this context, it is clear that in order for the third condition, that is the urgency of the situation, to be decided, the state of being related to public interest and public order should be parallel to the other two conditions mentioned in the article... "

"(...) In this sense, in the absence of a state of urgency that would necessitate the urgent expropriation of the immovables, the [decision] of the urgent expropriation of the immovables in the case is not lawful."[337] As seen, State Council ruled that urgent expropriation shall only be lawful if the president decides on the urgency of a situation which is "indeed" urgent.[338]

---

336 For a detailed examination of urgent expropriation, see Cenk Şahin, *Acele Kamulaştırma* [*Urgent Expropriation*] (İstanbul: On İki Levha, 2018).

337 SC 6th C., M. 2012/6974, D. SE, 30.05.2013.

338 In the same direction: SC 6th C., M. 2008/6014, D. 2010/4866, 17.05.2010, www.lexpera.com.

Within the scope of urgent expropriation, an immovable may be seized upon request of the related administration from the court (other necessary acts to be made afterward except determination of the expropriation payment amount) by depositing the expropriation payment amount to the bank which the court shall determine through experts within 7 days.[339]

3.5.1.6. Seizure Without Expropriation

Administration sometimes uses an immovable without complying with the method of expropriation through occupation or such actions. This situation is called "seizure without expropriating."

Constitutional Court has defined this notion in one of its decisions: "Contrary to the article 46 of the Constitution and Law no 2942, the virtual or legal seizure of the immovables subject to private law, wholly or partially, without payment, by the State, public corporate bodies, public institutions, real and private legal persons on whose favor expropriation is possible in case of public interest... is defined as 'seizure without expropriation.'"[340]

De facto seizure refers to the situations in which administration seizes or occupies immovables that are subject to private law, without a duly expropriation act. Since there is no legal basis regarding *de facto* seizure and such seizure is totally undue, the action is no longer accepted to be an administrative action and becomes a "tortious action" within the meaning of civil law.[341] Therefore, disputes arising from the issue of de facto seizure are handled before civil jurisdiction.

Seizure without expropriating is not only valid in case of *de facto* seizure. Administration may as well violate property right of the persons by using the authorities granted to it with legislation and thus obstructing or limiting the owner to benefit from its property right. In this situation, legal seizure is in question.[342]

Within this scope, in a decision of Court of Cassation, it was ruled that "it cannot be said that administration, who obstructs the enjoyment of the owner

---

339 Şahin, *Acele Kamulaştırma*, 146–161.

340 CC 1st Sec., Mustafa Demirbaş, AN 2013/2002, 30.12.2014, §36, www.anayasa.gov.tr.

341 Akyılmaz, Sezginer, and Kaya, *Türk İdare Hukuku*, 670; Erhan Tutal, "Kamulaştırmasız El Atma Davalarında Yargılama Sürecindeki Son Gelişmeler [Recent Developments in Prosecution Process of Cases of Confiscation Without Expropriation Cases]," *Court of Jurisdictional Disputes Journal*, no. 7 (2016): 1115–1116, https://dergipark.org.tr/tr/download/article-file/229933.

342 Akyılmaz, Sezginer, and Kaya, *Türk İdare Hukuku*, 674.

by not expropriating the immovable in dispute which is allocated as school area in the construction plans for a long time, or by not giving another immovable to the plaintiff through barter, respects property right of the individual."[343] Court of Jurisdictional Disputes indicated that administrative judiciary has jurisdiction on the matters concerning legal seizure.[344]

3.5.2. Procedure of Transfer

An immovable property that is under the ownership of a public corporate body cannot be expropriated by another public corporate body.[345] For these situations, procedure of transfer may be in question. Accordingly, the public corporate body which is in need of an immovable assesses the value of the property and makes a written application to another administration by indicating the value.

If these two public corporate bodies agree, then the property is transferred. If they do not, upon the application of the administration which demands the property, the related circuit of State Council decides on the dispute within two months. State Councils decision is final. In the event that the parties agree during the case, State Council rules that there is no necessity to decide on the matter since there is no dispute at hand.[346]

Upon the decision of State Council, purchaser administration implements the procedure laid down in the article 10 of Expropriation Act. Namely, administration applies to civil court of first instance for the determination of the price. The procedure prescribed in article 10 of the Law is mentioned under the title of "3.5.1.1.2. Phase of Expropriation."

A property, resource, limited real right, which is obtained in this way, is counted as being expropriated. Therefore, the obtained good cannot be used for a purpose other than the aim of transfer or outside the will of transferor administration.

Lastly, we should mention the administrations which are authorized to establish acts of transfer. Above, we mentioned that not every public corporate body can expropriate. According to State Council, not every public corporate body has the authority to make a "transfer" as well. For instance, in a case that is subject to a dispute before State Council, a foundation university (according to law,

343 Court of Cassation, General Assembly of Civil Chambers, M. 2010/662, D. 2010/651, 15.12.2010, www.lexpera.com.tr.

344 CJD, M. 2011/238, D. 2012/63, 09.04.2012, www.hukukturk.com.

345 Akyılmaz, Sezginer, and Kaya, *Türk İdare Hukuku*, 653.

346 SC 1st C., M. 2016/1192, D. 2016/108, 22.06.2016, www.kazanci.com.

foundation universities do not have authority of expropriation) applied to another public corporate body for the transfer of a property. Since the parties could not agree, the dispute was reviewed by State Council. High Court reached the conclusion that not being authorized to expropriate also prevents the public corporate body—which is not authorized—from being a party to "transfer acts."[347]

3.5.3. Requisition

Requisition is a method, in which administration is authorized to acquire the right to use or own the property of movables and to temporarily use immovables of private law persons or to force citizens to work for administration.[348] That is to say, through the act of requisition:

- Administration may acquire the right to own or use a movable belonging to a private law person,
- Administration may acquire solely the right to temporarily use the immovable belonging to a private law person,
- Administration may impose forced labor to citizens.[349]

---

347 The related part of the decision is as follows: "Considering these evaluations on the subject and the paragraph added to the additional article 7 of the Higher Education Law no 2547, foundation higher education institutions will not be able to acquire an immovable subject to private property through expropriation, even if it is for a public duty such as education. Therefore, it would be contrary to the purpose of the legislator to state that a foundation higher education institution, which does not have the opportunity to expropriate even a privately owned immovable when the public interest is in question, can take over the immovable belonging to another public corporate body that is already functional for a public service." SC 1st C., M. 2013/1210, D. 2013/1120, 24.09.2013, www.kazanci.com.

348 Ramazan Yıldırım, *Türk İdari Rejimi Dersleri* [*Turkish Administrative Regime Lectures*] (Konya: Mimoza, 2014), 424.

349 In the article 7 of State of Emergency Law, it is laid down that "Public institutions and corporations as well as legal and real private law persons, who are within the area in which state of emergency is declared due to natural disaster and dangerous epidemic diseases, are obliged to give land, territory, facility, vehicle, equipment, food, medicine, medical equipment, clothing and other items that are requested from them or which are subject to obligations." According to the article 16 of the Law, "(1) A document is given to the persons concerned in return for the work done and for the goods received or used. (2) Upon the application of obligees of property and labor to the relevant authorities with these documents, the price, rent, fee, or compensation of the goods purchased or the work done is duly paid according to the local market or sales price, as determined and appreciated by the emergency boards or bureaus. (3) In cases of

Unlike in the situations that necessitate expropriation, it is most of the time possible for administration to purchase a movable property that it needs. Likewise, it is also possible for the administration to find people that desire to work in public service. Therefore, requisition is principally only an available method during state of "emergency" when it is hard for administration to find sufficient personnel or to obtain movable property. In times of emergency, it may also be necessary to confiscate an immovable for a temporary period. For instance, in case that a hospital collapses due to a severe earthquake, an immovable nearby may be confiscated to cure the wounded.

In the article 119 of the Constitution, it is prescribed that, in state of emergencies, financial, material or labor obligations to be imposed on citizens shall be regulated by law. Provisions concerning requisition can be found in the laws that are implemented during state of emergencies (such as Law on National Defense Obligation Law no. 3634, Turkish National Protection Law no. 3780) and especially in the State of Emergency Law no. 2935.

In principle, an equivalence is paid to the relevant persons in return for the requisition.[350] This payment does not have to be in advance. As a matter of fact, related laws prescribe that the payment in return for these obligations shall be made after the end of state of emergency.

3.5.4. Nationalization

Through nationalization, movable and immovable properties in the possession of private law persons can be transferred to administration. According to the article 47 of the Constitution, private law undertakings that are of the nature of public service can be nationalized.

Nationalization enables the transfer of undertakings as a whole—with its movable, immovable properties, receivables and debts—which are carried out by private law persons but are in the nature of a public service or has become public service over time. Of course, such a transfer can only be possible if prescribed by law. In addition, the Constitution lays down that a private undertaking can only be nationalized in case that it is compulsory due to public interest. Legislature

---

delayed payments or payments with instalments or are settled in installments, these receivables are paid together with additional legal interest. (4) Interested parties may apply to the civil jurisdiction against the price, rent, fee or compensation that is appreciated in accordance with the general provisions."

350 Ahmet Yayla, *Türk İdare Hukukuna Göre İstimvalin Rejimi* [*The Regime of Requisition Pursuant to Turkish Administrative Law*] (Ankara: Yetkin, 2016), 190.

has the authority to determine whether nationalization is compulsory. However, from the Constitutional provision, it is understood that, to nationalize an undertaking, the public service carried out by the private law persons should be in the qualification of a monopoly and establishment and operation of this service by administration should be extremely difficult due to present conditions. Otherwise, right to property may be breached.

In fact, according to the article 2 of Law no. 3082 on Nationalization,[351] nationalization is only possible in case that three cumulative conditions are met. Firstly, the service or production of private person constitutes public service nationwide. Secondly, there is no way to provide this service or production through control, competition, substitution or other ways. Thirdly, in case that the service or production is slowed down or ceased, the public will confront great harm.

The reverse process of nationalization is privatization. Likewise, privatization is only possible if prescribed by law and through the procedures laid down in the law. As a matter of fact, the Law no. 4046 on Implementation of Privatization is enacted for this purpose.

351 Law no. 3082 on Procedure and Substance of Nationalization of the Private Undertakings Which is in the Characteristics of Public Service in Situations where Public Interest Obliges, dated 20.11.1984, OG 01.12.1984–18592.

Section II: Activities of Administration

Abstract
To realize public interest, administration has two main activities, namely, public service and police. The activity of police is aimed at realizing "public order" by restricting fundamental rights and freedoms. Under the subject of "police" we will firstly detail the elements of public order, namely, safety, well-being, general health and other elements. Secondly, we will elaborate the essential distinctions concerning police, which also has effects on the determination of jurisdiction. Thirdly, we will touch upon administrative policing procedures. Within policing procedures, an activity may be free, subject to notification or permission, or may be totally prohibited. Fourthly, we will implement article 13 of the Constitution, in which lawfulness criteria of restriction of fundamental rights and freedoms are shown, to the activities of police. Lastly, we will indicate that policing powers expand in times of emergency in which public order is more distorted compared to ordinary times.

The other main activity of administration, which is public service, aims to realize common needs and thus public interest. Under the subject of "public service," we will first detail the principles of public service: continuity, regularity, adaptation, equality, impartiality and gratuitousness. Secondly, we will elaborate the establishment of public service. Thirdly, public service will be handled according to the person who will carry out the service, with which monetary resource and employee. Accordingly, public service may be carried out by the administration itself or by a private law person through a unilateral assignment of administration or an agreement.

Keywords: police, public order, proportionality, public service, principles of public service, public interest

1. Police (Law Enforcement)

Law enforcement refers to the notion of "police." The term "police" meant the administration of provinces and organization of states beforehand. Later on, it meant the administration of state and the activities of the government. Today, police bear a narrower scope and refers to a specific activity of the administration.[352]

When we use the term "police," the activities of gendarmerie and police organization come into mind. However, in public law, police refers to an activity of the administration in a broad manner. In other words, police does not only cover the activities of gendarmerie or police (officer), but all the activities carried out to secure public order.[353] In this sense, activity of police emerges in numerous fields. The activities of Information Technologies and Communication Authority, Capital Markets Board, Competition Authority, Radio and Television High Council, acts of municipalities regarding licenses in the field of labor or business and hunting ban on endangered animals are a few examples within this regard.

The fundamental aim of all administrative activities is to actualize public interest. Public order which is the aim pursued by policing is a narrower and a particular aim compared to public interest. Police serves public interest by maintaining public order.[354] Public service is also an activity aimed at public interest.[355] The main difference is that while public service introduces performance (such as public works building roads, bridges), police introduces prohibitions and implements sanctions to protect public order.

While public service enables persons to use their rights, police restricts fundamental rights and freedoms to provide security, protect public health and so forth. Due to this difference, it can be put forward that administration has two distinct activities. However, it is also possible to state that there is only one activity of administration which is public service by accepting the activities such as providing security and peace, protecting health within the scope of introducing performance.

---

352 Onar, *İdare Hukukunun Umumi Esasları V. III*, 1476.

353 Yves Gaudemet, *Traité De Droit Administratif Tome I* (Paris: LGDJ, 2001), 721.

354 Özge Okay Tekinsoy, "Kolluk Faaliyetleri [Policing Activities]," in *İdare Hukuku*, ed. Turan Yıldırım (İstanbul: On İki Levha, 2022), 609.

355 Gözler, *İdare Hukuku V. II*, 252.

As seen, the final aim of both public service and police is public interest. Therefore, it is accepted in the doctrine that policing is also a public service. As a matter of fact, Gözler defines policing as "an activity of public service seeking to introduce public order."[356] A definition by Onar also points to the same conclusion.[357]

In substance, it may be put forward that public service and police have been mixed within administration and these two services have been interlocked. As a matter of fact, as Onar states, each service organization has the authority to prevent the conducts which violates order, and which opposes the processing of that public service via its own means.[358] In other words, each service has its own police.[359]

For instance, activities carried out by universities are activities which introduce services. In other words, performance of "education and training" is introduced to students who enroll to these institutions. Therefore, universities are institutions which provide public service. However, universities are also granted with authorities to take measures providing order to guarantee that this service is procured properly. Restraining students who make noise during the classes or who disturbs the activity of education may be counted within this regard. As seen, public service and police are carried out side by side most of the time.

Some authors also add "restriction of fundamental rights and freedoms" which is the result of policing to its definition. Pursuant to such a definition, administrative policing is "restrictions to rights and freedoms by public institutions aimed at providing public order."[360]

---

356 Gözler, *İdare Hukuku V. II*, 477.

357 "It shows the corpus committee (sum of) of public or individual measures taken by administration to secure the inner peace and security, health and order of a nation and to avoid the assaults against persons and posessions and which are confirmed and provided with a variety of sanctions and services carried out for this purpose." See Onar, *İdare Hukukunun Umumi Esasları V. III*, 1476.

358 Onar, *İdare Hukukunun Umumi Esasları V. III*, 1478.

359 "General police" becomes involved when the policing measures within the public service are not sufficient. Maybe, it would be appropriate to call police as a "procedure" belonging to the process of public service. See Onar, *İdare Hukukunun Umumi Esasları V. III*, 1474–1475.

360 Atay, *İdare Hukuku*, 608–609.

1.1. Public Order

The aim of policing is to provide public order.[361] Then, what is public order? According to Sancakdar, public order is "the status of maintenance of the lives of the society in peace, confidence and development."[362] According to Okay, order is the concrete order opposing disorder and refers to "the lack of disorder."[363] A society comprising of unknown number of persons whose injury will affect the entire society is required in order to call this order as "public order."[364]

According to Yayla, order is lack of confusion and disorder in a place and the validity of an environment where people live by feeling themselves and their relatives safe.[365] Likewise, according to Atay, public order is procurement of order and regularity in a specific place, in other words lack of confusion and disorder and the validity of an environment where people carry out their lives feeling safe and remote from danger and threat.[366] Another definition by Yayla includes the notion of public sphere: "public order as people and their relationships to be in regularity and a safe environment where they gather with other people, families, fellows or as a folk, in other words, in 'public sphere.'"[367]

Considering these definitions, public order may be defined as "lack of confusion and disorder in public sphere." In this situation, the notion of public sphere should also be elaborated. Is public sphere the place where private life begins? Or is it inside our home? Reaching an exact definition is not possible within this regard. Sometimes, it is seen that private life and public sphere coincide. For instance, campus of a university may be counted within public sphere. However, pictures and information in a cell phone of a student who steps into the campus is related to her private life and should be protected.

As public sphere and private life coincides, sometimes administration is required to interfere with the private life of a person. For instance, some people collect everything which they find outside and cannot throw these away. Houses of these people transforms into garbage house in time, and they disturb others to a significant extent with the formation of smell, insects, etc. In this situation,

---

361 Gilles Lebreton, *Droit Administratif Général* (Paris: Dalloz, 2013), 187; Akyılmaz, Sezginer, and Kaya, *Türk İdare Hukuku*, 589.

362 Sancakdar, Önüt, Doğan, Turhan, and Seyhan, *İdare Hukuku*, 759.

363 Okay Tekinsoy, "Kolluk Faaliyetleri," 609–610.

364 Okay Tekinsoy, "Kolluk Faaliyetleri," 610.

365 Yayla, *İdare Hukuku*, 36.

366 Atay, *İdare Hukuku*, 609.

367 Yayla, *İdare Hukuku*, 36.

administration may interfere with the garbage house. Likewise, a person who listens to loud music at night may disturb their neighbors and administration may interfere with such a situation.

As seen, it is hard to specify the exact boundaries of public sphere. According to doctrine and judiciary, public order is comprised of three elements: safety, well-being and general health. Maybe, these three elements may help to concretize or materialize the notion of public order.

1.2. Elements of Public Order

It is accepted that public order has three elements:

1. Safety
2. Well-being (public peace)
3. General health

Below, we will elaborate these elements of public order.

1.2.1. Safety

Safety is procurement of safety of life (physical integrity, honor, decency and so forth) and property. Safety of life also encompasses safety of relatives. Safety of property encompasses both property rights and other rights related to possession.

It should be noted that national security is not equivalent to safety. In national security-related matters, there is a danger aimed at the nation from inside or outside. This danger is aimed at the country and its indivisible integrity with its nation. Despite that some activities or incidents may damage public order, these may not danger national security.[368]

State Council ruled that "protection of persons' safety of life and property is a fundamental duty of the state. Administration is required to establish police organization and provide required means and possibilities to carry out this duty and provide public order and well-being timely."[369]

1.2.2. Well-Being (Public Peace)

The negation such as smoke, bad smells, garbage and noise which can disturb the public peace should be removed.[370] For instance, making noise in a specific place

---

368 Atay, *İdare Hukuku*, 614.

369 SC 10th C., M. 1994/7359, D. 1995/3559, 12.07.1995, www.kazanci.com.

370 Sancakdar, Önüt, Doğan, Turhan, Seyhan, *İdare Hukuku*, 763.

after a certain hour may damage well-being. The notion of well-being changes according to time and place. In other words, it is relative. For instance, while loud music may be allowed until 00.00 in a holiday resort, in other places the allowance may be until 10.00 p.m. Likewise, a certain conduct which disturbs well-being of a society may not disturb well-being of another society. Sacrificing an animal in a garden of a house in Germany may disturb well-being of that society. The notion of well-being may also change with time. For instance, sacrificing in the garden of apartment blocks or in the street is not allowed in our country today.

Administration may use its policing authorities in situations which affect well-being in the city life negatively. For instance, State Council has found that the decision of metropolitan municipality, regarding removal of sand deposit which exposes sand and smoke to a certain place outside of the city, is unlawful. In this decision, the Court made its assessments depending on the element of well-being.[371] Likewise, State Council has found an administrative fine charged to a hospital lawful, since the hospital which did not take due precautions, polluted the environment through the smoke from its chimney.[372] In another dispute, license given by administration to an enterprise which exposes dust and smoke and which was situated in an area full of olive trees was found to be unlawful.[373]

However, decisions taken by administration depending on the element of "well-being" may not be lawful all the time. For instance, a decision of the municipality regarding the removal of a lightened advertising board in front of a furniture shop was found to be unlawful.[374]

1.2.3. General Health

It is important to know that each person's health does not concern public health.[375] Health of each individual may be handled within the scope of public service. Hospitals usually deliver such public service. The health that concerns police, on the other hand, is the health of the society, in other words, general health. For instance, combat of health ministry with swine influenza, Ebola, AIDS and corona virus may be accepted as protection of general health.

---

371 SC 8th C., M. 1992/2310, D. 1993/2419, 17.06.1993, www.kazanci.com.
372 SC 6th C., M. 1999/4388, D. 1999/4681, 12.10.1999, www.kazanci.com.
373 SC 8th C., M. 2009/8976, D. 2010/3225, 04.06.2010, www.kazanci.com.
374 SC 6th C., M. 2005/1905, D. 2005/4944, 21.10.2005, www.kazanci.com.
375 Akyılmaz, Sezginer, and Kaya, *Türk İdare Hukuku*, 599.

To protect general health, it is possible to restrict fundamental rights and freedoms.[376] For instance, entrance may be restricted to places under quarantine because of a contagious disease. Freedom of residence and movement may be restricted.

Combat against addiction to drugs or alcohol may as well require administration to take police actions regarding general health.[377] Likewise administration may scrutinize and take police actions if required regarding the usage of devices which has been a part of social life with technological developments and which may damage persons' health. The most recent examples within this scope are cell phones, base stations[378] and wireless network.

---

376 However, administration shall obey some standards while restricting fundamental rights and freedoms for general health. Otherwise, the restriction would be unlawful. For instance, in a case, a primary school teacher was suspected that she does not have mental health due to her behavior and speech during her defense for an investigation which was aimed at her, and it was decided to transfer her to a healthcare facility at the end of the investigation. Transfer decision was implemented obligatorily by the police officers since the mentioned teacher refused to go to the healthcare facility. State Council has ruled that right to liberty and freedom was infringed via obliging a person to go to somewhere even though the administration does not have a base in the law. SC, 2nd C., M. 2011/9468, D. 2013/8021, 13.11.2013, www.kazanci.com.

377 Sancakdar, Önüt, Doğan, Turhan, Seyhan, *İdare Hukuku*, 764. Subarticle (e) of article 5 of ECHR on right to liberty and security lays down that "the lawful detention of persons for prevention of the spreading of infectious diseases, of persons of unsound mind, alcoholics or drug addicts or vagrants" do not infringe this right. Even though freedom of persons of unsound mind who creates danger for society can be restricted, as laid down explicitly in ECHR, it is required that the subject is laid down in law and the act is carried out legally by institutions which is authorized by this law.

378 "Accordingly an expert report is necessary on whether base stations are required to be established in the residential district, whether the same working performance will be valid in case that it is established in a place other than the residential district, whether it will damage persons' health in case that it is established in the residential district. If it is put forward that the mentioned base station will not damage persons' health if it is established in the residential district, then a further expert report is also required on the grounds that if the base station possesses the conditions laid down in the by-law..." SCPSCAC, M. 2005/3419, D. 2008/966, 03.04.2008, www.kazanci.com.

1.2.4. Other Elements of Public Order

In doctrine, it is put forward that some other elements are added to the mentioned three elements (safety, well-being and general health) of public order:[379] Human dignity, protection of individuals against themselves (for instance, obligation to fasten seat belt), public morality,[380] public esthetics (for instance, ensuring that the buildings are in the same color, not permitting structuring that disarrays the landscape of the city or clearing advertisement boards off streets)[381] and so forth.[382]

Administration may be authorized by law to take measures on removal or reorganization of the structures which cause eyesore to provide public aesthetics.[383] Administration may interfere with the area of private property by using this authority.[384] On the other hand, administration itself should not eliminate public aesthetics. State Council has approved the findings of the administration court which annulled the decision of the municipal council regarding structuring of

---

379 Gözler states that while modern approach (unlike classical approach) adds new elements other than the three mentioned within the notion of public order. Gözler, *İdare Hukuku V. II*, 479; SC 6th C., M. 1988/477, D. 1988/646, 09.05.1988, www.kazanci.com.

380 Sancakdar, Önüt, Doğan, Turhan, and Seyhan, *İdare Hukuku*, 764.

381 6th Circuit of the State Council confirmed the decision of the administrative court on acknowledgment of a municipality's act on not allowing an advertisement board to be placed at the roof of a building. SC 6th C., M. 1998/3936, D. 1999/4131, 21.09.1999, www.kazanci.com.

382 It is pointed out that in France, a new public order element as "respect to necessities of cohabitation" (le respect des exigences du vivre-ensemble) has been emerged. Accordingly, activities that are contrary to basic values of French society and republic can be prohibited. As an example to the implementation of this element, prohibition of "concealing face in society" is accepted to be legal. Lebreton, *Droit Administratif Général*, 194–195.

383 Lebreton, *Droit Administratif Général*, 188.

384 For instance, article 40 of the Construction Law is as follows: "(1) The people concerned shall be notified that they must eliminate the issues of and prevent emergence of debris and heaps in landlots, houses and other places, facilities that generate noise and smoke, private gutters, sewers, pits, wells, caves and similar things which violate public safety and hygiene and are objectionable in respect of urban planning, aesthetics or traffic. (2) If the notification is not respected within the time allowed in the notification, the municipality or governorship shall eliminate such problems and collect the costs with a 20% surcharge from the landlot owner; and suspend the activity which gives rise to such issues."

parking lot and bazaar to Güvenpark which is situated in Ankara, considering the element of "aesthetics."[385]

Administration should also make plans regarding public aesthetics beforehand and consider the facts that would be in question in advance, such as number of expected immigrants and emerging new technologies. State Council has emphasized this point stating that "It is clear that implementation and preparation of the construction plan should precede urban growth."[386]

Administration is also responsible to prevent persons to self-harm. For instance, obligations regarding the drivers to fasten seat belts or motorcycle drivers to wear helmet is a result of policing activity aimed at this objective. Convincing a person not to commit suicide or preventing her by using force may also be an example on this regard.

Prevention of staining one's dignity or prevention of activities causing one to be humiliated in public or prevention of someone to be humiliated, who accept to be humiliated may also be regarded within the scope of public order.[387] For instance, the character played by Kemal Sunal in a movie called "Şark Bülbülü" accepts to be beaten to get money in return. According to a national gazette news, this film came true, and a person began to earn money by being beaten.[388] In those kinds of situations, it may be admitted that administration needs to take precautions to protect public order.[389] French State of Council also approved the

---

385 SC 6th C., M. 1988/477, D. 1988/646, 09.05.1988, www.hukukturk.com.

386 SC 6th C., M. 1996/5362, D. 1997/3020, 17.06.1997, www.kazanci.com.

387 Lebreton, *Droit Administratif Général*, 192–194.

388 http://www.hurriyet.com.tr/gundem/ekmegimi-dayak-yiyerek-kazaniyorum-19775885.

389 State Council approved the court of first instance which decided "to dismiss the action on the grounds that the act in dispute is not unlawful since it is understood that in the broadcast which is the subject of the dispute, the presenter of the program Mehmet Ali Erbil used element of humor in the program, brought seven persons who have several disabilities and who among one of them was dressed soldier cloths on the stage, gave instruction to raise their hands by giving them various orders just like in the military service, the genitalia of the person was displayed on the screen in consequence of the presenter's move who quickly lowered the pants of a person among the seven by getting behind them, the disabled persons were used as a figure by the nature of the program and the situations which is arisen from the persons being disabled as an element of humor, the mentioned situation originated affects tarnishing the persons' dignity with respect to a great deal of disabled persons and their families even though it is accepted that these persons has participated in the program willingly and the broadcast in dispute violates the principle of broadcasting laid down in the

administrative act which prohibited a game that involved throwing very short adult people away in a discotheque.[390]

Meanwhile, administration itself should not dishonor or insult any person. For instance, it is brought forward that a person was walked around with a head of sheep on hand after being caught by police with the allegation of stealing a sheep and this subject was published in several newspapers.[391] After the mentioned person acquitted of the criminal case, compensation suit was brought before (full remedy action) the administrative jurisdiction. In this dispute, State Council ruled that even though it emphasized that the fact could not be proved with the evidence, in the event that the fact was real, the intentional and malicious activities of the police were not related to public service, and they were responsible with their individual faults. Therefore, State Council ruled that in such cases the rules regarding the protection of public officials were not applicable.[392]

It should be stated that additional elements such as human dignity, preventing persons to self-harm and public aesthetic may be considered within the scope of three elements we mentioned at the beginning.[393] For instance, preventing persons to self-harm and public aesthetic may be associated, respectively, with safety and well-being. Likewise, human dignity may also relate to public well-being.

1.3. Essential Distinctions Regarding Police

The activity of policing is subjected to several distinctions. First, police activities are subject to a distinction according to the area it concerns. Secondly, it is further divided into two considering the characteristic of the activity.

---

subparagraph (s) of article 4 of the Act no 3984." See SC, 13th C., M. 2008/3035, D. 2009/4642, 27.04.2009, www.kazanci.com.

390 Conseil d'État, N° 136727, ECLI: FR: CEASS:1995: 136727.19951027, 27 octobre 1995; http://arianeinternet.conseil-etat.fr.

391 Constitutional Court has decisions regarding human dignity. For a decision stating that especially "exposure" and "beating" is contrary to human dignity, see Pertev Bilgen, *İdare Hukuku* [*Administrative Law*] (İstanbul: Filiz, 1996), 33 (summary of the CC decision M. 63/75).

392 SC 12th C., M. 1969/2245, D. 1971/2418, 28.10.1971, reciter Yüksel Esin, *Danıştay'da Açılacak Tazminat Davaları, İkinci Kitap, Esas* [*Compensation Actions Before State Council, Second Book, Merits*] (Ankara, 1973), 247–248.

393 Okay Tekinsoy, "Kolluk Faaliyetleri," 614.

1.3.1. General Administrative Police—Special Administrative Police

Safety, well-being and general health which compromise public order cannot be provided via only usual police personnel and methods. This is because, firstly preventing some infringements of public order requires expertness. Secondly, some infringements show their results on the long term (erosion, nuclear waste and some other environmental pollutions). These can only be prevented with measures prepared by expert staff.

Therefore, it is beneficial to make a distinction between general administrative police and activities that require different expertness and organization. A variety of subjects such as protection of forests, protection of cultural and natural properties, scrutinization of development and housing, control of customs, scrutinization of stock market and markets are within the scope of special administrative policing.

It should be noted that the branches in the general administrative police as a result of division of labor should be distinguished with the special administrative police. For instance, the activities of the branches or departments such as smuggling, action force, children police and narcotics within the police department are examples of general police. Therefore, the police which works at narcotics is required to take action when witnessing a crime is committed which is not within the area of expertise. However, tourism police cannot interfere in case of murder at a hotel. Its expertness is auditing the hygiene and maintenance of hotels, etc.

Gözler emphasizes that the main difference between general administrative police and special administrative police relies on the "subject-matter competence."[394] Indeed, in special administrative police, expertness in a particular subject and exercising power only on this subject are in question compared to general administrative police. Additionally, in case of special policing, types of procedures are different from general policing.[395]

It is debated whether the activities of local administrations (special provincial administrations, municipal districts and villages) regarding police falls within general or special policing. Dominant view on this regard accepts policing activities of local administrations as general police.[396] It is important to know here

---

394 Gözler, *İdare Hukuku V. II*, 500.

395 Okay Tekinsoy, "Kolluk Faaliyetleri," 621.

396 Gözler, *İdare Hukuku V. II*, 505. For dissenting view, see Akyılmaz, Sezginer, and Kaya, *Türk İdare Hukuku*, 607.

that the elements of well-being and health are on the focus within the scope of policing activities carried out by local administrations. Exceptionally, there are some provisions in statutes regarding local administrations to provide safety (obligations of municipals to remove things that can cause accidents and to prohibit these with this purpose).

In brief, general police is authorized and responsible to execute police acts and actions on every activity and everybody in the area which it is authorized.[397] Its authorized area does not have to compromise the whole country. Even the private security in the university is accepted to be general police since it can execute vast number of policing acts in order to maintain the public order. In contrast, special police is authorized in the area of particular activities[398] (like banking, tourism and protection of forests) or particular groups and persons (e.g., policing on hunting only concerns hunters).

1.3.2. Judicial Police—Administrative Police

Both judicial police and administrative police are carried out by the same administration and personnel.[399] However, the difference of these activities is their characteristic. Basically, while administrative police prevents distortion of public order, judicial police concerns actions regarding prosecution of crimes.

However, the organization and personnel are the same. In other words, both judicial police and administrative police are carried out with the same personnel and organization, which are police officers and gendarmerie. While police officers take actions regarding prosecution of crimes under the orders of public prosecutors, they also are under the order of ministry of the interior, governorship and security general directorate due to their administrative policing activities.

Gendarmerie has three duties: military duties, duties regarding judicial policing and administrative policing. The distinction is important since the jurisdictions differ according to this distinction. Administrative law applies to administrative policing and disputes are resolved by administrative jurisdiction. On the other hand, judicial policing relates to criminal law and arising disputes in this area are resolved in criminal jurisdiction.[400] This distinction between

397 Sancakdar, Önüt, Doğan, Turhan, and Seyhan, *İdare Hukuku*, 765.

398 Sancakdar, Önüt, Doğan, Turhan, and Seyhan, *İdare Hukuku*, 765.

399 Akyılmaz, Sezginer, and Kaya, *Türk İdare Hukuku*, 602; Okay Tekinsoy, "Kolluk Faaliyetleri," 617.

400 Gözler, *İdare Hukuku V. II*, 490; Sancakdar, Önüt, Doğan, Turhan, and Seyhan, *İdare Hukuku*, 761.

judicial police and administrative police is made with two criteria: prevention-suppression criterion and criterion of being related to a crime.

1.3.2.1. Prevention-Suspension Criterion

According to the prevention-suspension criterion, administrative police is in a preventive character, whereas judicial police is in suppressive character. In other words, while administrative police aims to prevent public order to be damaged, judicial police aims to sanction the actions which have already damaged public order.

While administrative police acts before public order is distorted and crimes are committed, judicial police acts after crimes are committed. Judicial police aims to identify offenders, gather evidence and deliver defendants to judicial authorities to enable a criminal suit on defendants after the crime is committed.

Constitutional Court explained judicial police as "the activities towards pursuing a committed crime, gathering evidence, prosecuting offenders and catching them."

1.3.2.2. Criterion of Being Related to a Crime (Intent)[401]

Criterion of being related to a crime is developed by French State Council and French Court of Jurisdictional Disputes.[402] Accordingly, if an activity of police relates to a specific crime, then judicial police is in question. Otherwise, administrative police is at hand. Here, what is important is the aim of the activity of police. This aim is in fact the intention which police officer has commencing its policing duty. If this intention is related to investigation or prosecution of a crime, then judicial police is in question. If not, administrative policing prevails.[403] For instance, if police officer searches the offender of a crime which is committed in the area implicitly during a routine alcohol control to drivers, judicial policing activity is invalid since the main intention is prosecution and investigation of a crime.

In doctrine, Zabunoğlu criticizes the mentioned criteria due that "their boundaries are not explicit" and defends that the distinction should be made according to the provisions of Law of Police Powers.[404] It may be

---

401 Gözler, *İdare Hukuku V. II*, 485.
402 Gözler, *İdare Hukuku V. II*, 485.
403 Gözler, *İdare Hukuku V. II*, 485.
404 Zabunoğlu, *İdare Hukuku*, 544.

concluded that the provision in Law of Police Powers lays down both criteria.[405]

1.4. Administrative Policing Procedures

1.4.1. Freeness

Freeness refers to the ability of persons to execute any activity freely on condition that it does not disturb public order. In other words, it refers to carrying out activities without facing any condition like notification or obtaining permission. In a pluralist and liberal democratic law system, freeness regime is what is essential.[406]

Activities that are not subject to permission or not prohibited by laws such as traditional meetings or marriage ceremonies are in principle free. However, exceptionally these activities may be prohibited if they disturb public order. In these situations, administration should choose the least restrictive and the most libertarian measure.

For instance, according to Environmental Law and related regulations, local environment board has the authority to designate or prohibit the areas which marriage ceremonies can take place. We think that the administration should allow marriage ceremonies to take place in places where the damage to the environment would be less instead of prohibition. In other words, power to "designate" should be prior to prohibition with a libertarian approach.

According to the Constitution (article 33), associations (legal societies) may be established without getting a permission. It is also not required to obtain a permission or to notify an office to publish a book.

However, it should also be noted that carrying out a practice without notifying or obtaining a permission does not grant a right to carry out unlawful practices. If an unlawful practice is in question, predetermined sanctions may be implemented.

---

405 According to the provision, duty of the police is "a) to obviate following the provisions of this law before the actions being committed contrary to laws, ordinances, directives, government orders and public order, b) to fulfil duties written in Law of Criminal Procedure and the other laws after a crime is committed." The word "obviate" and "to fulfil duties regarding a crime" seem to encompass criteria of prevention-suppression and "being related to a crime."

406 Atay, *İdare Hukuku*, 644–645.

1.4.2. Notification Procedure

For some activities, notification is obliged. In this case, it is not necessary to obtain a permission. However, to execute a practice, it is obligatory to notify the administration that is laid down in the related law.[407]

The difference between permission procedure and notification procedure is that while in the prior it is not possible to carry out the activity without a permission, in the latter notification is sufficient to carry out such activity. In other words, in the notification procedure, administration does not establish an act. Administration also shall not hamper the activity by "not taking" the notification.

For instance, obligation to notify governorship or district governorship is laid down in the Law on Meetings and Demonstrations.[408]

However, notification does not mean that the administration can no longer intervene when the public order is distorted.[409] In such cases, administration may apply sanction by using its policing authority.

1.4.3. Permission Procedure

According to the permission procedure, in order to carry out some activities, it is obligatory to obtain a permission from the administration.[410]

In Turkey, many activities are subject to permission. To name a few: According to Law on Police Powers, opening places of entertainment is subject to the permission of administrative chief (provincial governor and local governor). Such places that are opened without a permission are closed down by the police officers (article 7). Again, permission is obligatory to construct a building and after that inhabitancy permission is needed according to the Zoning Code (articles 21 and 30).

---

407 Okay Tekinsoy, "Kolluk Faaliyetleri," 639; Sancakdar, Önüt, Doğan, Turhan, and Seyhan, *İdare Hukuku*, 780.

408 According to the article 34 of the Constitution, "Everyone has the right to hold unarmed and peaceful meetings and demonstration marches without prior permission." In a recent Constitutional Court decision, a provision of Law no. 2911 on Meetings and Demonstrations was annulled due that it was amounting to a permission procedure for meetings and demonstrations. Therefore, the Court found that these provisions were contrary to articles 13 and 34 of the Constitution. CC, M. 2018/137, D. 2022/86, 30.06.2022, OG 12.01.2023–32071.

409 Atay, *İdare Hukuku*, 646.

410 Okay Tekinsoy, "Kolluk Faaliyetleri," 638; Sancakdar, Önüt, Doğan, Turhan, and Seyhan, *İdare Hukuku*, 779–780.

1.4.4. Prohibition Procedure

Prohibition procedure means that legislature has prohibited a certain activity (on condition that it does not contradict with the Constitution and international treaties). According to the principle of a state governed by rule of law, administration cannot prohibit an activity which is not envisaged by law. In other words, administration cannot introduce a prohibition with an administrative act without basing on a law. Therefore, from the perspective of administration, prohibition procedure is the implementation of the prohibition envisaged by law.[411]

Prohibiting gambling in hotels, closing down private teaching institutions (dershane) and prohibiting smoking in closed areas[412] may be counted as examples to the prohibitions envisaged by law.

1.5. Lawfulness of Police Acts and Actions

According to article 13 of the Constitution, "Fundamental rights and freedoms may be restricted only by law and in conformity with the reasons mentioned in the relevant articles of the Constitution without infringing upon their essence. These restrictions shall not be contrary to the letter and spirit of the Constitution and the requirements of the democratic order of the society, the secular republic and the principle of proportionality."

Firstly, the notion of "restriction" in the article is important. The term "restriction" should not be interpreted as the elimination of fundamental rights and freedoms entirely. Since the legislator has chosen the word "restriction," an "area" should be left from the "right" to be benefitted from.[413]

Since policing activity restricts certain fundamental rights and freedoms, this activity should abide by the principles laid down in article 13 of the Constitution. These principles are explained below.

---

411 Atay, *İdare Hukuku*, 647.

412 Okay Tekinsoy, "Kolluk Faaliyetleri," 636–637.

413 "The word 'restriction' should be interpreted as the narrowing down of the norm area (assurance area) of fundamental rights and freedoms by legislature. In other words, the opportunity to benefit from a certain right or freedom should continue even after it is restricted." SC, 10th C., M. 2006/946, D. 2008/6084, 15.09.2008; www.kazanci.com.

1.5.1. Restriction Must Have a Basis Provided by Law

It is only possible for the administration to restrict a right or freedom, only if it has a basis in the law. Administration cannot introduce a prohibition which is not envisaged by law.

For instance, Student Selection and Placement Center (ÖSYM) had issued a bylaw regarding taking fingerprints of the candidates and methods on retinal scanning to provide security and confidentiality of exams. State Council highlighted that a law regarding protection of personal data had not been come into force at the time of this act yet and administration should not regulate such an area with a bylaw.[414]

1.5.2. Restriction Must Be in Conformity with the Reasons Mentioned in the Relevant Articles of the Constitution

Restriction cannot be based on a reason other than the mentioned reasons in the relevant articles of the Constitution. A reason mentioned for the restriction of a right or freedom cannot be used for the restriction of another right or freedom.

For instance, in the article 23 of the Constitution, freedom of residence and movement is regulated. According to the third paragraph of the article, "freedom of movement may be restricted by law for the purpose of investigation and prosecution of an offence, and prevention of crimes." Accordingly, freedom of movement cannot be restricted due to, for instance, "general health." In fact, in Turkey, curfews which were implemented during COVID-19 pandemic were highly criticized,[415] since Constitution does not allow freedom of movement to be restricted due to the reasons of "general health."[416]

---

414 SCPSCAC, SE 2013/819, 06.03.2014, www.ido.org.tr/lib_upload/files/Danistay%20 karari.pdf.

415 In Turkey, state of emergency was not declared due to pandemic.

416 See Seçkin Yavuzdoğan, "Tehlikeli Salgın Hastalık Sebebiyle Alınan Sokağa Çıkma Yasağı Kararları Üzerine Birkaç Not [A Few Notes on Curfew Decisions Due to Dangerous Epidemic Diseases]," *Adalet Dergisi* 1, no. 2 (2020): 134, https://dergipark.org.tr/tr/download/article-file/1205205; Zeynep Şahin, "Pandemi Dönemindeki Kısıtlamaların Hukukiliği [Legality of Restrictions During Pandemics]," *KHAS Hukuk Bülteni*, June 17, 2021, https://hukukbulteni.khas.edu.tr/bulten/89; Gözler, "Korona Virüs Salgınıyla Mücadele İçin Alınan Tedbirler Hukuka Uygun Mu? (2) [Are The Measures Taken For The Fight Against Corona Virus Pandemic Lawful?]," 6.07.2020, https://www.anayasa.gen.tr/korona-2.htm.

1.5.3. Restriction Must Not Be Contrary to the Letter and Spirit of the Constitution

The letter of the Constitution means the "text" of the Constitution. The condition of being in line with the letter of Constitution especially gains more importance when the Constitution introduces an additional guarantee for a right.[417] For instance, in the article 21 of the Constitution, it is stated that no domicile shall be entered unless there exists a decision duly given by a judge.[418] Therefore, a police officer cannot enter a domicile without obtaining a court decision.

The spirit of the Constitution is a debated expression.[419] In general, we can interpret this notion as the principle of a state governed by law.

1.5.4. Restriction Must Not Infringe the Essence of the Fundamental Rights and Freedoms

The essence of a right is interpreted by the Constitutional Court. Accordingly, acts which constrain a fundamental right or freedom to a great extent and which lefts no place for the implementation of a right and freedom are accepted to infringe the essence of the right and freedom.[420]

1.5.5. Restriction Must Not Be Contrary to the Requirements of the Democratic Order of the Society

Democratic order of the society should be "libertarian and pluralist democracy." Within this scope, a decision of State Council may be mentioned. The dispute before the Court was related to the decision of the governor, who did not permit putting up of posters of a political party. State Council evaluated the expression of "Yankee Go Home with Your Soldier-Bases and Hamburgers" on the posters. State Council ruled that the decision of the governor is unlawful as the expression on the posters are of the characteristic of the reflection of plurivocality which is natural in a democratic and libertarian system.[421]

---

417 Gözler, *İdare Hukuku V. II*, 585.

418 This article has an exception in cases where delay is prejudicial.

419 Tanör and Yüzbaşıoğlu indicate that "the spirit of the Constitution" cannot be defined objectively. Tanör and Yüzbaşıoğlu, *1982 Anayasası*, 160.

420 CC, M. 2012/108, D. 2013/64, 22.05.2013, OG 12.07.2013–28705.

421 SC 10th C., M. 2004/7627, D. 2006/2380, 12.04.2006, www.kazanci.com.

1.5.6. Restriction Must Not Be Contrary to the Principle of Proportionality

The principle of proportionality necessitates proportionate measures to be taken to prevent distortion of the public order. State Council ruled that "according to the principle of proportionality, the measure used must be suitable to achieve the aim, the aim and measure must not be within an immoderate proportion. The principle of proportionality assures fundamental rights and freedoms, and it is aimed that a balance between restriction and rights and freedoms should be achieved, and restricted rights and freedoms are damaged to the minimum extent possible. In other words, the measure must be suitable and necessary and in a reasonable proportion to the aim."[422]

The sub-principles of the principle of proportionality are adequacy (suitability), necessity and reasonableness (proportionality *stricto sensu*). State Council explicitly mentions these sub-principles when evaluating the legality of the police act or actions.[423]

---

422 SC 10th C., M. 2009/13450, D. SE, 12.04.2010, www.kazanci.com.

423 SC 10th C., M. 2006/946, D. 2008/6084, 15.09.2008, www.kazanci.com. The related part of the decision is as follows: "The principle of proportionality, which is laid down in the 13th article of the Constitution and which is one of the criteria on restriction of fundamental rights and freedoms, indicates that a reasonable relationship should be valid between the aim and the measure, in other words an equitable balance should be valid between the restriction and the benefit provided. This principle has three sub-principles in the scrutinization of the relationship between the measure of restriction and aim of restriction, as 'adequacy' related to the determination of whether the legal measure is suitable to reach the aim of restriction, 'necessity' searching whether the restrictive measure is necessary in respect to reaching the aim of restriction and democratic public order, 'reasonableness' determining whether the aim and measure comprises an unreasonable proportion and therefore determining whether an unproportionate obligation is specified.
In the restriction of the freedom assembling a meeting, the aim is to protect national security, public order, general health and public moral and rights and freedoms of others and to prevent commitment of crime; the measure is to postpone or prohibit the meeting. In case that the aim becomes impossible to realize (for instance, providing public order or preventing commitment of crime) in case that the meeting is held, the necessity of the prohibition or postponing the meeting may be in question. In addition, in order that the proportionality principle is satisfied, the necessity is not sufficient and as mentioned above, a reasonable proportion between the aim and the measure should be valid. Within this scope, in case that the pursued aim is satisfied by postponing the meeting, banning it constitutes contradiction to the principle of

1.5.6.1. *Adequacy (Suitability)*

According to the sub-element adequacy, the measure applied in the restriction should be suitable to realize the aim of restriction.[424] In other words, the measure should contribute to the aim (public order).[425]

1.5.6.2. *Necessity (Imperativeness)*

Necessity of police acts or actions requires "the most suitable and lenient measure" (or the least restrictive measure) to be chosen. In a decision of the Constitutional Court, this sub-principle is explained as: "... Necessity-imperativeness inquires whether restrictive measure is imperative in order to reach the aim of restriction."[426] As highlighted by the High Court, the measure is accepted to be proportionate only if the measure is imperative to protect public order and if there is no other solution. If the aim would be achieved by a more lenient measure, this measure should be chosen primarily.[427] For instance, in case that establishment of a barrier is sufficient, pepper gas should not be used by the police during a protest.[428]

---

proportionality and article 13 of the Constitution." Also see MHAC, 1st C., M. 2008/1019, D. 1989/27, 26.05.2009, www.kazanci.com.

424 Okay Tekinsoy, "Kolluk Faaliyetleri," 645.

425 Yücel Oğurlu, *Karşılaştırmalı İdare Hukukunda Ölçülülük İlkesi* [*Principle of Proportionality in Comparative Administrative Law*] (Ankara: Seçkin, 2002), 168.

426 CC, M. 1988/50, D. 1989/27, 23.06.1989, OG 04.10.1989–20302.

427 Oğurlu, *Karşılaştırmalı*, 165.

428 We think that the sub-principle necessity-imperativeness also incorporates situations where administration has more than one authority to use in a particular case. In that case, administration must use the least restrictive authority. In addition, the principle of proportionality should also be valid when the authority of law enforcement is not used on persons. In a dispute subject to the decision of State Council, a person released her dog without a leash (even though otherwise is alleged, evidence could not be gathered that the dog was on a leash). At this point, the team of municipality who have received orders to kill stray dogs and cats thought that this dog was stray and killed it. State Council ruled that administration is not responsible in this specific case. We think that administration should have taken a different measure other than killing the dog since killing act and action was not necessary to reach the aim pursued. Therefore, we think that administration did not obey the principle of proportionality. However, it should be indicated that this decision belongs to the year of 1984. See SC 8th C., M. 1982/2638, D. 1984/690, 16.04.1984, www.kazanci.com. In those years, such an activity by administration would be reacted normally. Therefore, the element of time should also be considered within the scope of the principle of proportionality.

1.5.6.3. *Proportionality* Stricto Sensu

According to the sub-principle of proportionality *stricto sensu*, an unreasonable proportion between the aim and the measure must not be valid. In other words, if fundamental rights and freedoms are restricted to a great extent for a rather unimportant aim, this would be contrary to the principle of proportionality.

All the three sub-principles must be satisfied in a particular case. In other words, consistency to one of these principles is not sufficient. In case that a measure is adequate and imperative, but not proportionate, then the principle of proportionality is violated. Considering judicial decisions, it is understood that the third sub-principle (proportionality *stricto sensu*) is valued the most.[429]

An example may be found in the decisions of State Council regarding "Dağlıca Assault." As a consequence of an assault of the terrorist group to the military station in Dağlıca, a lot of soldiers were killed. Publication regarding this incident was banned by a decision signed by deputy prime minister and several ministers. However, the duration and scope (which publications was within the ban) was not determined by the decision. State Council found that restriction to right to information indefinitely was contrary to proportionality *stricto sensu*.[430]

A measure which is seen necessary in a period of time may not be seen necessary in a different period of time. Consequently, there are some old laws still in force having provisions contrary to the principle of proportionality. Firstly, the question may be avoided by answering that the lawmaker would abolish these laws if it thought so. Secondly, it can be alleged that using these powers may be unlawful based on the contemporary notion of state governed by law.

429 SC, 15th C., M. 2016/6791, D. SE 12.10.2016, www.kazanci.com. In the concrete case subject to this decision, administration implemented a regulative act in which it stated that employees authorized to give courses on driving cannot be given duties on qualifying examinations for one year in case that they commit an action contrary to the regulations. The High Court annulled this act since a reasonable proportion between the aim pursued and the measure which is not gradual regarding the severity of the action and which bears a consequence in which an action within the scope of all the regulations are subject to such sanction. Even though State Council mentioned all three sub-principles, it based its decision on the proportionality *stricto sensu*. We think that in this dispute, it should also be highlighted that the measure (restriction for one year from the service) is not necessary or imperative to prevent "actions contrary to all kinds of regulations." Secondly, it should also be stated that this measure is not adequate to prevent the aim which is directed to prevent traffic accidents.

430 SCPSCAC, M. 2009/1637, D. 2013/1160, 01.04.2013, www.kazanci.com.

Likewise, in a dispute regarding the losses during police force toward the rebellion in Diyarbakır jail, State Council highlighted that the measure in question became necessary to secure the order in jail after it examined the evidence. However, State Council evaluated that the sub-principle of proportionality *stricto sensu* was violated since "excessive force" was used which did not comply with the aim pursued.[431]

Lastly, we should mention that the notions of "location and time" are also important on the assessment of whether police acts and actions are compliant with law. The scope of supervision on police activities is broader in public places. Entering houses or workplaces is only possible in case of requests of help, prevention of crime or validity of a danger such as fire or water flood. Likewise, policing powers are broader at night compared to daytime.

1.6. Expansion of Police Powers

Sometimes, there may be situations such as natural disaster, economic crisis or extensive act of violence. In those situations, ordinary legal system may not be sufficient to suppress these emergencies, or the dangers originated from these emergencies. In other words, in state of emergencies, public order confronts dangers which are more severe compared to ordinary times.

In these situations, national sovereignty is at stake, beyond distortion of public order. This is why, police activities expand in state of emergency regimes in parallel with the broadening of distortion of public order. We may summarize what is meant by the expansion of police powers as "more restriction to freedoms and restriction to more freedoms."

Likewise, there is difference between the standard on compliance with law of the police activities in ordinary times and in state of emergencies. An act or action, which is accepted to be contrary to law in ordinary times, may be accepted to be in conformity with law in state of emergencies. Then, is expansion of police powers unlimited? What is meant by state of emergencies? We will answer these questions below.

There are laws in Turkey which one may not be aware of since they are suspended (like the sword of Demokles) during ordinary times: "state of emergency laws." These laws are not implemented during ordinary times. However, at the moment when the conditions are fulfilled, these laws become effectuate. They incorporate provisions which restrict fundamental rights and freedoms

---

431 SCPSCAC, M. 2010/2741, D. 2013/4312, 02.12.2013, www.kazanci.com.

to a considerably high extent. Below, we will explain state of emergencies, consequences of state of emergencies and the limits of policing during state of emergencies.

1.6.1. State of Emergencies

State of emergency is laid down in the article 119 of the Constitution. This article incorporates two kinds of state of emergencies within itself.

Firstly, state of emergency may be declared "in the event of war, the emergence of a situation necessitating war, mobilization, an uprising, strong rebellious actions against the motherland and the Republic, widespread acts of violence of internal or external origin threatening the indivisibility of the country and the nation, emergence of widespread acts of violence aimed at the destruction of the Constitutional order or of fundamental rights and freedoms, serious deterioration of public order because of acts of violence."

In the past, this type of state of emergency was declared due to loss of lives and properties in consequence of terrorism and the coup attempt on July 15. State of emergency was declared in certain parts of the country due to terrorism rather than in the whole country, while in the whole country during the coup attempt.

Secondly, state of emergency may be declared "in the event of occurrence of natural disasters, outbreak of dangerous epidemic diseases or emergence of a serious economic crisis." Recently, state of emergency has been declared covering 10 cities in Turkey due to the destructive earthquake centered in Kahramanmaraş for a duration of three months.[432]

State of emergency law shall become valid with the declaration of state of emergency by the President. This decision shall be published in the Official Gazette and shall be submitted for approval to the TBMM on the same day.

State of emergency is limited with time. The emergency shall not exceed six months; however, it may be extended. State of emergency is also limited with the location.[433] It shall only embody the location in which the reasons necessitating state of emergency emerges. In other words, if the reasons to declare state of emergency are only valid for a certain part of the country, then, state of emergency shall not be declared involving the whole country.

---

432 Presidential Decision no. 6785, OG 8.02.2023–32098; https://www.resmigazete.gov.tr/eskiler/2023/02/20230208-1.pdf.

433 Tanör, and Yüzbaşıoğlu, *1982 Anayasası*, 423.

1.6.2. Consequences of Declaring State of Emergency

The main consequence of declaring state of emergency is that fundamental rights and freedoms may be suspended partially or entirely. According to the first paragraph of article 15 of the Constitution, "In times of war, mobilization, a state of emergency, the exercise of fundamental rights and freedoms may be partially or entirely suspended, or measures derogating the guarantees embodied in the Constitution may be taken to the extent required by the exigencies of the situation, as long as obligations under international law are not violated."

In state of emergencies, administration may impose "monetary obligations and obligations regarding right to property and labor."[434] In ordinary times, forced labor is not possible according to article 18 of the Constitution. However, in some types of state of emergencies, labor may be forced. For instance, in the event of declaration of state of emergency due to earthquake, legal and real persons may be obliged to take duties such as debris removal.

In some types of state of emergencies, right to property may be restricted. Administration may seize a private property. For instance, administration may convert a house into a health center for the treatment of injured. Or administration may seize personal properties such as off-road cars in earthquake locations. However, the state shall compensate damages afterward.

As a second consequence, PDs may be issued during state of emergency. These PDs are not limited on subject unlike PDs issued in ordinary times.[435]

---

434 Article 119/5 of the Constitution lays down that "The monetary obligations, and obligations regarding right to property and labor to be imposed on citizens … shall be regulated by law." According to the article 5 of State of Emergency Law, "In case that state of emergency is declared due to the occurrence of natural disasters, outbreak of dangerous epidemic diseases; money and all kinds of movable and immovable property, which cannot be provided and which is needed in order to save persons effected by the disaster, necessary works, compensation of damages and losses occurred, shall be procured by obligations regarding money, assets and workforce." According to article 7 of the aforementioned law, "Legal persons and real persons who are within the location in which state of emergency is declared due to occurrence of natural disasters and outbreak of dangerous epidemic diseases are obliged to provide the land, plot, building, facility, vehicle, tool, food, pharmaceutical and medical device, cloth and other materials requested from them or they may be requisitioned."

435 Article 119/6 of the Constitution lays down that "In the event of state of emergency, the President of the Republic may issue presidential decrees on matters necessitated by the state of emergency, notwithstanding the limitations set forth in the second sentence of the seventeenth paragraph of the Article 104. Such decrees which have

In addition, judicial review of state of emergency PDs is limited. For instance, during state of emergency declared in Turkey due to terrorism, Statutory Decree no. 285 was issued, providing that the acts of governors on the location subject to state of emergency could not be reviewed by the courts. Due to this regulation, administrative courts had to dismiss the files against the mentioned acts without reviewing the legality of the act.[436]

1.6.3. Limits of Policing in State of Emergency

During state of emergency, policing powers expand. However, there are also limitations to be respected according to the law. According to the article 15 of the Constitution, first, obligations under international law must not be violated. Secondly, principle of proportionality must be respected. Thirdly, some fundamental rights shall be protected. The individual's right to life shall be inviolable except where death occurs through acts in conformity with law of war. The integrity of individual's corporeal and spiritual existence, freedom of religion and conscience, presumption of innocence, freedom of thought and opinion, retrospectivity of crimes and punishment prevails.

It is also important to know how or whether judicial review is possible in state of emergency regimes. We may answer this question in four steps. First, is decision to declare state of emergency subject to judicial review? During the term of the former Constitution (dated 1961), "Council of Ministers" decision to declare state of emergency was accepted to be an administrative act. However, State of Council ruled on lack of jurisdiction, since the decision turned into a legislative act with the approval of TBMM.[437] In case that the same approach is adopted for "the decision of the President to declare state of emergency," administrative judiciary will not be able to review this act.

Secondly, is approval of the Assembly subject to judicial review? Approval of the Assembly may not be brought before the Constitutional Court, since the

---

the force of law shall be published in the Official Gazette, and shall be submitted for approval to the Grand National Assembly of Turkey on the same day."

436 SCPSCAC, M. 2000/785, D. 2002/714, 18.10.2002, www.hukukturk.com; SC, 10th C., M. 1995/8209, D. 1996/8630, 24.12.1996, www.kazanci.com.

437 SC Plenary Session of the Chambers, M. 1970/389, D. 1970/442, 03.07.1970; recited from Kazım Yenice, "Sıkıyönetim İlanı Kararı ve Yargısal Denetimi Sorunu [Declaration of Martial Law and the Problem of It's Judicial Review]," *State Council Journal* 1, no. 2 (1971), https://www.danistay.gov.tr/assets/pdf/yayinlar/dergi/2021-02-24-11-59-8164234.pdf.

Court in the past found that this approval does not belong to legislative function. The Court ruled that this approval is only a "condition act" which provides state of emergency laws to be implemented.[438]

Thirdly, are PDs of state of emergency subject to judicial review? Article 148/1 of the Constitution lays down that "… presidential decrees issued during a state of emergency or in time of war shall not be brought before the Constitutional Court alleging their unconstitutionality as to form or substance." The same provision was adopted for decrees having force of law before the constitutional amendment in 2017.[439] When decrees having force of law of state of emergency times were before Constitutional Court, the Court ruled that in case a decree having force of law of state of emergency is not within the scope of the subject, the place and the time of state of emergency, this decree is also not within the review prohibition laid down in article 148. In other words, the Court did not bind itself with the "name" of the regulation and reviewed the constitutionality of decrees in case that they are not in the characteristics of "state of emergency decrees."[440]

However, after the attempted coup on July 15, 2016 in Turkey, state of emergency was declared and Constitution Court have changed its practice for the decrees adopted in this state of emergency.[441] In these decision, the Court bounded itself with the "name" of the regulation and ruled on lack of jurisdiction.[442] On the other hand, these decrees are debated and decided in TBMM according to the Constitution (article 119/end) and Constitutional Court has jurisdiction to review these laws.[443] When reviewing such laws, Constitutional Court emerged a new practice and examined the context of these laws. Accordingly, in case that the provision is within the time and the aim of state of emergency, then this law should be reviewed pursuant to article 15 of the Constitution which set limits to the suspension of fundamental rights and freedoms. If not, the law should be reviewed pursuant to article 13 of the Constitution which sets limits to the restriction of fundamental rights and freedoms in ordinary times.[444]

---

438 CC, M. 1970/44, D. 1970/42, 17.11.1970, OG 30.03.1971/13794.

439 With the constitutional amendment, decrees having force of law have been removed from the Constitution and PDs have been adopted.

440 CC, M. 1990/25, D. 1991/1, 10.01.1991, OG 05.03.1992–21162; CC. M. 1991/6, D. 1991/20, 3.7.1991, OG 08.03.1992–21165.

441 Tanör, and Yüzbaşıoğlu, *1982 Anayasası*, 441.

442 CC, M. 2016/166, D. 2016/159, 12.10.2016, OG 04.11.2016–29878; CC. M. 2016/171, D. 2016/164, 02.11.2016, OG 08.11.2016–29882.

443 Tanör and Yüzbaşıoğlu, *1982 Anayasası*, 442.

444 See for instance, CC, M. 2018/73, D. 2019/65, 24.07.2019, OG 29.11.2019–30963.

While this approach has prevented the results of unconstitutionality of decrees to some extent,[445] it may make such a review ineffective since unconstitutional decree would not be reviewed until it is decided by TBMM. Since the governing rules of PDs did not change on judicial review, we may state that these precedents are also valid for "state of emergency PDs."

Fourthly, are acts of state of emergency administrations subject to judicial review? For instance, can one file a suit against the acts of state of emergency governors? This is possible in theory since the Constitution does not ban such a review. However, the Constitution has a provision regarding restriction of suspension of execution. Accordingly, "the law may restrict the issuing of an order of suspension of execution of an administrative act in cases of state of emergency…." It should be noted that this provision alone is sufficient to make judicial review ineffective. This is because, even though a file is submitted before judiciary, administration will be able to implement the act in question until this act is annulled. Until the time of annulment, legal consequences of the act will come into existence and damages that cannot be compensated may occur. In fact, some laws regarding state of emergencies envisage provisions which prevent judicial review of administrative offices.

In brief, it would not be wrong to state that judicial review in state of emergencies is least possible from the perspective of positive law.

445 Tanör and Yüzbaşıoğlu, *1982 Anayasası*, 442.

2. Public Service

Public service is hard to define in administrative law. For the sake of a definition within the scope of positive law, a statement frequently made by the Constitutional Court may be considered:[446] "By its broader definition, public service is continuous and regular activities which are carried out by the state or other public corporate bodies or under the supervision and scrutinization of them in order to fulfil common needs and provide public interest."[447]

We can reach five conclusions from this definition. At first, since the state is also a public corporate body, the expression of "by the state or other public corporate bodies" may be shortened to "by public corporate bodies."

Therefore, a public corporate body may carry out a public service. Of course, the biggest public service provider is the state public corporate body. At this point, it should be noted that the activities carried out by legislature and judiciary, which do not possess a public personality, but are within the public personality of the state, are also public services.[448]

Secondly, in the definition it is stated that public services may be carried out under the supervision and scrutinization of public corporate bodies. But this definition lacks the person who can carry out the service. The person, who carries out public services under the supervision and scrutinization of public corporate bodies are private law persons.[449] Constitutional Court highlighted that

---

446 Another definition of State Council in a dispute should also be mentioned: "Activities, which are subjected to a regime of superiorities and obligations by the legislative power because of public interest and impossibility of their being provided by private persons and their responsibility and scrutinization to be undertaken by a public corporate body are accepted to be public service." SC 13th C., M. 2012/1871, D. 2013/276, 06.02.2013, www.kazanci.com.

447 CC, M. 2004/13, D. 2007/85, 17.05.2007, OG 21.11.2007–26707. This definition is the same with the definition of Onar in the doctrine. See Onar, *İdare Hukukunun Umumi Esasları V. I*, 13.

448 "Judicial activity which are carried out by courts are also public services and this service to be carried out free of charge is a fundamental principle." MHAC, M. 2004/1360, D. 2005/264, 03.02.2005, www.kazanci.com.

449 "... An important point that should be indicated for the public service to be operated by private law persons is that even though the service is operated by private law persons, the characteristics and principles related to the service do not change. Specifically, the principles of public service preserve its existence and the responsibility

the obligation of administration to carry out public service by itself changed due to the developments on social life.[450]

The abovementioned two types of legal persons generate the organic conditions of the public service. In conclusion, organic condition of public service is public service to be carried out by public corporate bodies or private law persons subject to the scrutinization of public corporate bodies.

Thirdly, the expression of "under the supervision and scrutinization of them" in the definition also draws attention. The meaning of this expression is that private law persons cannot be self-ordained when carrying out public service and should be subject to specific rules. This is because public service is in question and this service must be carried out properly. Being carried out properly means this service to be continuous, to be at a certain standard, to be not so expensive. In brief, public service needs to be carried out in accordance with the principles of public service, as we will explain below. Therefore, to secure that public service is carried out accordingly, private law persons need to be under scrutinization and supervision of administration. This activity of scrutinization and supervision is performed by administration.[451]

---

of administration holds." SC 1st C., M. 2008/744, D. 2008/834, 03.07.2008, www.kazanci.com.

450 CC, M. 1990/4, D. 19990/6, 12.04.1990, OG 17.06.1990–20551.

451 It is alleged that some activities which are carried out by private law persons without a bound with administration (like an administrative act or licenses related to public service) may also be in the characteristics of public service. In doctrine, these activities are called as virtual public service. See Peiser, *Droit Administratif*, 191; Onur Karahanoğulları, *Kamu Hizmeti* [*Public Service*] (Ankara: Turhan, 2015), 270 ff. In our opinion, if the public order deteriorates and the state would be obliged to step into this activity in case that private law persons abandon to carry out the activity, a "veiled" public service may be in question. For instance, when the "mini-busses" (dolmuş) which are operated by private law persons, went on strike, public life was effected to a great extent. Reverse was the case when taxicabs went on strike. From this perspective, it may be alleged that the activity of minibus drivers is public service, while passenger transportation via taxicabs is not. According to the first subparagraph of article 47 of the Constitution, "Private enterprises performing services of public nature may be nationalized in exigencies of public interest." From this expression, it may be concluded that some private enterprises carry out public service. (A connection may be found between the approach of Constitutional Court as "*the activity which deteriorates public life when absent*" and Gülan's approach in doctrine regarding the principles of public service being perceived even before the activity carries off the characteristic of public service. See Aydın Gülan, "Borcunu Ödemeyen Devlete Karşı Ne Yapılabilir? [What Can Be Done Against the State Which Does Not Pay its Debt],"

In France, it is highlighted that the definition of public service transformed to activities toward public interest performed by private law persons who do not use the privileges of public force under the control of administration.[452]

For instance, even though electricity distribution is carried out by a private law person, it is a public service.[453] Administration makes private law persons perform this activity via "procedure of licensing." The first step of supervision and scrutinization is to determine the persons who are going to perform this activity. Administration determines this private law person according to the criteria envisaged by law (for instance, possessing the financial capacity necessary to carry out public service). Accordingly, supervision and scrutinization begins in this stage. License is only granted to persons who can perform public service as it needs to be. Likewise, administration attains the authority to supervise and scrutinize via license or contract. In addition, administration may use its general policing authority.

In one of its decisions, State Council has highlighted about electricity public service that "activity of electricity distribution is of the characteristics of public

Journal of Administrative Law and Administrative Sciences 13, no. 1, 11 (1995): 105, https://dergipark.org.tr/tr/pub/iuihid/issue/57855/14642). In other words, it may be concluded that if private law activity is not performed continuously, in an even and impartial manner, resulting the deterioration of public life, the existence of a "veiled" public service may be in question. In case that this activity is not carried out properly, the state interferes in and nationalizes this private enterprise if necessary. In other words, the state takes over it with the whole facilities, receivables and debts. In our opinion, this take over must be performed through nationalization by law. A counter approach alleging that administration is authorized to convert a private activity into a public service, would mean granting administration with establishment of public services without any borders. This conclusion would be contrary to the principle of legal administration and public service being established by law. In doctrine, it is asserted that administration may interfere in activities which are virtual public services by bringing some obligations. We think that, even though "veiled" public services which are carried out by private law persons may be valid, it may not be asserted that administration has a general authority to interfere in such activities. As Gülan puts forward in doctrine, "administration to interfere with private law activities solely based on its own assessments by counting itself as the watchman of public service" is inconvenient. (See Aydın Gülan, "Kamu Hizmeti Kavramı [The Notion of Public Service]," *Journal of Administrative Law and Administrative Sciences* 9, no. 1–3 (1988): 157, https://dergipark.org.tr/tr/pub/iuihid/issue/1251/14697).

452 Lebreton, *Droit Administratif Général*, 133–134.

453 CC, M. 1994/43, D. 1994/42–2, 09.12.1994, OG 24.01.1995–22181.

service that is subject to superior privileges and regime of obligations apart from private activities, and which is also in the last instance under the responsibility and scrutinization of a public authority…"[454]

High Court ruled on the subject of inner-city transportation that "the municipality, is the principal provider of inner-city transportation service which is undeniably a public service in nature. Municipality has the duty and authority to regulate, scrutinize and sanction that originates from it being the principal provider of this service, in case that it does not perform this service itself and makes others perform it with several procedures."[455]

Therefore, the responsibility also belongs to the administration in public services carried out by private law persons via a license or an administrative contract. Administration would be responsible and sentenced to compensation in case that it does not supervise and scrutinize private law persons for the service to be performed regularly and does not sanction when necessary and a damage is born thereof.[456]

Fourthly, the definition involves the expression of "providing public interest." A public service which is not beneficial for public cannot be thought.[457] Public interest compromises the material condition of public service. Then, what is public interest? It is hard to define this notion. Moreover, this notion changes according to time and location, in other words it is not static.[458] In doctrine, several approaches, discussions are brought forward to define this notion. What we can do here is to approach the matter from positive law and indicate that the activities which are accepted as public service by legislature or competent organs of local administrations are toward public interest.

Lastly, the definition involves the expression of "continuous and regular activities." In fact, continuity and regularity are two of the principles of public service. There are more principles as we will mention below. In our opinion, the reason why these principles are within the definition is that these are the most important among them. An activity, which is not continuous and regular, does not make any sense. For instance, if electric service is delivered on only certain times

454 SC, 13th C., M. 2012/1871, D. 2013/276, 06.02.2013, www.kazanci.com.

455 SC, 8th C., M. 2011/3811, D. 2016/4474, 28.04.2016, www.kazanci.com.

456 For instance, State Council ordered indemnification of the damage born by ruling shared liability of Capital Markets Board and Banking Regulation and Supervision Agency which could not prevent a bank from making a transaction that was forbidden. See SC, 13th C., M. 2005/2625, D. 2005/5753, 02.12.2005, www.kazanci.com.

457 Peiser, *Droit Administratif*, 191.

458 Akyılmaz, Sezginer, and Kaya, *Türk İdare Hukuku*, 3.

of the day, this service being delivered on an equal manner or by benefitting from the best technologies would not be important.

On the other hand, are these principles obliged to be within the definition? The answer to this question is negative. In case that the organic and material condition is realized, then there is a public service and this service is needed to be performed in conformity with the principles of public service.

Özay in doctrine also mentions within the context of public service that if the need could not be fulfilled, disturbance in society would emerge.[459] Likewise, Constitutional Court highlighted that noncontinuity and irregularity on deliverance of public service makes public life turn upside down.[460] In our opinion, definitions of Özay and Constitutional Court also demonstrate that continuity and regularity are more important compared to other principles.

There is no hesitation that the activities which are designated in Constitution as public service are public services. These activities are "constitutional public services."[461] For instance, the activity of education is characterized as public service in the Constitution explicitly. In a dispute, State Council ruled that "the fact that a service which is designated as public service in Constitution or in the laws that are performed by real or legal persons who are subject to private law norms or performed by employees of these persons does not change the characteristic of this activity being a public service and the employee being a public service employee."[462]

2.1. The Principles of Public Service

The main principle of the public service is the obligation to carry out public service. Administration is obliged to carry out public service that it is responsible of. That is to say, administration cannot abstain to carry out a public service.

A dispute before State Council may be given as an example within this regard. In this dispute, an application to make a water supply contract was rejected by İSKİ (Istanbul Water and Drainage Authority) since the pre-subscriber who was the last resident in the premises did not pay the debts. The first instance court ruled that the rejection decision was unlawful since İSKİ shall not avoid

---

459 Özay, *Günışığında*, 182.

460 CC, M. 1994/71, D. 1995/23, 28.06.1995, OG 20.03.1996–22586; CC, M. 1994/43, D. 1994/42-2, 09.12.1994, OG 24.01.1995–22181.

461 Martine Lombard, Gilles Dumont, and Jean Sirinelli, *Droit Administratif* (Paris : Dalloz, 2013), 320–321; Karahanoğulları, *Kamu Hizmeti*, 264 ff.

462 SC 10th C., M. 2009/11303, D. 2009/8021, 15.09.2009, www.kazanci.com.

providing public service. State Council approved the decision of the first instance court.[463]

As seen, administration cannot avoid providing public service it is obliged to carry out. At the same time, this public service is needed to be performed according to certain principles, in other words, as it is needed to be performed. Principles of public service are mentioned as Rolland Principles in French administrative law.[464] Below, we will explain these principles.

2.1.1. The Principle of Continuity

Public service needs the establishment and operation which fulfills the need as long as the need continues.[465] However, public service is not required to be performed uninterrupted.[466] What is important is that public service should be delivered when needed.[467]

Some services must be uninterrupted.[468] Otherwise, we cannot say that there is a public service which is delivered as it needs to be delivered. Electricity public service is an example on this regard. For instance, suppose that an operation could not be performed due to power cut in a hospital. This service fault can result in a violation to right to life.

On the other hand, we cannot state that being uninterrupted is a must for all public services. For instance, state opera and ballet or museums deliver public service. However, these services may be available at certain hours of a day. This feature does not mean that this service is not continuous. What is important is that the service must be delivered when needed.[469]

---

463 SC 8th C., M. 2002/4145, D. 2003/3056, 23.06.2003, www.kazanci.com.

464 Lebreton, *Droit Administratif Général*, 168 ff.

465 Gaudemet, *Traité De Droit Administratif*, 749.

466 Melikşah Yasin, "Kamu Hizmeti [Public Service]," in *İdare Hukuku*, ed. Turan Yıldırım (İstanbul: On İki Levha, 2022), 557.

467 Lombard, Dumont, and Sirinelli, *Droit Administratif*, 325.

468 M. Gözde Atasayan, *Kamu Hizmetlerinin Süreklilik ve Düzenlilik İlkesi* [*The Principle of Continuity and Regularity of Public Service*] (İstanbul: On İki Levha, 2012), 83–84.

469 "...Public transportation service is explicitly an activity in the characteristics of public service which meets a need for public interest and therefore needs to be carried out continuously and regularly. This continuity does not mean that public service should be performed all the time. It is fundamental that public service should be uninterrupted when the need arising from public service emerges." SC, 8th C., M. 2007/8336, D. 2009/2995, 06.05.2009, www.kazanci.com.

State Council ruled that being in conformity with the principle of continuity in health services is a right at the same time, since it is related to right to life.[470] This right is to benefit from and reach to health services when needed. As seen, individuals have rights on certain services to be provided continuously. It is an obligation or duty for administration to provide such a service continuously.

There are some consequences of this principle. First of all, strike is prohibited for public employers due to possibility of service being interrupted.[471]

Secondly, a theory called unpredictability theory (imprevision) is implemented for concession agreements. Accordingly, a private law person, who carries out public service by making concession agreement with administration, has to provide public service continuously even in circumstances which are unpredictable to occur and impossible to prevent causing economic losses. However, administration has to compensate private person's losses. This approach is the same in permission procedure and in other methods in which private law persons perform public service. Administration can oblige private law persons to continue performing public services even if it is financially disadvantageous.

Thirdly, daily works are obliged to be carried out. For instance, resigned government or public employer has to perform daily works until new government or public employer takes over. Otherwise, public service would be hindered, and the principle of continuity would be violated. This fact would end up being service fault.

Lastly, non-seizability of public property is also related to continuity of public service. Public service which needs the usage of public property would be hindered in case that these properties were able to be seized because of debt. For instance, in case that medical device in a public hospital was seized, providing health service would not be possible.

2.1.2. The Principle of Regularity

The principle of regularity refers public service to be delivered in a certain quality and standard.[472] While providing natural gas continuously via natural

---

470 SCPSCAC, M. 2007/1884, D. 2011/88, 24.02.2011, www.kazanci.com.

471 Lombard, Dumont, and Sirinelli, *Droit Administratif*, 324–325; Yasin, "Kamu Hizmeti," 557; Atasayan, *Kamu Hizmetlerinin*, 165.

472 State Council highlighted that public service in question must be provided regularly, evaluating the problems related to teachers leaving the duty temporarily, delay of new appointments or nonexistence of teachers as follows: "Education service, provided by Ministry of National Education, is one of the services needed to be delivered regularly due to its characteristics and which is essential, irrecusable, non-substitutable from

gas pipelines is related to the principle of continuity, providing natural gas at a certain pressure and intensity is related to the principle of regularity. Likewise, while providing electricity continuously is related to the principle of continuity, voltage of electricity descending or arising is related to the principle of regularity. For a third example, changing opening hours of museums daily may be given as an example where the principle of regularity is not obeyed.

2.1.3. The Principle of Adaptation

The principle of adaptation necessitates public service to change, renew and adapt according to the change in public needs.[473] For instance, in case that registers of persons would be kept in notebooks today like before, it would be contrary to this principle. Or even though electricity is invented, if streets were lighted by gasolier, this principle would not be obeyed.

Just as the change in public needs may require technology to be developed, administration shall also adopt to cultural, economic or social changes.[474] For instance, if sacrificing animals in street makes persons uncomfortable in time, a related regulation should be brought into force. Or if the country gets through an economic crisis, some saving measures regarding public administration may be taken.

According to the State Council, the principle of adaptation is "both a duty and authority of administrations to re-regulate and change the practices in the areas which they have the authority to regulate in conformity with the public needs and the contemporary necessities."[475]

The principle of adaptation has some consequences on private law persons, beneficiaries of the service and personnel performing the service.

Firstly, this principle has several consequences on private law persons who carry out public service under the supervision and scrutinization of administration. Administration may request from private law persons who carry out public service via concession agreement or license procedure to adapt the service to current conditions. In case that administration makes such a request unilaterally

---

the perspective of existence of persons, the public and public peace." SC, 2nd C., M. 2008/3392, D. 2011/15944, 30.11.2011, www.kazanci.com.

473 Gaudemet, *Traité De Droit Administratif*, 749; Lombard, Dumont, and Sirinelli, *Droit Administratif*, 327.

474 Yasin, "Kamu Hizmeti," 559.

475 SC, 15th C., M. 2014/6132, D. 2018/2209, 06.03.2018, www.hukukturk.com; SC 15th C., M. 2017/287, D. 2018/6547, 02.10.2018, www.hukukturk.com.

and with the idea of public interest to the contracting private law person, this person cannot object. Moreover, administration may annul the contract unilaterally by compensating private law person if conditions necessitate so. In license procedure, usually the principle of adaptation is inherent in the status generated by laws and other regulative acts. In other words, in this procedure, administration requests from private law persons to meet the principle of adaptation based on related regulations, instead of administrative agreement. Sometimes, license itself may incorporate such provisions.

Secondly, this principle also has consequences on the beneficiaries of the service. Administration may always change the conditions regarding benefitting from the service based on the principle of adaptation. In this case, acquired rights cannot be in question easily.[476] For instance, in case that a common exam

476 In administrative law in our country, it is nevertheless possible to benefit from acquired rights. SCPSCAC defined acquired rights referring to doctrine: "In doctrine, acquired right is defined as a right which is acquired in conformity with the current law and bears favorable lawful consequences specific to persons and which should be protected by the legal system even in the existence of circumstances such as withdrawal of the act or legislative amendment." SCPSCAC, M. 2015/1130, SE, 12.11.2015, www.lexpera.com; SCPSCAC, M. 2015/1134, SE, 12.11.2015, www.lexpera.com. As seen, in order to rule on acquired rights, the right in question should be born "in conformity with the current law." 8th Circuit of State Council has highlighted that a right which is obtained unlawfully is not protected by the legal system: "…In order to rule on acquired right, this right should be obtained lawfully. A right which is acquired unlawfully cannot be thought to be protected by the legal system. As a matter of fact, in the decision of the Board of the Unification of Case Laws dated 22.12.1973, Merits numbered 1968/6, 1973/14, which is also mentioned in the decision of the court, it is envisaged that in case of deception and sham declaration of the interested person, the payment may be retrieved without seeking for time limit." SC, 8th C., M. 2004/1570, D. 2004/3441, 27.09.2004, www.hukukturk.com; SC, 8th C., M. 1999/2720, D. 2000/8365, 19.12.2000, www.hukukturk.com. Also see Duran, *İdare Hukuku Ders*, 424; Hakan Yumuşak, "İdari İşlemin Kaldırılması ve Geri Alınması [Abolishment and Withdrawal of Administrative Act]" (master's thesis, İstanbul Medipol University Social Sciences Institute, 2018), 38.

State Council rules on protection of acquired rights in condition that the right is obtained lawfully due to the principle of administrative stability. While acquired rights are not protected in case of statuses obtained unlawfully, "subjective gains" (acquisitions) obtained until status is ended by administration are accepted to be protected. 5th Circuit of State Council concluded: "However, it should be accepted that this protection provided based on administrative stability, is no longer valid when it reaches a consequence which distorts public order and accordingly public interest, and this

is brought by law to perform advocacy, a university may adapt its education service to the new exam system by making changes in its bylaw. In this case, the new bylaw will be implemented to the students who have not been graduated yet and who will get into the faculty thereafter. The allegation of acquired rights, of students who have not been graduated yet, will not be accepted by judiciary.

Another example is making changes in tariffs of public service. For instance, administration can raise the sale price of natural gas if its cost increases.

What is important on the implementation of the principle of adaptation is that the changes should only affect future legal consequences. In other words, administration cannot collect increased prices from users retrospectively.

Another important issue on this principle is that the need to adapt should emerge factually. In other words, administration cannot make changes in service arbitrarily.[477]

Thirdly, this principle has consequences on the personnel which carries out the service. Since public employees are in a status that is predesignated by laws or other regulative acts, administration may adapt working conditions of public employees to the changing conditions of service. For instance (on condition that it is not contrary to related legal norms), administration may change working hours or places. The same fact is also valid for contract employees. However, contract employee may request compensation in case that administration aggravates the working conditions indicated in the contract.

---

protection should be limited to the personal gains born until the illegal act is corrected. More clearly, in case that status attained with an administrative act, and acts and actions based on this status bear consequences and effects regarding the public, this status will not be protected; however, personal gains obtained by relevant person until administrative corrects the mistaken act shall be untouchable." SC, 5th C., M. 1994/7834, D. 1997/2030, 09.10.1997, www.lexpera.com.

477 State Council evaluated administration's act regarding the unition of subbranches of "Child Hematology" and "Child Oncology" into one subbranch called "Child Hematology and Oncology" requiring three years of education, based on the principle of adaptation. State Council made it clear that "even though making changes, re-regulating in accordance with the necessities of the time and needs of society is both a duty and authority for the administration due to the principle of adaptation, it is obligatory for administrations to use this authority in conformity with law and to present the facts concretely which necessitates the regulation that will realize public interest and is fundamental for the change." State Council found that the regulation is unlawful since administration could not present the facts necessitating the regulation. SC, 8th C., M. 2010/106, D. SE, 18.05.2010, www.kazanci.com.

Likewise, administration may control whether public employees work as required in condition that it does not breach the principle of right to privacy and protection of personal data. State Council, on a dispute regarding supervision of public employees with technological methods, indicated that "it is necessary to react naturally to the usage of developing technology by administration in public area for the purpose that it has an easing effect on public service being carried out effectively and productively."[478]

2.1.4. The Principle of Equality

According to article 10 of the Constitution,

> Everyone is equal before the law without distinction as to language, race, color, sex, political opinion, philosophical belief, religion and religious denomination, or any such grounds. (…)
>
> State organs and administrative authorities are obliged to act in compliance with the principle of equality before law in all their proceedings.

The principle of equality includes both "equality on entering public service" and "equality on benefitting from public service."[479] Article 70 of the Constitution lays down the right to enter public service. Accordingly, "Every Turk has the right to enter public service. No criteria other than the qualifications for the office concerned shall be taken into consideration for recruitment into public service." In one of its decisions, State Council indicated that "…conditions preventing to enter public service based on discrimination on gender are contrary to the principle of equality..."[480]

The principle of equality on benefitting from public service prohibits discrimination between persons who are in the same situation.

In Turkish legal system, "relative equality" is adopted instead of absolute equality both on entering and benefitting from public service.[481] Article 10 of the Constitution adopts the principle of relative equality. Practices of Constitutional

---

478 SC, 12th C., M. 2005/6811, D. 2006/1959, 15.05.2006, www.kazanci.com.

479 Akyılmaz, Sezginer, and Kaya, *Türk İdare Hukuku*, 567.

480 SC, 12th C., M. 2004/4382, D. 2006/539, 22.02.2006, www.hukukturk.com.

481 Turgut Tan, and Bahar Bayazıt, *İdare Hukuku* [*Administrative Law*] (Ankara: Turhan, 2021), 342. For same approach in France, see Lombard, Dumont, and Sirinelli, *Droit Administratif*, 325–326.

Court and State Council also favor relative equality.[482] According to relative equality, in case of "significant difference on circumstances" or circumstances where "public interest" requires, discrimination on persons are in accordance with the law. For instance, giving priority to seriously damaged patients is as such. In case that a specific service is charged differently based on income level, it can be accepted that the principle of equality is not breached due to public interest. In a dispute, State Council did not see "contrariness to the necessities of service and public interest on adopting of the rule of demanding a certain payment by the defendant institution from persons having sufficient economic power who are physically and psychologically handicapped and/or have mother and father, when providing service considering the cost of the service."[483] From the antonym of the decision, it is understood that administration may make a distinction between persons who have sufficient economic power and those who have not, considering the principle of relative equality.

Judiciary may annul the administrative act when it reaches the conclusion that the service is carried out contrary to the principle of equality. For instance, State Council found the decision of central administration regarding entombing Yusuf Bozkurt Özal to Süleymaniye Mosque contrary to this principle. The related part of the decision is as follows: "… Article 10 of the Constitution lays down that "Everyone is equal before the law without distinction as to language, race, color, sex, political opinion, philosophical belief, religion and religious denomination, or any such grounds. No privilege shall be granted to any individual, family, group or class." Even though there is not any extraordinary situation to discriminate, [the decision], which allows … to be buried in another place other than the graveyard of municipality and therefore which privileges him on this regard, cannot be said to be in compliance with the principle of equality laid down in the mentioned article."[484]

State Council also annulled an administrative act which caused churches not to benefit from usage of free water because of contrariness to the principle of equality: "There is no doubt that the Protestant church of which the complainant

482 CC, M. 2011/26, D. 2012/41, 15.03.2012, OG 26.06.2012–28335; SC, 13th C., M. 2019/4415, D. 2021/532, 17.02.2021; www.lexpera.com; CC, M. 2018/73, D. 2019/65, 24.07.2019, OG 29.11.2019–30963.

483 SC, 10th C., M. 1998/1582, D. 1999/2239, 06.05.1999, www.kazanci.com.

484 SC, 10th C., M. 2002/4723, D. 2004/5434, 09.06.2004, www.hukukturk.com. This decision is also approved by SCPSCAC. See SCPSCAC, M. 2005/16, D. 2005/1118, 05.05.2005, www.hukukturk.com.

is in charge, is one of the places of religion mentioned in the assembly decision in question. The fact that places of worshipping belonging to other religions or beliefs than the ones counted in the decision, does not mean that the decision is a specific decision made only for places of worship belonging to specific religions. It cannot be accepted that the municipality, which is obliged to regulate and arrange the common and civilized local needs of city residents can make discrimination between religions when delivering service. In this situation, the decision of administrative court, regarding dismissal of the action filed with the request of annulment of the decision, is not seen to be right, since the act is not in conformity with the rules of equality and equity, while the protestant church, of which the complainant is in charge, is needed to be benefitted from the right to use free water due that it is one of the places of religion within the scope of municipality assembly decision mentioned above."[485]

2.1.5. The Principle of Impartiality

Pursuant to the principle of impartiality, administration is obliged not to discriminate between persons via its acts and actions.[486] In fact, impartiality refers to the obligation of obeying the principle of equality by the administration in its relationship with persons. In other words, this principle represents the duties of administration.

Three methods are mentioned to provide public service impartially:

- Impartiality through avoidance:[487] In this method, administration avoids making acts and actions which could bear the consequence of the administration to behave partially. For instance, during a time when allegations of bribery against a senior public official is on the media, a university administration may prohibit or postpone a scientific meeting regarding bribery.
- Impartiality through pluralism:[488] In this method, administration provides impartiality by giving opportunity for every opinion to be delivered. For instance, giving voice equally to both demonstrators and police or related administrative offices in a meeting related to human rights violations arising from the interference to meetings and demonstrations may be an example in this regard.

485 SC, 8th C., M. 2004/4350, D. 2005/809, 22.02.2005, www.danistay.gov.tr.

486 Yasin, "Kamu Hizmeti," 556.

487 Gözler, *İdare Hukuku V. II*, 322.

488 Gaudemet, *Traité De Droit Administratif*, 750.

- Impartiality through objectivity:[489] In this method, administration exhibits attitude related to the service without being under influence of any political, religious, social factor, etc. For instance, in a study conducted by a university related to communism, impartiality would be achieved through objectivity by only referencing scientific publications and also considering opposing views.

2.1.6. The Principle of Gratuitousness

According to the principle of gratuitousness, public service needs to be provided without a fee.[490] However, it would not be wrong to state that public service being gratuitous is no longer a principle today. State Council ruled that "Even though it is accepted principally that public service is gratuitous in doctrine, due to increase on public services undertaken by administration and number of beneficiaries in parallel, with the aim to prevent charging the burden of services which are delivered gratuitously to nonbeneficiaries of that service it is also accepted that a co-payment is possible considering the ability to pay of beneficiaries of certain services."[491] As seen, High Court highlights the satisfaction of equality between beneficiaries and nonbeneficiaries of the service. In other words, by charging beneficiaries, equality is satisfied. For instance, the cost of a bridge in a certain city is only charged to beneficiaries of that bridge and is not reflected to the persons living in other cities via taxes. Some authors in doctrine also put forward the same view.[492]

Court of Jurisdictional Disputes indicated that "Constitution assigned the state primarily on the subjects of social and economic rights and duties. However, state will carry out this duty within the boundaries laid down in the article 65 of the Constitution, within the capacity of its financial resources. As a consequence of this understanding, the notion of public service, in which being gratuitous is the first condition in classic administrative law changed eventually and the practice, in which contribution to the costs to be requested from beneficiaries in proportion to their ability to pay in return of the service, has gained wide currency."[493]

Thus, a certain amount of fee may be taken in return of the service. However, some public services are still performed without charge. For instance,

---

489 Gözler, *İdare Hukuku V. II*, 323.
490 Akyılmaz, Sezginer, and Kaya, *Türk İdare Hukuku*, 569.
491 SC, 8th C., M. 2011/7969, D. SE, 18.01.2012, www.legalbank.net.
492 Akyılmaz, Sezginer, and Kaya, *Türk İdare Hukuku*, 569; Yasin, "Kamu Hizmeti," 561.
493 CJD, Law Branch, M. 2003/36, D. 2003/41, 16.06.2003, www.kazanci.com.

procurement of safety of life and property (policing may also be accepted as a public service) is carried out by police without a fee. For another instance, the article 42/5 of the Constitution states that "Primary education is compulsory for all citizens of both sexes and is free of charge in state schools." Likewise, State Council ruled that taking fee in return of social services is contrary to the principle of social state.[494]

The most important subject within the principle of gratuitousness is related to the meaning of fee. It is alleged that the "price" of public service should not be construed of profit added to the cost.[495] In other words, it is accepted that a profit cannot be gained when public service is provided. Accordingly, the price should not overtake the cost of the service.

At this point, some authors make a distinction between administrative public services and financial, industrial and commercial public services.[496] Accordingly, in case that administration delivers a service with operating procedures of private sector (and the service in question is similar to an activity carried out by private law persons and the financing of it is provided by fees taken from beneficiaries) or the law predetermines this (for instance, when law explicitly lays down that the provisions of private law may be implemented to the relationship between provider of the service and beneficiaries and authorizes civil jurisdiction in disputes arising from this relationship), making profit is possible. On the contrary, fee taken from the service should not overtake the cost in case there is an administrative public service.

An important rule regarding this principle is that a fee cannot be taken without providing a service. For instance, in case that administration takes fee from owners of enterprises in return of "waste collection" and it does not carry out this activity by establishing necessary facilities, requesting for fee would be illegal. In other words, a fee cannot be taken in return of an undelivered service.

---

494 "Since social services aim to eliminate material, moral and social deprivation and meet needs, to prevent and resolve social problems and improve and to enhance standard of living, it is no doubt that social services cannot be provided in return of a fee, therefore the services in question should be benefitted by everyone in need and who are disabled due to the principle of social state laid down in the Constitution. Within this scope, it is not lawful to dismiss the action, … the act in question and article 32 and 47 of the by-law mentioned which is the base of the act should have been annulled..." SCPSCAC, M. 2000/401, D. 2000/938, 03.07.2000, www.kazanci.com.

495 Akyılmaz, Sezginer, and Kaya, *Türk İdare Hukuku*, 570.

496 Gözler, *İdare Hukuku V. II*, 345.

Likewise, in case that a public service is a fundamental service which should be procured without charge, requesting for a fee in return would be unlawful.[497] For instance, one of the fundamental duties of municipalities is to scrutinize whether restaurants are operated sanitarily. Administration cannot charge for this service.

State Council also ruled that "considerably low" prices in public service activities carried out by private law legal persons may also be unlawful. In a related dispute, High Court concluded that taking a fee which is lower than the cost of gasoline that will be used during courses by a private driving school may impair the service.[498]

It is indicated that new principles such as accessibility, participation, being qualified and transparency are added to the principles of public service along with the mentioned ones.[499] In our opinion, these new principles may be considered under the mentioned classic principles. Therefore, we are of the opinion that these principles are not needed to be handled separately.

In doctrine, Karahanoğulları highlights regarding the definition of public service that activities of state are "immune to the rules of market forces to a certain extent."[500] We believe that the essence of the principles we mentioned above is this sentence.

2.2. Establishment of Public Service

In principle, public service shall be established by law. This rule is based on the idea that the freedom of "free working and establishing private enterprises" would be restricted by the state establishing public service.[501] This is because

497 Gözler, *İdare Hukuku V. II*, 347.

498 "...Evaluating the file, since, in consequence of the examination of the defendant administration, it is understood that the fees designated and published by the institutions in question are even lower than the price of gasoline that is used by a student during the course and do not meet the cost, it is a fact that the institutions operating at a loss cannot improve the standard of education laid down in the article 2 of the Law no 625, will cause to unfair competition along the lines that they cannot provide qualified education and as a consequence of unqualified education of motor vehicle driver schools, traffic accidents resulting with deaths and exhaustion of national wealth is inevitable." SC, 8th C., M. 1992/3042, D. 1993/3670, 19.10.1993, www.kazanci.com.

499 Lebreton, *Droit Administratif Général*, 176.

500 Karahanoğulları, *Kamu Hizmeti*, 397.

501 Onar, *İdare Hukukunun Umumi Esasları V. I*, 38; Gözler, *İdare Hukuku V. II*, 358.

when a public service is established, the state either prohibits activities of private law persons in the area which is subject to public service (it carries out the activity as a monopoly) or gets into competition with them.[502] Since fundamental freedom and rights can only be restricted by law, public service can only be established by law. At the same time, public service necessitates a certain organization. Therefore, the Constitutional provision ruling that administration shall be established by law makes it obligatory for public service to be established by a law.[503] Necessary budget for organization, personnel and property for the established public service is based on a decision of TBMM.[504]

On the other hand, as already mentioned, according to the article 123 of the Constitution, public corporate bodies may also be established by a PD. Since public corporate bodies are established to provide public service, it would be not wrong to state that public service may as well be established by a PD.[505] On the other hand, it may again be alleged that PDs cannot establish public services, since this establishment restricts the freedom of "free working and establishing private enterprises." We may state that a PD cannot establish a public service in case it will create a monopoly. However, where state gets into free competition with the other providers and concrete restrictions are not imposed on this regard to private law persons, PDs may establish public service.

In addition, a public service may as well be established by an administrative act, in condition that it is bases on a law or a PD and the framework is determined by law or PD.[506] Some authors indicate that only local public services

---

502 Günday, *İdare Hukuku*, 322 ff; Ebru Zeybek Cebeci, *Kamu Hizmetlerinin Gördürülmesine İlişkin Sözleşmeler: (Kamu Hizmeti Anlayışındaki Değişim Ekseninde)* [*Agreements Regarding Making Public Service Performed: (From the Perspective of Changes in Public Service Understanding)*] (Ankara: Seçkin, 2021), 44.

503 Akyılmaz, Sezginer, and Kaya, *Türk İdare Hukuku*, 563.

504 Onar, *İdare Hukukunun Umumi Esasları V. I*, 39.

505 Yasin, "Kamu Hizmeti," 539.

506 Onar, *İdare Hukukunun Umumi Esasları V. I*, 38; Yayla, *İdare Hukuku*, 85; Günday, *İdare Hukuku*, 333. "... Public service with its modern meaning, is a service provided to public via either a public institution itself or a private entrepreneur under a close supervision of a public institution. In addition, to suppose a service to be public service, it is not needed to be carried out as a monopoly. It is an authority of legislator to establish a public service or transform a private activity to a public service. A public service may be established by law directly or by executive organ based on the authority given by law." SC 1th C., M. 1992/232, D. 1992/294, 24.09.1992, www.kazanci.com.

which are not national in characteristics can be established by an administrative act.[507]

Last but not least, if the Constitution obliges a public service to be established by law, this public service may only be established by law. For instance, according to article 130 of the Constitution, universities can only be established by the state and by law.

In principle, it is also possible for an administration which primarily has the duty to establish and operate a public service to hand over the establishment and operation of the public service to a private person for a certain time via an administrative contract (not private law contracts)[508] or a unilateral act (such as license and permit).[509] For instance, public service concession agreements or activities which are carried out by private law persons with a license (electricity and natural gas distribution activity) given by administration is as such.

It is also possible to abolish a public service with the procedure of its establishment when public no longer needs it. Abolishment of public service is provided through the principle of parallelism in procedure and authority. Therefore, principally the office which established the public service is authorized to abolish it. However, we should note that a public service cannot be abolished with a hierarchically lower norm than the norm which is the base of the establishment. Likewise, a PD cannot abolish a public service that is established by a law while a law can abolish a public service established by a PD due to article 104/17.[510]

2.3. Operating Procedures of Public Service

Operating procedures of public service refers to the matters related to the person who will carry out the service, with which monetary resource and employee. Different scenarios may occur regarding whether the public service is carried out by

---

507 Gözler, *İdare Hukuku V. II*, 369–371; For the differing views, see Yasin, "Kamu Hizmeti," 543.

508 "… Administrative contracts which are executed to establish or operate public service are distinguished from private law contracts since they grant some authorities based on public force to the executors of the service in order for the service to be carried out also providing the administration to have the authority of supervision and scrutinization in order for the service to be carried out regularly and steadily." SC 13th C., M. 2008/5151, D. 2008/6509, 28.11.2008, www.kazanci.com.

509 Lebreton, *Droit Administratif Général*, 158 ff.

510 Gözler, *İdare Hukuku V. II*, 377–379.

a private law legal person or a public corporate body and via monetary resource and personnel of one of these.

Within this scope, first, public service may be carried out by administration itself. Secondly, a private law person can perform public service when the private person is unilaterally assigned or gets into an agreement with the administration.

2.3.1. Secure Modality

Secure modality refers to the situations where public service is carried out by a public corporate body via its own organization, personnel and assets.[511] A substantial part of public services being performed by central administration such as national defense, justice services and health services are carried out via secure modality. Local administration may as well provide public service through secure modality.

A public corporate body (both local administrations and public institutions) which is certainly not within the state may also carry out a public service with its own organization, sources and personnel, in other words, via secure modality.[512] In this case, since a separate public corporate body is established by law to perform public service, some authors handle this procedure as a separate procedure called "establishment of public institution modality."[513] In public institution modality, public service is performed by public corporate bodies which are not within central administration and autonomous financially and administratively. General Directorate of Highways, General Directorate of State Theatres, Scientific and Technological Research Council of Turkey, İstanbul Electric Tramway (Streetcars) and Tunnel Establishments, state economic enterprises are as such.

2.3.2. Public Service Being Performed by a Private Law Person

According to Constitutional Court, public service is "continuous and regular activities which possess the aim of public interest carried out by the state or other public corporate bodies or private law persons which are subject to supervision and scrutinization of the state or another public corporate body."[514] As seen,

511 Onar, *İdare Hukukunun Umumi Esasları V. I*, 43; Yasin, "Kamu Hizmeti," 566.

512 Onar, *İdare Hukukunun Umumi Esasları V. I*, 43; Yasin, "Kamu Hizmeti," 567.

513 Gözler notes that public institution modality is in question where a public administration (either state or local administrations) establishes a separate public corporate body to provide a public service. Gözler, *İdare Hukuku V. II*, 394.

514 For instance, see CC, M. 2013/88, D. 2014/101, 04.06.2014, OG 22.07.2014–29068; CC. M. 2012/27, D. 2012/173, 08.11.2012, OG 28.03.2013–28601.

public service can be both provided by a public corporate body or private law person (in condition that it is scrutinized).

At this point, it should be evaluated whether private persons can operate all kinds of public services. As already mentioned, article 128 of the Constitution indicates that "The fundamental and permanent functions required by the public services that the State, state economic enterprises and other public corporate bodies assigned to perform in accordance with principles of general administration shall be carried out by public servants and other public employees." Accordingly, the fundamental and permanent functions, that are performed in accordance with the principles of general administration, must be performed by public servants and other public employees, which is the administration.[515]

On the other hand, according to the article 47/4 of the Constitution, legislature shall decide which services will be carried out by real or legal persons through private law agreements. Therefore, while fundamental and permanent functions that are performed in accordance with the principles of general administration shall be carried out by administration, the other public services which can be carried out according to the principles of private management can be carried out by private persons.

Within this scope, it should be indicated that public services which are directly related to sovereignty cannot be performed by private law persons. For instance, it is not possible for private law persons to carry out the activities performed by the "armed forces" or "judiciary."[516]

It is also not possible for a private law person to undertake a public service by itself. State or other public corporate bodies need to assign or authorize the private person. This assignment or authorization may be realized in two ways: via a law, an administrative act or via an administrative contract. In other words, "unilaterally" or "bilaterally" (sometimes also multilaterally).

2.3.2.1. Unilaterally Assignment of Private Law Persons to Carry Out Public Service

The administration may assign a private person to carry out public service unilaterally. Unilateral assignment may be seen when the administration establishes a private law person. Secondly, the administration may grant a private law person

515 Akyılmaz, Sezginer, and Kaya, *Türk İdare Hukuku*, 575.
516 Yayla, *İdare Hukuku*, 88.

the status of public interest association. And at last, the administration may grant licenses to private law persons. Below, we will elaborate on these procedures.

2.3.2.1.1. Establishment of Private Law Person by Administration

State or local administrations (special provincial administrations, municipal districts, villages) may entrust private law persons to carry out a public service by firstly establishing the private law person with their financial sources.

In this case, the person performing public service is subject to private law. However, sometimes these may be granted with some public force privileges (such as ability to conduct unilateral acts and *ex officio* execution). If these persons have acts regarding using public force, these acts are regarded as in administrative characteristics and arising disputes are resolved by administrative judiciary.

2.3.2.1.2. Granting the Status of Public Interest Association

Administration may convert the activity performed by a private law person to public service by granting the person a different status and augmenting scrutinization and supervision on it. According to the article 27 of Law of Associations, central administration may grant an association the status of "public interest association." This decision is not an act of licensing. However, it may be regarded as unilaterally assignment of private law persons to carry out public service.

2.3.2.1.3. Licensing Procedure

Public corporate bodies may assign private law persons to perform a public service via licensing procedure.[517] In fact, in this procedure, application of private law person and acceptance of this application is in question. Then, may it be alleged that a two-sided act is valid? The answer to this question is not affirmative since the determinant will is the will of administration in licensing procedure. In other words, administration has the final say whether to grant a license to a private law person.

Assets, personnel and liability of private law persons who are assigned to perform a public service via license are subject to private law and disputes thereof are resolved in civil judiciary. However, private law persons, who obtained a

517 Ali Ulusoy, *Kamu Hizmeti İncelemeleri [Reviews of Public Service]* (İstanbul: Ülke, 2004), 37–38.

license, may also be granted with public force privileges. In cases where these use public force, their acts are in characteristics of administrative acts.

At this point, a further distinction is needed. Some licenses are related to policing activity of the administration aiming to maintain the public order. On the other hand, there are licenses concerning the undertaking of a public service by a private person.[518] These licenses should be distinguished from each other. The fundamental difference between the two is that public service principles do not apply when licenses regarding policing is in question. Reverse is the case when there is a public service taken over by a private person with a license. In other words, "scrutinization and supervision" mentioned in the public service definition of Constitutional Court are strictly and completely implemented in case of public services performed via licensing procedures. This supervision and scrutinization incorporates "public service principles." In doctrine, this "supervision and scrutinization" is mentioned as "a content-wise inspection" or corresponding expressions.[519]

2.3.2.2. Making Private Law Persons to Carry Out Public Service via Contract

A private law person may make a contract with Administration to undertake a public service as long as the contract is in administrative character.[520] There are

518 Yasin, "Kamu Hizmeti," 572.

519 Özay, *Günışığında*, 249; Akyılmaz, Sezginer, and Kaya, *Türk İdare Hukuku*, 581; The authors preferred the expression of "beyond the police scrutinization." Ulusoy preferred the expression of "internalized scrutinization"; Ulusoy, *Kamu Hizmeti İncelemeleri*, 31. Gülan suggested the expression of "operational scrutinization"; Gülan, "Kamu Hizmeti Kavramı," 150.

520 "A significant point that needs to be indicated for the procedures of performing public service by private law persons is that, even though the operation of service is transferred to private persons, the qualification and principles of the service do not change. Especially, the existence of public service principles is preserved and responsibility of administration regarding the services holds." SC 1st C., M. 2008/744, D. 2008/834, 03.07.2008, www.hukukturk.com. "... Actually, usage of superior powers by private law persons which is needed to perform public service is in question in case of concession agreements, which transfer establishment and/or operation of public service to a private entrepreneur. In other words, "privilege" which is situated within the structure of public service, is transferred to private law person who is given public duty and used by this person in case of concession agreements." SCPSCAC, M. 1996/79, D. 1996/83, 03.10.1996, www.kazanci.com.

no restrictions regarding the types of contracts. The most commonly preferred agreement are concession agreements. Since the procedures such as "common secure modality"[521] and "tax-farming"[522] are abandoned as of today, we will not mention these. We will only explain the essentials of the procedures which are exercised today.

2.3.2.2.1. Concession Agreement

The emergence of concession agreements is based upon the increase in the number of public services and massive financial burden for the establishment and operation of these services. For instance, for establishment and operation of "cell phones" service, expensive infrastructure as well as expert, well-paid personnel is needed. Therefore, instead of establishing itself, the state may prefer to allow a private person to establish a public service and to reap its profits for a certain time. By this means, the state does not spend excessively, the service is provided and after a certain time the service will be transferred to the state.[523]

---

521 In common secure modality, administration establishes public service organically, with its own facilities and possibilities. Via this procedure, administration makes a private law person to carry out a public service, in which the damage belongs to the administration and the private law person is paid with a share from the revenue. Akyılmaz, Sezginer, and Kaya, *Türk İdare Hukuku*, 580.

522 In the era of Ottoman Empire these contracts were related to land and farming but then their area of application broadened and changed. For further information see Ömer Can Baş, "İdare Hukukunda İltizam Usulü ve İltizam Sözleşmeleri [Tax-farming Procedure And Tax-farming Contract In Administrative Law]," *Marmara Üniversitesi Hukuk Fakültesi Hukuk Araştırmaları Dergisi* 26, no. 2 (2020): 1019–1031, https://dergipark.org.tr/en/download/article-file/1330752. Gözler indicated that tax-farming contracts refer to the contracts in which private law person undertakes to carry out public service on its own profit and loss in return of a price. Gözler, *İdare Hukuku V. II*, 74.

523 "... However, the most decisive feature of concession procedure is that the public service is established by the owner of concession and the funds, investment goods, tools and all other equipment necessary to perform the service is provided by the owner of concession. In case that necessary facilities are established or provided by administration, another procedure distinct from concession procedure is put into implementation. This procedure may be characterized as secure modality, common secure modality, or tax farming according to an evaluation on the provisions of the contract.
Besides, in concession procedure, in case that the owner of concession retards public service, administration may carry out the public service by temporarily replacing the owner of concession according to the provisions of contract provided that the risks

Concession agreements are usually concluded between administration and a private person. However, exceptionally, some authors in France argues that a concession agreement may also be made between two public corporate bodies.[524]

2.3.2.2.2. Definition of Concession Agreement According to the Constitutional Court

Constitutional Court indicated that "... In administrative law, the term concession is seen as a procedure of performing public service. Performance of public service by private law persons under the supervision and scrutinization of administration pursuant to a supposedly long term 'administrative agreement' where the fund, profit, loss, and harm is on private person is called concession. Multiplicity of administrative works in the presence of needs or difficulty of finding resource oblige this procedure to be implemented and result in public service to be carried out by a private entrepreneur. Agreements on transferring of establishment and/or performance of public service to a private person are defined as 'public service concession agreements.'"[525]

Additionally, according to the Court, "... It can be determined whether a service is 'public service' and an agreement 'concession agreement,' by examining its nature, not by looking at the law. In case that a public service will be performed by a private entrepreneur for a long duration, the agreement is qualified as concession agreement."[526]

In consideration of doctrine and judicial decisions, the features of concession agreements may be summarized as follows:

1. The subject of the agreement shall be establishment and operation of a public service (as well as only operation),[527]

---

and losses are on the owner, and the goods allocated to the public service are needed to be transferred to or shared with administration by the owner of concession as envisaged in the contract at the end of concession..." SC 1th C., M. 2006/203, D. 2006/719, 06.07.2006, www.kazanci.com.

524 Lebreton, *Droit Administratif Général*, 159.

525 CC, M. 1994/43, D. 1994/42-2, 09.12.1994, OG 24.01.1995–22181.

526 CC, M. 1994/43, D. 1994/42-2, 09.12.1994, OG 24.01.1995–22181.

527 Günday indicates that the agreements solely covering the establishment of public services are accepted to be private law agreements, not as concession agreements by the judiciary. Günday, *İdare Hukuku*, 344; On the contrary: Akyılmaz, Sezginer, and Kaya, *Türk İdare Hukuku*, 582.

2. The owner of concession (private law person who is the contracting party) may be granted certain public force privileges,
3. Beneficiaries are the financial source of the public service,
4. The service is carried out under the supervision and scrutinization of administration.

Contracting administration is entitled with the following authorities:

(a) *To be able to make unilateral modifications on the contract:* In case that a new situation emerges that necessitates the contract to be revised according to the new circumstances, administration may request from private person to bring the service in compliance with the new circumstances.[528] However, in case that this unilateral modification increases the obligations of private person and deteriorate the financial balance of the contract, administration shall compensate it.[529] Likewise, administration cannot change the provisions in the contract concerning the price unilaterally.[530]
(b) *To have the authority to annul the contract unilaterally:* In case that private person cannot fulfill the requirements of the contract with its gross fault, administration may annul the contract unilaterally. In this case, administration is not needed to compensate the private person. On the other hand, even though the private person bears no fault, social conditions may require this concession agreement to be annulled. In this case, a legal term called *rachat* would be in question. *Rachat* refers to a procedure where administration purchases the concession granted to private person along with the facilities in return of its price.[531]
(c) *To carry out inspections and conduct sanctions:* Administration shall scrutinize whether the private person performs public service "in compliance with the principles of public service." In case that administration detects that the service is not performed properly, it may implement sanctions such as temporal seizure, requesting a certain amount of money based on penal clause.

The contracting private person is authorized to request from administration to preserve the financial balance of the contract.[532]

---

528 SCPSCAC, M. 2009/1533, D. 2009/1729, 16.09.2009, www.kazanci.com.
529 Günday, *İdare Hukuku*, 347.
530 Akyılmaz, Sezginer, and Kaya, *Türk İdare Hukuku*, 583.
531 Günday, *İdare Hukuku*, 347.
532 Günday, *İdare Hukuku*, 348.

Section III: Acts of Administration

Abstract
To realize public service, administration needs to establish acts. Unilateral acts of administration, which are established by using public force, are referred as administrative acts. In this section, we will detail the features of administrative acts, which are unilateral, executable, final, and which are subject to presumption of legality and judicial review. Secondly, we will focus on the types of acts according to their material division, number of intents which establish such acts and their feature of being explicit or implicit. Thirdly, we will handle the elements of administrative acts which are resorted when determining the legality of such acts. These elements are authority, form/procedure, motive, subject and aim. Fourthly, we will assess termination of administrative acts, specifically the cases where administration abolishes and withdraws its act. Lastly, we will detail judicial review of administrative acts which are null and void.

Administration may as well conduct agreements to carry out public service. However, all agreements of administration are not subject to administrative law. Therefore, within the title of "Agreements of Administration," we will assess the notion and criteria of administrative agreements. Secondly, we will detail the types of administrative agreements which mostly appear, that are public service concession agreements and administrative service agreements. Thirdly, we will touch upon how administrative agreements may be terminated. Fourthly, we will assess the principles applied when the financial balance of the agreement is disturbed. Lastly, we will handle the private law agreements of administration.

Keywords: administrative acts, administrative agreements, elements of administrative acts, private agreements of administration

1. Administrative Acts

Administration should also be able to establish "acts" like private law persons to carry out public service. Since public corporate bodies are accepted to be "persons" by the legal system, it is possible for them to possess rights and take on debts like private law persons can do.

On the other hand, administration may use public force unlike private law persons. Legal system has granted public corporate bodies superiority compared to private law persons in order for them to act for the "public interest" and carry out "public services." This is because, sometimes an activity which serves to the interests of the greater part of the society may be contrary to the interests of some persons. For instance, the interest on establishing an elementary school may be superior to the interests of landlords who own the land that the school will be established on. On the other hand, sometimes, it may be necessary to value the interest of specific persons over the interest of the general. For instance, it may be necessary to block or stop traffic to rush a seriously wounded person to hospital. In these situations, the activity should be carried out even though it would be contrary to the interests of some people. This would hardly or not be possible if administration had the same legal status as private law persons. Therefore, administration is granted with the authority to use public force.

In brief, administration can both carry out private law acts just like private law persons and acts which necessitate the use of public force. Therefore, acts of administration are the sum of private law acts and acts carried out by using public force. The acts of administration, carried out by using public force, are "administrative acts."[533]

Then, how can one distinguish administrative acts among legal acts? It is accepted that some features of administrative acts distinguish them from other legal acts. The following decision of the State Council may be instructive on this regard: "The characteristics of administrative acts, which do not have a definition prescribed by a law, is determined by doctrine and the decisions of administrative jurisdiction. Accordingly, in order to acknowledge that a disposal or a decision is an administrative act, it should be established by a public body or an administrative office which is within the organization of administration, and it should be related to an administrative activity of administration in the field of

533 Akyılmaz, Sezginer, and Kaya, *Türk İdare Hukuku*, 349.

administrative law. Widely accepted features and characteristics of administrative acts may be counted as unilaterality, legality and executability."[534]

The criterion of "being established by a public body or an administrative office which is within the organization of administration" refers to administrative acts organically.[535] From an organic point of view, acts carried out by administration are acts which are carried out by state (central or provincial organization) and other public corporate bodies (provincial special administrations, municipalities, villages and decentral organizations in service).

On the other hand, the criterion of "being related to the activities in the field of administrative law" associates with "the function of administration."[536] It should be stressed that organic criterion is sometimes insufficient.[537] Some acts of legislature or judiciary may as well be related to the function of administration and these acts should also be accepted as administrative acts.

Indeed, there are such acts of legislature and judiciary which cannot be considered as a legislative or judicial activity.[538] Likewise, administration may carry out acts which are not within the function of administration. A decision of State Council is important in this regard: "The notion of 'administrative function,' which is an important element on designation of administration and the field of administration, possesses an important place and all of the acts of offices within administration may not be related to administrative function, and the acts of legislative and judiciary organs which are not within administration may be related to administrative function. From this point of view, the acts which are not related to judiciary function cannot be counted as judiciary acts even though they are established by councils composed of judges or courts or even only judges. The acts related to administrative function should be counted as administrative acts irrespective of the office which establishes them and should be reviewed by administrative judiciary. As a matter of fact, the acts and activities of judicial offices, which can be separated from acts and activities that are established only because of the characteristic of being a court and carried out in this capacity, constitutes administrative activity or administrative act."[539]

---

534 SC 12th C., M. 2005/6811, D. 2006/1959, 15.05.2006, www.hukukturk.com.

535 Akyılmaz, Sezginer, and Kaya, *Türk İdare Hukuku*, 341.

536 Özay, *Günışığında*, 416.

537 Akyılmaz, Sezginer, and Kaya, *Türk İdare Hukuku*, 341.

538 Yayla, *İdare Hukuku*, 426–427; Akyılmaz, *İdari Usul İlkeleri*, 37; Çağlayan, *İdare Hukuku Dersleri*, 318.

539 SC 5th C., M. 1995/4416, D. 1996/1911, 17.05.1996, www.kazanci.com.

In this regard, State Council found that appointment of a member to Radio and Television High Council by legislature is within administrative function and decided that this appointment is an administrative act.[540]

In another case, a person who fell from a high place died in the hospital she was taken to. After the accident, with an order by prosecutor a search was carried out in the minibus the person was living in and some personal information and a cell phone were found. However, this person was decided to be buried in cemetery of the nameless by the prosecutor who did not make any effort to reach to the relatives of the person. In the dispute before State Council, filed by the relatives of the person, High Court underlined that the acts regarding necessary search in order to reach the relatives of the person are related to administrative function. Therefore, State Council annulled the decision of the first instance court that had reached the conclusion that ministry of justice could not be held responsible of the consequence of a judicial function.[541] According to State Council, the first instance court should have investigated whether service failure was committed, considering that the prosecutor carried out an administrative activity.

Likewise, a private law legal person may be granted to establish administrative act by using public force.[542] In those cases, the acts of a private law legal person, which cannot be accepted to be within administration organically since it is not a public corporate body, should be accepted as an administrative act.[543] State Council ruled that the acts of the management of Organized Industrial Sites by using public force are administrative acts even though they are private law persons.[544] Likewise, State Council ruled that some acts of a private person who

540 SC 5th C., M. 2005/5627, D. 2007/72, 24.01.2007, www.kazanci.com; However, we may state that the decisions of administrative courts are not consistent. For instance, in a decision of State Council, it is indicated that "In order for an act to be called as 'administrative act,' this act should be established by an administrative office. In our Constitution, which adopted the principle of separation of powers, the duties and powers of TBMM is regulated in the section of 'Legislature.'" Therefore, State Council rejected to evaluate the act of TBMM and did not dispute whether the act is functionally administrative. SC 10th C., M. 2006/1095, D. 2007/5137, 13.11.2007, www.hukukturk.com.

541 SC 10th C., M. 2009/9560, D. 2013/8793, 09.12.2013, www.danıştay.gov.tr.

542 Akyılmaz, Sezginer, and Kaya, *Türk İdare Hukuku*, 343.

543 Yayla, *İdare Hukuku*, 427–428; Mehmet İnanç, *Özel Hukuk Tüzel Kişilerinin İdari İşlemleri* [*Administrative Acts of Private Law Persons*] (İstanbul: On İki Levha, 2018), 427–428.

544 "Administrative acts, which are defined as transactions related to administrative function and bear legal consequences based on unilateral declaration of intent, are

carries out public service via a concession agreement are administrative acts.[545] Court of Jurisdictional Disputes has also found that some acts of private law legal persons are administrative acts in some disputes.[546]

Lastly, it is also notable that administrative acts and administrative actions differ. Administrative action may be defined as a factual change, movement or fact which occurs in the material world (it can also occur in the moral world as is in pressure and threat[547]). Most of the time, administrative action emerges from an administrative act being implemented. For instance, "demolition decision" is an act; demolition of a house by municipality employees as a consequence of implementation of this act is an "administrative action." In some cases, administrative action emerges without an administrative act beforehand. In these cases, it is accepted that a "plain action" is in question.[548] For instance, a plain action

---

principally introduced by the offices of administration. However, acts—which bear legal consequences with unilateral declaration of intent and are self-executable—of private law legal persons—who are authorized to use public power and procedures regarding administrative function exceptionally by explicit legislation—should also be regarded as administrative acts. This is because, the distinctive element on whether an act is an administrative act is that it is carried out in an area related to administrative function and by using public power and procedures, in other words the acts are subject to the principles and rules of administrative law." SC, 10th C., M. 2009/5590, D. 2009/10533, 16.12.2009, www.hukukturk.com.

545 SCPSCAC, M. 2011/55, D. 2011/205, 07.04.2011, www.kazanci.com.

546 CJD, Law Branch, M. 2011/55, D. 2011/205, 07.04.2011, www.kazanci.com.

547 For instance, mobbing, in other words abuse at work, actions toward tiring out and discouraging, bear its consequences in moral world. State Council approved the first instance court which decided on compensation of the damage caused due to mobbing of a lecturer in medicine faculty. SC 8th C., M. 2008/10606, D. 2012/1736, 16.04.2012, www.kazanci.com.

548 State Council explained the difference between administrative act and plain action in one of its decisions as follows: "Administrative acts are unilateral and self-executable legal transactions related to the administrative activities of administrative offices and authorities and which are established within administrative law. On the other hands, a physical work, move, operation and studies which an administrative decision or act does not lie behind are administrative actions. While administrative acts reflect declaration of intents which makes and bears change, administrative actions only bear legal effects and consequences in condition that the relevant persons use their rights and authorities." SC, M. 1994/6053, D. 1995/3611, 18.09.1995, www.hukukturk.com. In another State Council decision, plain administrative action is defined as follows: "Administrative actions refer to a move, fact, attitude during the functioning of administration and to only material disposals which are not related to administrative

is in question when a bulldozer belonging to General Directorate of Highways damage a private car during a road repair. This is because this action has not emerged from an administrative act being implemented. At this point, it may be thought that an administrative decision is held beforehand, and the damage has occurred while this decision regarding road repair is being implemented. However, what we mean here is that there is not an administrative act regarding damaging that person's car. Otherwise, every administrative action is possible to be linked to an administrative act.

In conclusion, we can state that at first, organic perspective is not enough. Persons other than administration (even private law persons in condition that law has authorized) can establish administrative acts. Therefore, a functional assessment should also be carried out along with an organic assessment. Secondly, we can state that acts of administration are not equivalent to administrative acts. Administration can establish acts other than the ones that are related to administrative function, namely, private law acts.[549] Finally, we may propose a definition of administrative act in the strict sense as "Declaration of intents which affect the legal situations of persons or objects irrespective of the consent of the other party, which are related to administrative function, and which are established by a public corporate body or a private law person if authorized."

1.1. Features of Administrative Acts

Administrative acts have some distinct features to differentiate them from other acts, namely, administrative acts are unilateral, executable as of the moment they are established, final, presumed to be lawful and subject to judicial review. Under this title, we will explain these features of administrative acts.

---

decision and acts, in other words, which an administrative act and decision does not lie behind." SC, 15th C., M. 2015/7308, D. 2017/555, 07.02.2017, www.kazanci.com.

549 In the doctrine, Akyılmaz defines administrative acts inclusively as such: "Administrative acts are unilateral declaration of intents which are of public nature and affect legal situations of persons or objects belonging to them irrespective of their content and which are established by using public force by administration or by private law persons acting on administration's behalf." See Bkz. Akyılmaz, *İdari Usul İlkeleri*, 30–31. Even though this definition is inclusive to a considerable extent, we think that this definition is open to criticism since it does not incorporate administrative acts of legislature and judiciary. The word "administration" should not be interpreted from an organic point of view and should be understood as "administrative function."

1.1.1. Unilateralism

Administrative acts (the expression of administrative decision is also used in doctrine)[550] are established with unilateral declaration of administration. This means that, in principle, administrative acts make changes in legal situations notwithstanding the consent or intent of the other party.[551] Between the relationship of administration and governed, superiority of public administration is relevant rather than the equality of the wills (such as in expropriation decision, implementing disciplinary punishment, issuing a bylaw).[552] In private law, most of the time the situation is reverse. In private law, for a legal act to emerge, the wills of the parties should comply with each other in principle.[553] In sum, unilateralism refers to the nonnecessity of the other party's acceptance for the act to bear legal consequences.

In some cases, individuals shall demand an administrative act to be established. For instance, if a person wants to be an officer, she needs to lodge an application. Similarly, an application is necessary to obtain a construction license. Within this scope, it may be born in mind that a contract is formed as a consequence of the offer and the acceptance just like in private law contracts. However, here, the decisive intent is the intent of administration.[554] The reciprocity of intents, that exists at the moment of the request of the person, gives its place to the unilateral intent of the administration and the supremacy of this intent.[555]

---

550 Individual administrative acts are also called as "administrative decisions." See Gözler, *İdare Hukuku V. I*, 787. The term "administrative decision" may be preferred in order to exclude individual administrative acts that do not bear legal consequences. See Turan Yıldırım, "İdari İşlemler [Administrative Acts]," in *İdare Hukuku*, ed. Turan Yıldırım (İstanbul: On İki Levha, 2012), 451. We do not make such a distinction.

551 Günday, *İdare Hukuku*, 124.

552 Gözler, *İdare Hukuku V. I*, 776.

553 Gözler, *İdare Hukuku V. I*, 776.

554 "… Administrative law is a part of public law and a status law which regulates administration. In administrative law, there are statuses designated beforehand by laws and rules, in other words general legal situations. To get in and out of this status usually depends on the intent of the person in question. However, the person in question does not have the ability to designate the conditions of the status she intents to get in and negotiate. This status is not contractual and voluntary, but legislatorial and statutory…" MHAC 2nd C., M. 2003/517, D. 2003/939, 03.12.2003, www.kazanci.com.

555 Akyılmaz, Sezginer and Kaya indicate that the intents of the private person regarding establishment of the act should be evaluated as procedural acts which do not possess legal effect, rather than the "fundamental intent." Akyılmaz, Sezginer, and Kaya, *Türk İdare Hukuku*, 350.

In doctrine, it is indicated that unilateralism has the same meaning with executability.[556] This is only true when we speak of administrative acts in the strict sense, since preparative acts are unilateral, but not executable. State Council finds that "executability" and "unilateralism" are distinct from each other in meaning and scope.[557]

Unilateralism does not mean that the administrative act should be the consequence of only one intent. The important issue here is the direction of the intents. In other words, acts of administration may be the consequence of more than one intent like in municipal board's decision. However, the decision only belongs to the administration, and there are related persons on the other side who will be affected by this decision. Even though more than one will takes part on the establishment of the act, the outcome is the act of only one party, namely, administration.

Unilateral act may also be established by more than one administration.[558] State Council has found that a protocol between Social Insurance Institution and Turkish Pharmacists' Association (which is one of the professional organizations having the characteristics of public institutions) is a "unilateral" administrative act conducted by more than one administration: "... It is known that the fundamental characteristics and features of administrative acts are counted as unilateralism, legality and executability. The feature which is important for the protocol in question is the feature of unilateralism. Unilateralism as a notion is not a single declaration of intent. Unilateralism does not refer to the intent of only one person or organ, but the single declaration of intent of more than one administrative organ. Therefore, while the intent in administrative act may be declared by only one office or organ, it is also possible that more than one administrative office and organ may unite for a single declaration of intent and in all these situations it is accepted that the administrative act is unilateral."[559]

1.1.2. Executability

Executability of administrative act means that the act has the power to be effective "as of the moment it is established." This does not mean that administration must implement this administrative act. Administration may withdraw or abolish the act. What is important here is that the act has the power to be

---

556 Günday, *İdare Hukuku*, 112; Gözler, *İdare Hukuku V. I*, 776.

557 SC, 5th C., M. 1995/4416, D. 1996/1911, 17.05.1996, www.kazanci.com.

558 Akyılmaz, Sezginer, and Kaya, *Türk İdare Hukuku*, 350.

559 SCPSCAC, M. 2006/4286, D. 2007/60, 08.02.2007, www.hukukturk.com.

executed as of the moment it is established even if the other party lacks intent thereof. As a matter of fact, in a decision of State Council, it is indicated that "the most obvious feature of administrative act is that it may affect the legal status of the related person by administration's unilateral intent, notwithstanding the persons request."[560]

Executability originates from administrative acts being aimed at public interest and being based on public power.[561] Authorization to conduct unilateral and executable acts is one of the most important privilege that is granted to administration to carry out public service.[562]

It should be indicated that all unilateral acts are not executable. Acts that do not affect the legal situations of persons or objects and which do not make a difference in the legal world are not executable.[563] Differentiating executable acts from nonexecutable acts are important since acts that are not executable cannot be subject to an action for annulment. As a matter of fact, pursuant to Administrative Judicial Procedure Act, "executability" is counted among one of the first aspects (preliminary) which administrative court shall examine.[564] In case that there is not any "executable act" in question, then the suit will be rejected before considering the merits.

Within this scope, explanatory acts, warning acts, preparatory acts and internal acts may be given as examples to acts which are not executable. Firstly, "explanatory," "indicator" or "indicative" acts are not executable.[565] These acts

---

560 SC 5th C., M. 2006/2586, D. 2006/5740, 28.11.2006, www.hukukturk.com; SC 5th C., M. 2005/4897, D. 2006/666, 21.02.2006, www.hukukturk.com.

561 Gözler, *İdare Hukuku V. I*, 777.

562 Gözübüyük, and Tan, *V. I*, 373.

563 Akyılmaz, Sezginer, and Kaya, *Türk İdare Hukuku*, 352.

564 According to the third subparagraph of article 14 of the Administrative Judicial Procedure Act, "In State Council, a judge rapporteur assigned by the president of the Division, in administrative and tax courts, the president or a member assigned by him, shall examine the following aspects of the petition respectively:

a) Jurisdiction as to subject-matter and venue,

b) Encroachment upon administrative authority,

c) Legal capacity,

d) Whether there is a final administrative act that must be executed, which can be a subject of administrative suit,

e) Statute of limitation,

f) Indication of adverse party,

g) Compliance with articles 3 and 5."

565 Akyılmaz, Sezginer, and Kaya, *Türk İdare Hukuku*, 342.

only suggest a view or intent of the administration on a specific subject.[566] While these acts may be established upon one's request,[567] administration may also establish these acts on its own motion.

Likewise, warning acts are not executable. However, if administration orders a person to do something in a certain time limit with the warning of a sanction, such act is assumed to be executable.[568]

Preparatory acts are not executable as well.[569] These are acts like a research, examination conducted before the final and executable act.[570] For instance, security intelligence is gathered for the police school applicants who desire to attend to the entrance examination. Related inspection authority may decide on the applicant to attend to the examination or not. However, pursuant to the legislation, this decision needs to be sent to the Security General Directorate ("SGD") and SGD makes the final decision on whether the applicant can attend to the exam. Here, the decision of related inspection authority is a "preparatory act." In case that a file is suited against this act, the case will be rejected before viewing the merits. Administrative court will rule that a suit should be filed after the executable act is established, which is the act of SGD.[571]

Internal acts are also not executable. Administration may establish acts like circular, declaration or notice, which concerns its own organization. State Council indicated that such acts are directly related to the internal structure of administration.[572] Here, the important issue is to determine the "qualification"

---

566 Yıldırım, "İdari İşlemler," 451.

567 On the other hand, requests of administration may not be executable as well: "… The acts of institutions, that they make a written request to the related offices of chief public prosecutor, pursuant to the authorities and duties based on the laws they are subject to, are acts which administration conducts within the area of criminal procedure, which forms the beginning of criminal investigation and does not create changes concerning the legal position of related persons, and therefore which are acts that cannot be subject to administrative suits. In this situation, since Board's decision on making request to office of chief public prosecutor regarding the plaintiff, does not have the characteristic of a final and executable act, there is not any possibility to evaluate the merits of the case." SC 13th C., M. 2011/1527, D. 2011/2296, 16.05.2011, www.danistay.gov.tr.

568 Gözübüyük, and Tan, *V. I*, 376–377.

569 Akyılmaz, Sezginer, and Kaya, *Türk İdare Hukuku*, 352.

570 Gözübüyük and Tan, *V. I*, 377; Yıldırım, "İdari İşlemler," 451.

571 SC 8th C., M. 2004/6063, D. 2005/3078, 20.06.2005, www.kazanci.com.

572 Gözübüyük and Tan, *V. I*, 374.

of the act, not to the "title" of it.[573] For instance, under the title of "circular," an executable act may be established. Why is this important? This is important since that administration may establish executable acts under the title of internal acts to avoid judicial review. Therefore, by only looking at the title of an act, it should not be concluded that the case will be rejected without considering the merits.

In one of the decisions of the State Council, following sentences draw attention: "In the established case law of State Council, it is accepted that circulars cannot be subject to administrative suits, which informs the organizations of the administration about current legislation understanding, which shows the proceedings to them, and which do not violate third persons' rights and interests. However, in case that such acts bring a new element to the field of law, and therefore violates the related persons' subjective rights, interests, these acts can be subject to administrative suits."[574]

It should be noted that "executability" and "*ex officio* executability" are different notions.[575] *Ex officio* executability of an administrative act refers to the situations where administration has the ability to implement its act. *Ex officio* executability is not possible in private law. Vigilantism, in other words, obtaining one's right on its own, is prohibited. In private law, persons need to resort to courts or offices of execution to obtain their rights. If laid down by a law, there is no obligation for administration to resort to court or office of execution to implement its own decision.

The difference between *ex officio* executability and executability is that while executability is about emerging of the act, *ex officio* executability is about implementing it. When a decision is taken by administration, it is executable. In other words, the decision emerges with the power to make a change in legal status. However, implementation of this decision (transferring of this change to the real world)[576] is another issue.

In some situations, no action is necessary for the act to be transferred to the real world.[577] This happens by itself. In this case, it may be indicated that emergence of the act and transferring of it to the real-world interlace. For instance, this is the case when administration gives consent to some form of activity. The act will be reflected to the real world as of the moment the act emerges.

---

573 Yıldırım, "İdari İşlemler," 452.
574 SCPSCAC, M. 2006/3196, D. 2008/1179, 11.04.2008, www.kazanci.com.
575 Günday, *İdare Hukuku*, 113.
576 Günday, *İdare Hukuku*, 113.
577 Günday, *İdare Hukuku*, 113.

However, according to Gözler, administration principally is authorized to implement its own act unless otherwise is specified by law (for instance, in case that application to execution office is envisaged by law in order to implement a specific act).[578] Dissentingly Yayla and Günday stress that *ex officio* executability only exists if it is laid down by a law.[579]

Pursuant to the principle of rule of law, and the principle of legality of administration prescribed in the Constitution as an extension of the principle of the rule of law, administration itself shall not have the power to implement the act it has made. For administration to implement its own act, a law should authorize it.[580] In sum, we think that authorization by law regarding ex officio execution is necessary within the scope of the principle of rule of law.

1.1.3. Administrative Act Being "Final"

"Being final" is also considered as a feature of administrative acts in the decisions of administrative judiciary. The reason of this is that Administrative Judicial Procedure Act seeks an act which is final, and which must be executed, for the annulment actions not to be dismissed.

State Council has described this feature as follows: "... the features of 'executability' and 'being final' of an act are not identical and have quite different qualifications. From the perspective of the circumstances of the case, finality of administrative act is important with regard to the emergence of final act in the procedure of making administrative decisions. (...) In other words, finality means administrative act to be executable by being signed by competent administrative offices or organs and by being completed with all the stages prescribed for the administrative act to emerge."[581]

In brief, it may be concluded that "finality" and "executability" are evaluated as distinct features by the High Court. Among the decisions of the High Court, we could have found only one decision in which High Court rejects a suit without considering the merits since the administrative act does not possess solely "finality."[582] The same distinction is also made in doctrine. For example,

---

578 Gözler, *İdare Hukuku V. I*, 779.

579 Yayla, *İdare Hukuku*, 115; Günday, *İdare Hukuku*, 113.

580 Günday, *İdare Hukuku*, 113.

581 SC 5th C., M. 1995/4416, D. 1996/1911, 17.05.1996, www.kazanci.com.

582 SC 6th C., M. 1981/2932, D. 1983/988, 08.03.1983, www.kazanci.com. However, it can also be thought that High Court's approach is based on the distinction of administrative acts in broad terms (which are the sum of nonexecutable acts such as preparatory acts and executable acts) and administrative acts in the strict sense (which includes

Erkut highlighted that an administrative act may be final without being executable and may be executable without being final.[583]

1.1.4. Presumption of Legality

Administrative acts are presumed to be legal. However, illegality of administrative acts may be alleged since they do not constitute definite judgment like the decisions of the courts.[584] In other words, administrative act is presumed to be legal and implemented, till it is annulled by a court. Moreover, filing a lawsuit itself does not stop execution of the act.[585] Indeed, first paragraph of article 27 of Administrative Judicial Procedure Act provides that "Bringing an action to the State Council or administrative courts shall not prevent the execution of the administrative act which is the subject of the action."

Prevention of the execution of the administrative act before an annulment decision at the end of the proceedings is only possible when a "stay of execution" decision is taken by the administrative court. The conditions to decide on stay of execution are prescribed in the second subparagraph of article 27 of Administrative Judicial Procedure Act: "If the implementation of an administrative act should result in damages which are difficult or impossible to compensate for, and if this act is clearly unlawful, the State Council or administrative court may decide to stay the execution of the act, indicating the reasoning thereof, after obtaining the defense of the defendant administration or duration of defense expires. Stay of execution decision may be taken regarding acts which exhaust their effect through implementation before obtaining the defense of the administration, to be re-decided after obtaining defense. In stay of execution decisions, it is obligatory to indicate the reasoning that the administrative act is clearly unlawful and the damages which are difficult or impossible to compensate for in case the act is implemented. A stay of execution decision cannot be held, solely

---

only executable acts). From this perspective, it can be thought that acts which are not final refer to preparatory acts; and final acts refer to acts which are executable. In our opinion, from the wording of the decision, it is not possible to make a precise evaluation.

583 Celal Erkut, *İptal Davasının Konusunu Oluşturması Bakımından İdari İşlemin Kimliği* [*Identity of Administrative Acts As Constituting the Subject of Annulment Case*] (Ankara: Danıştay Yayınları no. 51, 1990), 118. See in the same direction: Kalabalık, *İdari Yargılama Usulü*, 147.

584 Günday, *İdare Hukuku*, 114; Özay, *Günışığında*, 407.

585 Özay, *Günışığında*, 408.

with the reasoning that an application has been made to Constitutional Court with the request to annul the related provision of the act."

Exceptionally, a law can provide that an application toward an administrative act shall stay the execution of this act.[586] For instance, according to subarticle 4 of article 27 of Administrative Judicial Procedure Act, "In the tax courts, bringing actions arising from tax disputes shall stop the collection of the disputed part of the imposed taxes, fees, duties and other similar financial obligations or increases and penalties concerning these obligations." As seen, according to the Act, bringing actions in tax courts has the effect of staying execution. In this case, a further stay of execution decision is not needed.

In brief, two exceptions may be counted to the presumption of legality. Firstly, administrative court may decide on stay of execution. Secondly, laws may grant a certain application the effect of staying execution of an administrative act.

1.1.5. Judicial Review

The principle of rule of law necessities all administrative acts to be subject to judicial review. According to Constitutional Court, "State governed by rule of law, indicated in the second article of the Constitution, is a state, based on human rights, which protects and strengthens these rights and freedoms, and it's acts and actions are in conformity with law, which establishes a judicious legal order in every field and maintains this by enhancing it, avoiding situations and stances in contrary with the Constitution, which makes law dominant over all state organs, which makes itself bound with laws and the Constitution and which is subject to judicial review…"[587]

State is comprised of legislature, executive and judiciary. Since administration is situated under executive in the Constitution, it is also within the notion of the state. In that case, a state that is subject to judicial review necessities administration to be subject to judicial review. In fact, the first subparagraph of article 125 of the Constitution is as follows: "Recourse to judicial review shall be available against all actions and acts of administration."

However, Constitution itself excluded some acts from judicial review. For instance, according to the second subparagraph of article 125 of the Constitution, recourse to judicial review is not available against acts of Supreme Military Council regarding promotion and retiring due to lack of tenure position.

586 Gözler, *İdare Hukuku V. I*, 783.

587 CC, M. 2012/80, D. 2013/16, 17.01.2013, OG 23.01.2013–28537.

Another example may be found in the tenth subarticle of article 159 of the Constitution. Accordingly, the decisions of the Council of Judges and Prosecutors shall not be subject to judicial review other than dismissal from the profession.

1.2. Types of Administrative Acts

Administrative acts are subject to several divisions in administrative law doctrine. Here, we will mention the divisions which are more important compared to others. Accordingly, the divisions of administrative acts may be gathered in four titles.

1.2.1. Administrative Acts According to Material Division

Administrative acts may be divided into two categories from the perspective of material division. Firstly, an administrative act may be "special," "concrete," "depleting by being implemented" and "personal." Secondly, an administrative act may be "general," "abstract," "constant" and "impersonal."[588]

1.2.1.1. Individual Administrative Acts

Individual administrative acts are acts which are individual and related to special situations.[589] In other words, these are acts related to specific persons, situations or objects.[590] For instance, expropriation of a real estate[591] or assignment of a person to an administrative duty are individual administrative acts. According to another definition, administrative acts are acts which are the consequences of regulatory administrative acts being implemented to a specific person, object or fact and create a valid situation only for this person, object, or fact.[592]

Individual administrative acts may be subject to a further division. Accordingly, an individual administrative act may be a condition act or a subjective act.[593]

---

588 Akyılmaz, Sezginer, and Kaya, *Türk İdare Hukuku*, 364.

589 See Louvaris, *Droit Administratif*, 80; Gözler, *İdare Hukuku V. II*, 769.

590 Günday, *İdare Hukuku*, 110; Yıldırım, "İdari İşlemler," 452.

591 "... when considering the legislations, it is understood that expropriation acts are individual acts related to property." SC, 6th C., M. 2001/3636, D. 2002/4849, 31.10.2002, www.hukukturk.com.

592 Gözübüyük and Tan, *V. I*, 360.

593 Akyılmaz, Sezginer, and Kaya, *Türk İdare Hukuku*, 368.

1.2.1.1.1. Condition Acts (Actes-Condition)

Condition acts are acts which put a person or an object into or out of an objective and impersonal legal situation (status) that is laid down beforehand.[594] In other words, there is a status which is constituted beforehand by a law (such as Public Servants Law) or other regulatory acts (such as bylaws related to the implementation of Public Servants Law) and administration puts a person or an object to this status through condition acts. From then on, the person or object will be subject to the laws or other regulatory acts regarding this status.

A typical example to condition acts is assignment acts on persons. Accordingly, State Council ruled that "assignment acts, which are in the characteristic of condition acts, carry the implementation of a power or authority which come from an objective rule within itself. The person enters into a status in which rights and duties, authorities and responsibilities are laid down beforehand via regulatory acts."[595]

Dismissal of a person from the occupation or termination of the duty of public servant are examples of condition acts which make persons exit from the status.

Administrative acts which provide transition between statuses, in other words, the acts which take a person or object from one status and put to another one, are condition acts as well.

Regarding objects, "allocation acts" may be given as an example to condition acts. Via an allocation act, a property belonging to administration which is legally in private property status enters into the status of "public property."[596]

1.2.1.1.2. Subjective Acts (Personal Acts)

Subjective acts are acts which puts certain persons or objects to a legal situation that's scope is determined by these persons or objects.[597] For instance, "tax assessment" is a subjective act. The tax that a person will pay in a year is determined by that person's income and other related characteristics. Therefore, the amount of tax payable differentiate from person to person.[598]

---

594 Günday, *İdare Hukuku*, 116; Gözübüyük and Tan, *V. I*, 362; Akyılmaz, Sezginer, and Kaya, *Türk İdare Hukuku*, 368; Odyakmaz and Kaymak, *İdare Hukuku*, 65.

595 SC 5th C., M. 2008/5015, D. 2008/6321, 19.12.2008, www.danistay.gov.tr.

596 Günday, *İdare Hukuku*, 117.

597 Günday, *İdare Hukuku*, 117; Akyılmaz, Sezginer, and Kaya, *Türk İdare Hukuku*, 369.

598 Gözler, *İdare Hukuku V. I*, 789.

Acts determining the score of an individual from an exam,[599] a disciplinary sanction,[600] seizure of a newspaper[601] and acts concerning public employees to benefit from social rights[602] are given examples to subjective acts in doctrine.

As seen, subjective acts differ from person to person.[603] Lastly, it should be noted that in administrative law, subjective acts are rare unlike in private law branches. Most administrative acts are in the characteristics of condition acts.

1.2.1.2. General Regulatory Administrative Acts

In public law, general regulatory administrative acts are used to refer acts which are general, abstract, nondepleting when implemented and which lay down a specific rule. These acts are also made by legislature since laws are also regulatory acts. General regulatory administrative acts of administration are acts which are made by competent offices within Turkish Republic administration. Bylaws are examples on this regard.

This type of acts are "general and impersonal."[604] In other words, these acts are not related to a certain person or situation, which establish abstract and general legal rules. These are acts which welcome new rules to the legal order or change or abolish an existing rule.[605] They do not deplete by being implemented and are implemented to related persons, objects or facts continually.[606] For instance, bylaws regarding students are implemented to all students who are registered to a school and these will be implemented to every student who will register to school in the following years unless these bylaws are abolished or amended.

In addition, there are acts which are general, but not regulatory. These are called as "general acts." These are acts which are implemented limited times (one or more than one time) to certain or determinable persons or situations and deplete by being implemented.[607] On the other hand, when general regulatory

599 Akyılmaz, Sezginer, and Kaya, *Türk İdare Hukuku*, 369; Odyakmaz and Kaymak, *İdare Hukuku*, 65.
600 Gözler, *İdare Hukuku V. I*, 789; On the other hand, in doctrine, some scholars state that disciplinary sanctions are within condition acts. See Akyılmaz, Sezginer, and Kaya, *Türk İdare Hukuku*, 368.
601 Gözübüyük and Tan, *V. I*, 363.
602 Günday, *İdare Hukuku*, 117.
603 Gözler, *İdare Hukuku V. I*, 789.
604 See Louvaris, *Droit Administratif*, 76; Gözler, *İdare Hukuku V. I*, 770.
605 Gözübüyük, and Tan, *V. I*, 360.
606 Yıldırım, "İdari İşlemler," 452–453; Akyılmaz, *İdari Usul İlkeleri*, 41.
607 Akyılmaz, *İdari Usul İlkeleri*, 42.

administrative acts are in question, there is no certainty on the properties mentioned.[608] For instance, in case that the governor decides on a two-day vacation in a certain province for elementary schools due to snowfall, this decision is a general act. But it is not regulatory. This is because, the number of schools which are in the scope of the decision is determinable and this act will deplete by being implemented. State Council rules in accordingly: "It should be also indicated that some administrative acts are general, but not regulatory. The determination on whether an act is a rule (regulation), is not made only by assessing the characterization of the doers of these, but also by assessing the contexts of these acts and legal consequences born."[609]

Lastly, it should be indicated that, administration does not have primary regulatory power unlike legislature. Constitutional Court is of the same opinion.[610]

1.2.2. Administrative Acts According to the Number of Intents

Administrative acts may be subject to a division concerning the number of intents and the way the intents are declared in three categories: basic, collective and combined acts.

Basic acts are acts which emerge by declaration of intent of only one public official.[611] For instance, grading a student by the professor is a basic act.

Collective acts are acts which are made by an administrative office comprising of more than one person.[612] These are acts in which more than one intent is declared at the same moment and in the same direction.[613] For instance, decisions of Boards are as such.[614] Here, collective acts are the decisions that are

---

608 A bylaw may be abolished as well after being implemented once. In this situation, the bylaw would be implemented to only a certain number of persons and deplete by being implemented. However, when the bylaw is brought into force, it is not decided that it would be implemented only once and deplete. The aim is that it would be implemented continuously for a long time to unpredictable number of persons or situations.

609 SC 5th C., M. 2007/7830, D. 2008/772, 13.02.2008, www.kazanci.com.

610 Yıldırım, "İdari İşlemler," 455.

611 Günday, *İdare Hukuku*, 118.

612 Yıldırım, "İdari İşlemler," 450.

613 Murat Sezginer, "İdari İşlem-İcrailik-Ayrılabilir İşlem-Yargısal Denetim [Administrative Act—Executability—Separable Act—Judicial Review]," *İl Han Özay'a Armağan, İstanbul Law Review* 69, no. 1–2 (2011): 243.

614 Günday, *İdare Hukuku*, 118. SC 13th C., M. 2006/883, D. 2006/4435, 22.11.2006, www.kazanci.com; The related part of the decision is as follows: "In the incident, the decision of Competition Board, which is the matter of dispute, is held by involvement of eight members. … Considering that decisions of Competition Board, in the

directly attributed to Boards, and which are isolated from the public employees who declare their intents.[615] Unlike combined acts, within the scope of collective acts, the intents do not form a line. In other words, in order for an intent to be declared, a subsequent intent is not necessary. Otherwise, the act will be considered as a combined act.

Lastly, combined acts are acts which emerge as a consequence of intents being declared following a line on the same direction and aim.[616] The intents of all administrative offices are decisive in the emergence of the act.[617] For instance, joint decrees are acts which emerge by the unification of intents of the president and related ministers.[618]

For these types of acts, "separable act doctrine" needs to be mentioned.[619] It is accepted that the acts, which "in its own" can bear legal consequences, among the declarations of intents within combined acts, can be separated from the other declarations of intent. Therefore, it is accepted that these acts can solely be subject to a lawsuit.[620]

---

characteristics of a collective act, are held with the involvement of intents more than one, after the gathered information and documents evaluated in the meetings and negotiations in accordance with the procedure determining obligatory procedures in inquisition and investigations in detail, and in consequence of the discussion of the views and opposing views brought forward by the ones who form the Board on the evidence put forward and allegations and pleas of the parties, pursuant to Law no 4054, it is an essential condition with regard to the form element of the act that the number of members are not uncertain and maximum and minimum number of members for convening and taking decisions of the Board is in accordance with the regulation incorporated in law."

615 Akyılmaz, Sezginer, and Kaya, *Türk İdare Hukuku*, 376.

616 Günday, *İdare Hukuku*, 119.

617 Akyılmaz, Sezginer, and Kaya, *Türk İdare Hukuku*, 375.

618 Yıldırım, "İdari İşlemler," 450.

619 "... In both doctrine and judicial decisions, it is accepted that the acts involved in legal procedures can also be subject to an annulment case, rather than the view that only the final act can be subject to an annulment case among the acts emerged in the procedure of taking administrative decisions. The main aim of 'separable act' doctrine is to provide judicial review for the acts within administrative procedures in case that they bear legal consequences." SCPSCAC, M. 2008/1357, D. 2009/2191, 12.11.2009, www.hukukturk.com.

620 For instance, before the amendment, the intents of "related universities," "Higher Education Council" and the "president" constituted assignment acts by following a line for the assignment of rectors in universities. Judicial review was not possible for the acts which were conducted solely by the president. However, in case that the intent of

In a dispute, administration prepared maps regarding an energy transmission project and expropriations that would be executed accordingly. A file was brought before administrative court for the annulment of the "energy transmission project." Administrative court rejected the case since expropriation did not take place and an executable act did not emerge. However, State Council decided that the transmission project is separable from the expropriation acts since the project itself is an executable act. In conclusion, State Council quashed the decision of the administrative court.[621]

Higher Education Council was separable, judicial review would be possible for its acts. In fact, in a dispute regarding the assignment of a rector, State Council ruled that the act of Higher Education Council can be subject to judicial review, by evaluating that, the intent of the Institution regarding elimination of three candidates, was a "separate" act: "... In the mentioned subparagraph, a three-stage procedure is envisaged for the selection of the rector, the first stage among these is the selection of 6 candidates for the nomination by the faculty members of universities; the second stage is the selection of three candidates among candidates for the nomination by Higher Education Council to be presented to the president; third stage is the assignment of the rectorship by the president among three candidates who are presented to the president. It should firstly be indicated that, the acts in the first and second stages of the procedure which ends with the appointment act of the president, can be separated from each other, and each constitutes an independent administrative act, even though they are in a close legal dependence with each other. Since the two of these acts create new legal situations and consequences independently from each other and from the final appointment act and limit the usage of authority in the next stage they bear the characteristics of being final and executable, it is clear that these acts cannot be accepted as preparatory acts which do not bear legal significance other than being enlightening and guiding for the authorized office as suggestion, recommendation, consideration and report submitted before the administrative act is taken. Therefore, these acts can be subject to a lawsuit without waiting for the final act or after the final act in condition that the time limit to file a lawsuit has not expired." SC 5th C., M. 1992/4035, D. 1993/3177, 16.09.1993, www.kazanci.com.

621 "... Energy transmission project, which is approved and finalized by administration, is a final and executable act; and judicial review of these acts which are separable from expropriation acts are carried out by the determination of whether a preparation is made suitable to public interest and to the necessities of the service. Since expropriation acts, which will be executed with regard to the energy transmission lines of which project preparation is done, are separable from the projects and are separate acts which will be dealt within the scope of Expropriation Code; the matter should be handled by considering merits in the suits filed against finalized projects. Thus, the decision—subject to appeal—is not lawful, since the case is rejected without examination with the reasoning that the act cannot be subject to a suit and since the

1.2.3. Implicit Acts

Administrative acts are mostly established via explicit declarations of intents of the related administration. Accordingly, administrative acts may be established in written, orally or via motion or with a signal.[622] These acts are called as explicit acts. However, in some situations, silence or omission (negligence) of administration may be attached with a legal consequence.[623] Firstly, omission may be related to an action. For instance, not scrutinizing an enterprise to prevent environmental pollution is an action of administration in the form of omission.[624] In case that a damage is caused through such omission, administration is obliged to compensate the damage. Secondly, legal order may deem the omission of administration to be an "administrative act." In this situation, "implicit rejection" or "implicit admittance" emerges.[625]

In case that an application is made to administrative offices for the execution of an act, an "implicit rejection act" emerges when the administration remains silent or fails to act within a certain time.[626] The person who made the application can file a suit against this rejection act.

The reason for this is to prevent administration from avoiding judicial review by remaining silent or failing to act. According to Administrative Judicial Procedure Act when applied to administrative judiciary, administrative court will evaluate whether there is an administrative act in question. In case that an administrative act is not in question, the court will reject the case. If a legal consequence was not envisaged for the omission, the administration would avoid making acts upon applications and a judicial review would not be possible since there is no act in question.[627] Thus, in case that administration can avoid judicial

decision should have been made by examining merits." SC 10th C., M. 2008/7771, D. 2009/19, 26.01.2009, www.kazanci.com. State Council also decided that the acts related to tender procedures of privatization are separable. See SC 10th C., M. 2004/8257, D. 2004/7618, 22.06.2004, www.kazanci.com.

622 Akyılmaz, Sezginer, and Kaya, *Türk İdare Hukuku*, 371.

623 Akyılmaz, Sezginer, and Kaya, *Türk İdare Hukuku*, 373.

624 SC 10th C., M. 2004/8703, D. 2006/2507, 18.04.2006, www.kazanci.com.

625 For instance, in the 10th article of Administrative Judicial Procedure Act (titled "Silence of the Administrative Offices"), it is provided that "(1) The persons concerned may request the administrative offices to implement an act or take an action that may be subject of a lawsuit. (2) If the request is not replied within thirty days, it shall be deemed to be dismissed."

626 Akyılmaz, *İdari Usul İlkeleri*, 25; Odyakmaz and Kaymak, *İdare Hukuku*, 67–68.

627 Gözler, *İdare Hukuku V. I*, 799.

review by remaining silent, it will be contrary to the principle of rule of law.[628] Pursuant to principle of rule of law, all acts and actions of administration should be brought to judicial review.

State Council summarized the subject as follows: "The notion of implicit rejection is accepted due to administration's avoidance to response arbitrarily. In administrative judiciary, it is essential that administration should be scrutinized by annulment cases and with the notion of implicit rejection, administration's evasion of the right to an effective remedy by not giving responses was eliminated."[629]

However, any application cannot give rise to an "implicit rejection act." For instance, in case that administration does not reply to a request of instruction or guidance, an implicit rejection does not emerge, since responses to these types of questions do not constitute executable acts. As we have already noted, only executable acts can be brought to administrative judiciary.[630] In other words, omission or silence of administration constitutes an implicit rejection act only if an application is lodged to administration in relation to an act or action that can be subject to an administrative suit.[631]

In principle, omission or silence of administration to an application demanding from the administration to make an executable act is an implicit rejection act.[632] However, exceptionally the law may foresee the reverse. In other words, law may set forth that silence or omission of administration amount to an "admittance." In this case, silence or omission of administration will constitute an "implicit admittance act."[633] An example for the implicit admittance act is envisaged in the article 30 of the Construction Law numbered 3194: "(…) Municipalities and governorships (…) must conclude the applications of the owners of the

---

628 Gözler, *İdare Hukuku V. I*, 799.

629 SC 6th C., M. 2013/673, D. 2015/1617, 18.03.2015, www.kazanci.com. In another decision, the following sentence draws attention: "...In administrative judiciary, the only tool to scrutinize administration is annulment cases. The existence of the concept of implicit rejection removes the possibility of administration not making an administrative act concerning the related person against which she/he may file a lawsuit in administrative courts by remaining silent." SC 6th C., M. 2014/6481, D. 2015/1906, 01.04.2015, www.lexpera.com.

630 Günday, *İdare Hukuku*, 121.

631 Günday, *İdare Hukuku*, 121.

632 Akyılmaz, Sezginer, and Kaya, *Türk İdare Hukuku*, 373.

633 Günday, *İdare Hukuku*, 121; Odyakmaz and Kaymak, *İdare Hukuku*, 67.

property within thirty days. Otherwise, the occupancy permit shall be deemed to be granted to the entire structure or the finished part."

State Council decided that administration to foresee an implicit admittance act through a general regulatory administrative act is illegal:

> ... In the provisions brought by the Covenant and Proclamation; health and safety of the volunteer is prioritized. All the procedures of clinical studies conducted on the persons are important and concerns the health of the volunteer closely. Therefore, for the changes in all procedures and subjects, positive opinion must be waited. Within this scope, implicit admittance brought by the mentioned provision does not comply with the provisions of the Covenant and Proclamation.
>
> For the mentioned reasons, clause (b) of the first sub-article of the article 20 of the Bylaw, which provides that: 'General Directorate is accepted to confirm the protocol changes in case that it does not present an opinion on the protocol changes within thirty-five days beginning from the day following the date of the application' is illegal and executability of this provision should be suspended...[634]

1.3. Elements of Administrative Acts

Administrative Judicial Procedure Act lays down that the determination regarding the legality of administrative acts is to be made within the scope of five elements: authority, form, motive, subject and aim. Each of these elements are explained below.

1.3.1. Authority (Power)

Turkish Constitution has two important provisions regarding the element of authority. Firstly, the Constitution states that no person or organ shall exercise any state authority that does not emanate from the Constitution. Administration is within "the executive branch of the state" and its ability to use public force is a state authority. Therefore, since administrative act is a declaration of intent aimed at a specific legal consequence, this declaration of intent must be made by persons or offices who are authorized to declare intent by law in respect to subject, place and time.

Secondly, according to the Constitution, the administration shall be regulated by law. Therefore, administration can only carry out acts and actions in case that it is authorized by law. However, this does not mean that every subject needs to be regulated by law. Laws which set fundamental principles, in other words lay

634 SC 10th C., M. 2009/3991, D. SE, 13.11.2009, www.kazanci.com.

down the general boundaries is sufficient. We should mention here that in cases where a "PD area" is provided in the Constitution (where exceptions to legality of administration is provided), an authority can also be granted to an administrative office via PDs. For instance, according to article 106/end of the Constitution, the duties and powers of the ministries shall be regulated by PDs. Therefore, below-mentioned explanations on the necessity of a "law" also holds true for PDs in cases of "PD areas."

Sometimes, a law may regulate authority explicitly. In these cases, "explicit authority" is in question.[635] On the other hand, sometimes a law grants administration a general authority since it cannot lay down every detail. In these cases, "implicit authority" is in question.[636] For instance, according to Law for Provincial Administration (law no. 5442), the governor has general policing authorities within the boundaries of the province. The governor may carry out administrative acts based on this general authority. The law does not lay down all the details regarding how and in which situations this authority shall be used since it is not possible. For instance, within the authority of general policing, the authority to prohibit bovine animals which are suspected to carry contagious diseases into the city to protect general health is an "implicit" authority.

On the other hand, administration should not go beyond the boundaries set by laws. In case that the administration goes beyond its authorization and makes an individual act or regulation by crossing over the limits set forth by the law, "trespassing of authority" is in question and the act shall be annulled by judiciary. For instance, in one of the cases before State Council concerning airline transport, a directive laying down administrative fines was evaluated. This directive envisaged administrative fine to airline operators which do not transport persons—who enter the country but are considered "inadmissible" passengers for several reasons—to other places in a specified duration. State Council annulled this directive by highlighting that administration did not bear the authority to regulate this area since there was no law which envisage and set borders for this administrative penalty.[637]

In sum, being authorized is exception and being unauthorized is the principle in administrative law.[638] The administration is only deemed authorized when

635 Akyılmaz, *İdari Usul İlkeleri*, 108.

636 Akyılmaz, *İdari Usul İlkeleri*, 108.

637 SC 10th C., M. 2003/4021, D. 2006/3011, 16.05.2006, www.kazanci.com.

638 "... 'Authority' in administrative law refers to the power to take decisions which are granted to administration by the Constitution or laws and compromises one of the most fundamental element of administrative acts. Authority, which is related to public

the authority is used by the offices and departments indicated by the law and in circumstances envisaged by law.

Generally speaking, in central administration the president is authorized to declare intent on behalf of the administration. In provincial organization, governor of provinces and district governors are authorized. In decentral administration, the decision-making body of the local administrations and public institutions are authorized. Other than the mentioned offices, the others are unauthorized in condition that a legally valid delegation of authority is not in question.

It should also be noted that an act that is not established by the authorized office shall not be deemed legal even with a later consent by the authorized office.[639] According to the State Council, "If the law has authorized the person performing the public service, … the authority must be used directly by that person. … Administrative acts must be established by authorized persons. The authorized person is the person who is authorized at the time of the establishment of the act. The consent given by the authorized person to an act made by an unauthorized person cannot be valid."[640]

It should also be indicated that the trespassing of authority may be "whole" or "partial."[641] For instance, the law may grant the administration with the authority to spend only 20 hundred liras from its budget for a certain act. In case that the administration decides to spend 25 hundred liras, the judiciary shall decide on the "partially" annulment of this act in respect of the surplus.

Lastly, there may be cases where the law grants the administration with the authority to make a certain act but does not grant the authority to make the contrary act like withdrawal or removal of this act. For these cases, a principle called "the principle of parallelism on authority" is evolved by jurisdiction. According to this principle, the office which is authorized to execute the act is also authorized to withdraw or abolish, in condition that the law does not authorize another administrative office to withdraw or abolish this act.[642] For instance, a law may

order, shall be used by the office or agency within the limits, designated by the law maker. Therefore, being unauthorized is the principle while being authorized is the exception in administrative law. Accordingly, rules regarding authority cannot be subjected to a broadening interpretation." SCPSCAC, M. 2007/2257, D. 2012/1117, 14.09.2012, www.kazanci.com; SC, 10th C., M. 2015/5095, D. SE, 09.02.2016, www.kazanci.com.

639 Akyılmaz, Sezginer, and Kaya, *Türk İdare Hukuku*, 382.

640 SC 5th C., M. 1989/2735, D. 1989/2286, 13.12.1989, www.kazanci.com.

641 Sarıca, *İdari Kaza*, 64.

642 Akyılmaz, Sezginer, and Kaya, *Türk İdare Hukuku*, 390.

grant the mayor of municipality with the authority to give license. In case that the law does not provide a provision on the authority to withdraw (revocation) or abolish this licensing act, the principle of parallelism on authority rules and the mayor may as well abolish or withdraw the license.[643] However, in case that the law grants the authority to abolish or withdraw the license to another office, the abolishment or withdrawal act of the mayor will be illegal in terms of authority.

The types of trespassing of authority may be classified from the severest to the lightest as "usurpation of function," "usurpation of authority," "serious and obvious trespassing of authority" and "trespassing of authority."

1.3.1.1. Usurpation of Function

Sometimes, administration may establish an act in the area of "legislature" or "judiciary." In this situation, a severe "trespassing of authority" emerges, which is called "usurpation of function."[644] Since this non-authorization is so severe; the act in which administration establishes by usurping the functions of legislature and judiciary shall be accepted to be "null."[645] In other words, the act is to be accepted as never born and not binding.[646]

In one of its decisions, State Council highlighted that "usage of judiciary power by administration" is usurpation of function: "The subject of judicial procedure which is in the area of the judicial function of the courts is out of the administrative area and shall be regarded as an exclusive subject of legislation. To accept that a subject laid down concerning judicial procedure to be in administrative area, it is a must that these matters and their boundaries to be shown

643 "It is undisputed that the administration, which is authorized to issue the licenses according to the law, is also the sole authority for the cancellation of these licenses, and since it is seen that there is no law prescribing the contrary, the mayor … should cancel the business and working license given by the mayor in accordance with the principle of parallelism in authority…" SC 8th C., M. 2010/3000, D. 2013/1929, 13.03.2009, www.kazanci.com.

644 Sarıca, *İdari Kaza*, 58; Çağlayan, *İdare Hukuku Dersleri*, 423; Odyakmaz and Kaymak, *İdare Hukuku*, 70.

645 Sarıca, *İdari Kaza*, 59; Odyakmaz and Kaymak, *İdare Hukuku*, 70.

646 It should be noted that in doctrine and administrative judiciary decisions, there is no unity on when "nullity" appears. General view suggests that nullity only appears in the elements of "authority" and "subject." In addition, within the scope of the element of "motive," the act is also accepted to be null when the illegality is so severe that it is noticeable at first glance.

explicitly by the lawmaker. The acceptance that administration can regulate the areas which legislature does not authorize it to regulate, means legislative authority being used by administration also referred as 'usurpation of function.'"[647]

1.3.1.2. Usurpation of Power (Authority)

When acts are established by persons who are unauthorized to declare intent on behalf of the administration, usurpation of authority is in question.[648] Persons who are not authorized on behalf of the administration

(i) May be within administration,
(ii) May be totally stranger to administration.[649]

The first situation concerns authority in terms of person. As we have mentioned, it is a condition that administrative acts should be established by persons who are authorized to establish acts on behalf of administration. Other than the authorized persons to act on behalf of administration, there are also persons such as servants, clerks or committees within administration, who do not possess the authority to declare intent on behalf of administration. In case that these persons declare such an intent, these intents are legally void due to usurpation of authority.

Secondly, usurpation of authority may also be in question in case that a total stranger to the administration establishes administrative acts. Within this scope, two possibilities may emerge. In other words, the person establishing the act may not have any bond with the administration. For example, when a person who is not a public officer makes an act as if she is a public officer, usurpation of power will be in question and the act will be declared null and void.

At this point, it should be questioned whether it would be fair that usurpation of power leads to nullity in all circumstances. Assuming that a registrar general of marriages has a twin, who replaces the registrar, it would not be fair to declare the marriage null and void due to usurpation of power. In these instances, the principle of "ostensible officer" is being implemented to protect the governed. As a consequence of the principle, the act is deemed to be valid. Likewise, in case that a citizen makes a payment to a fraudulent replacing a public officer

---

647 SCPSCAC, M. 2010/2072, D. 2010/1467, 04.11.2010, www.danistay.gov.tr.
648 SC 1st C., M. 1947/8, D. 1947/9, 15.03.1947, www.kazanci.com.
649 Çağlayan, *İdare Hukuku Dersleri*, 424; Odyakmaz and Kaymak, *İdare Hukuku*, 71.

authorized to make collections on behalf of administration, the citizen should be deemed to have made the payment.[650]

1.3.1.3. Serious and Obvious Trespassing of Authority

Serious and obvious trespassing of authority involves the cases where the trespassing of authority is heavier than the cases mentioned below, and which is understood from the first glance. In these cases, the illegality is based on the incompliance to the division of labor within the administration.[651] For instance, in case that the finance ministry takes decisions instead of health ministry, or ministry of education decides on an issue related to tax, serious and obvious trespassing of authority is in question.[652]

In these situations, an office is available which can declare intent on behalf of administration. In other words, there is a situation similar to the above-mentioned first type of "usurpation of power." The difference is that in "usurpation of power," the person within the administration is not authorized to declare intent on behalf of the administration. However, in "obvious and serious trespassing of authority," the person or office capable to declare intent on behalf of one administration establishes acts within the authority of another administration. Legal consequence of serious and obvious trespassing of authority is also nullity.[653]

1.3.1.4. Trespassing of Authority

Trespassing of authority may be subject to a division based on subject, location and time. Firstly, it should be indicated that it is unlawful if administration avoids using authority although it should from the perspective of subject, location and time. When the administration avoid using its authority, it may as well be alleged that there is an illegality related to the element of "subject" along with "authority."[654]

---

650 In doctrine, Gözler gives these examples from French jurisdiction: see Gözler, *İdare Hukuku V. I*, 852.

651 Sarıca, *İdari Kaza*, 59–62; Akyılmaz, Sezginer, and Kaya, *Türk İdare Hukuku*, 397.

652 Onar, *İdare Hukukunun Umumi Esasları V. I*, 302–303.

653 Odyakmaz and Kaymak, *İdare Hukuku*, 71.

654 Güher Ulu, *İdari İşlemin Yetki Unsuru* (Ankara: Seçkin, 2012), 287–288. The author thinks that while the illegality regarding element of subject is evident when the administration thinks that it is not authorized in a concrete case, "trespassing of authority" is valid when the administration avoids using its powers when it is aware of its authority.

1.3.1.4.1. Authority on Subject

The notion of "authority on subject" refers to the subjects that an administrative office may decide on. The situations in which the office is not authorized on subject may be handled in two categories: trespassing of authority within the same hierarchical order and trespassing of authority between offices belonging to different hierarchical orders. In addition, in case that the authority is delegated unlawfully, the element of authority will be erred on subject.

Trespassing of authority within the same hierarchical order may appear in several ways. Firstly, as we have mentioned in the related section, prohibition on replacement rules in hierarchical relations. Accordingly, while the inferior cannot decide by replacing her superior (for instance, in case that the district governor takes a decision that falls within the authority of the governor), the superior also cannot decide by replacing her inferior. The superior can only give orders to the inferior to make a decision on a certain way. It may seem illogical that the superior cannot replace the inferior when the superior can give orders to the latter to execute an act on a certain way. However, in case that the law only grants the authority to the inferior, the superior should not be deemed as authorized.[655] For instance, in case that the authority to inflict a disciplinary punishment to a research assistant belongs to the dean, the decision of the rector to give a disciplinary punishment to a research assistant will be illegal in terms of authority.[656]

As well as the prohibition of replacement, illegality in terms of authority may be observed between the different bodies of the same institution. For instance, in one of its decisions, State Council ruled that the tender is illegal in terms of authority since it was executed by mayorship instead of municipal committee.[657] Likewise, State Council ruled that the act in question is illegal due that the act, which should have been executed by the Higher Education Board (an organ of Higher Education Council), was executed by the president of the Institution.[658]

655 "Administrative decisions have to be made by the authorized organ, office or public servants who are granted authority by the Constitution and laws. According to the principles known in the administrative law on authority, the decision of an office in a lower level on behalf of an office in a higher level will render the act illegal, the decision of an office in a higher level on behalf of an office in a lower level will also render the act illegal in terms of authority." SCPSCAC, M. 2006/2042, D. 2010/448, 11.03.2010, www.kazanci.com.

656 SCPSCAC, M. 2006/2042, D. 2010/448, 11.03.2010, www.kazanci.com.

657 SC 8th C., M. 2005/2927, D. 2006/1138, 22.03.2006, www.kazanci.com.

658 SC 8th C., M. 2008/1501, D. SE, 10.03.2008, www.kazanci.com.

Trespassing of authority within the same hierarchical order is also in question when only one organ executes an act which should have been executed by more than one organ within an institution according to the law.[659] For instance, to give disciplinary punishment to a faculty member in a university, rector's decision is needed after the board decision. In case that the board decision is absent, the trespassing of authority will be in question.[660]

Trespassing of authority on subject may as well appear between offices belonging to different hierarchical orders. There are also several appearances of trespassing of authority in these cases too. Firstly, trespassing of authority occurs when an office under administrative tutelage does not present the act to the office that possess the authority of tutelage. For instance, suppose that the act envisages the authority of administrative tutelage of a minister over some acts of mayor of municipality. In case that the mayor does not present this act to the minister, trespassing of authority will be in question.

Likewise, in case that the office having the authority of tutelage executes an act on behalf of the office under tutelage (if the law does not envisage such an authority), the act will also be illegal concerning the element of authority. For instance, in case that the law authorizes "district" municipalities on determination of opening and closing hours of workplaces, the "metropolitan municipality" cannot execute acts on this regard.[661]

Lastly, the act would be illegal in terms of authority in case that an act should have been made by more than one office in different hierarchical, but only one office has made the act.

Even though the basic rule is that the act should be established by the authorized administrative office, an office within administration may delegate its authority to another office within administration. For a delegation to be lawful, two conditions are necessary to be fulfilled. Firstly, a law should envisage such a delegation. Secondly, this delegation should be conducted in compliance with the borders set out in the law.[662] In other words, delegation of authority should be "partial." In doctrine, it is accepted that an office cannot delegate all its powers

659 Akyılmaz, *İdari Usul İlkeleri*, 108–109.

660 SC 8th C., M. 2004/3101, D. 2005/4802, 23.11.2005, www.kazanci.com.

661 The district municipalities are not under hierarchy of metropolitan municipalities. The only mechanism to provide the integrity between these municipalities is administrative tutelage if envisaged by law, since each municipalities possess different corporate legal personalities.

662 SC 5th C., M. 2005/3947, D. 2007/4793,21.09.2007, www.kazanci.com.

to another office.[663] Turkish Constitutional Court also concluded that an office cannot delegate all its powers "including authorizations in scope of policing."[664]

There is a dispute between different circuits of the State Council on whether the delegation may be within the offices belonging different public corporate bodies. According to a decision of 8th Circuit, the delegation of authority should be within the same public corporate authority.[665] However, 14th Circuit ruled that delegation of authority is possible via different public corporate bodies.[666] We believe that such delegation should be valid in case that the law prescribes so.

State Council ruled that the delegation of authority will be ceased and return back to its original owner in case that the delegator's assignment ends, and another person replaces the office. According to the High Court, "… since the prior minister is not in office at the moment when the act is established, the authority of appointment by transfer no longer belongs to the undersecretary and it returns to the original owner who is the minister."[667]

In addition to delegation of authority, authority of signature can also be delegated. In this case, unlike delegation of authority, the authority of the delegator continues. The inferior who has the authority of signature may also establish acts on behalf of the delegator. Even though the signature is delegated, the original authorized can always use authority.[668]

In doctrine, in addition to delegation of authority and signature, the notions of "assignment by proxy" and "proxy" are also mentioned.[669] As we have previously stated, public service should be carried out continuously. However, an administrative office may become vacant due to some reasons such as retirement, resignation and annual leave. In such a case, the public service which should have been carried out by this person cannot be provided. In case that another public employee is granted with the authority to carry out this service, proxy is in question.[670] When "proxy" is in question, the assigned person should have the qualifications that are required to be assigned to that office.[671] On the other hand, "assignment by proxy" refers to the assignment of a person who has the

---

663 Çağlayan, *İdare Hukuku Dersleri*, 364.

664 CC, M. 2012/27, D. 2012/173, 08.11.2012, OG 28.03.2013-28601.

665 SC 8th C., M. 2015/4574, D. 2019/1943, 19.03.2019, www.kazanci.com.

666 SC 14th C., M. 2015/4896, D. 2018/1158, 07.03.2018, www.kazanci.com.

667 SC 5th C., M. 1989/2735, D. 1989/2286, 13.12.1989, www.lexpera.com.

668 Çağlayan, *İdare Hukuku Dersleri*, 366.

669 Çağlayan, *İdare Hukuku Dersleri*, 367 ff.

670 Akyılmaz, Sezginer, and Kaya, *Türk İdare Hukuku*, 178.

671 SC 11th C., M. 2001/481, D. 2003/5610, 22.12.2003, www.hukukturk.com.

closest qualifications for an office when a person with necessary qualifications is not available.

1.3.1.4.2. Authority on Location

The notion of "authority on location" refers to the geographical borders that an administrative office may use its authority in.[672] An administration may be authorized throughout the whole country. For instance, the President who is the head of central administration can use powers throughout the country.[673] In this case, trespassing of authority on location will not be witnessed.

However, there are administrations which can only use its authority within a limited area, such as local administrations or provincial organizations. In case that such an office exceeds this border, the act will be illegal in terms of authority. For instance, in case that the governor of Samsun executes an act related to the province of Erzurum, the act will be illegal.

1.3.1.4.3. Authority on Time

An administration must use its authority within the time limit it is authorized. Otherwise, trespassing of authority will be in question. For instance, in case that the deputy governor uses authority which can be used during period of deputation outside of this period, there will be trespassing of authority on time.[674] Likewise, an act established by an officer whose assignment process is not complete or whose assignment is expired will be illegal in terms of authority. For instance, in case that a rector whose assignment term expired, establishes an act by assembling the senate, it will result in trespassing of authority on time.[675]

A distinction should be made regarding the time limits provided by laws, in which the administration should establish the act. If this time limit is envisaged to assure the related persons rights, as in the disciplinary investigations, administration has to abide by it. Otherwise, the act will be illegal in terms of authority.[676] On the other hand, in case that the time limit aims to hasten the functioning of the administration, noncompliance to this time limit will not be accepted as trespassing of authority.[677]

---

672 Odyakmaz and Kaymak, *İdare Hukuku*, 72.

673 Akyılmaz, Sezginer, and Kaya, *Türk İdare Hukuku*, 383.

674 SC 2nd C., M. 2004/4638, D. 2006/510, 17.02.2006, www.kazanci.com.

675 SC 8th C., M. 2006/970, D. 2006/2893, 07.07.2006, www.kazanci.com.

676 Akyılmaz, Sezginer, and Kaya, *Türk İdare Hukuku*, 387.

677 SC 2nd C., M. 2008/3767, D. 2009/4866, 25.12.2009, www.kazanci.com. According to the High Court, such time limits aim to discipline administration. Likewise,

1.3.2. Form/Procedure

Even though Administrative Judicial Procedure Law only mentions the element of "form," it is accepted that this element also involves "procedure" which refers to the stages that should be followed when making administrative acts. In other words, the element of "form" is a wider notion which comprises the element of "procedure."[678] We prefer to evaluate these elements separately.

1.3.2.1. Form

The element of form is related to the "image" of the administrative act, or in which shape it is reflected to the world. Principally, administrative acts appear as written texts.[679] Exceptionally, administrative acts may as well appear in shapes of words, signs, voice and such. For instance, the motions of the police officer on a crossroad may be counted as an administrative act, which reflects to the world with signs. For another example, according to the Law of Police Powers, an oral decision may be held to disperse the illegal demonstration. Implicit acts, which emerge with the silence of administration to an application, are also not written by nature.[680]

In private law transactions, freedom of form principle is valid principally. On the other hand, certain form conditions are envisaged for private law transactions which bear severe consequences on persons. In order to motivate persons to think more on the consequences which the legal transaction will bear on these persons, certain transactions must be executed by following certain procedures and in certain forms. The reason why there are rules of form within the scope of administrative law is to protect the governed.[681]

SCPSCAC has used a similar distinction: "...The first point that should be noted in terms of the enforcement of the temporary article 3 of the By-Law is that the six-month period stipulated in the same article for the establishment of the proceedings is not a period of deprivation or entitlement for the parties, but has the quality to discipline the administration in an issue stipulated by law." SCPSCAC, M. 2002/219, D. 2002/686, 04.10.2002, www.kazanci.com.

678 Akyılmaz, *İdari Usul İlkeleri*, 67.

679 "... In administrative law, principally, the administrative acts shall be in written form..." SC 6th C., M. 2011/8290, D. 2012/1937, 24.04.2012, www.kazanci.com.

680 Odyakmaz and Kaymak, *İdare Hukuku*, 73.

681 "... As known, the reason why the legislation determines the administrative form and procure that is needed to be followed to make an administrative act is to provide guarantee for persons." SC, 10th C., M. 1999/1255, D. 2001/2029, 29.05.2001, www.hukukturk.com; "the fact that the rules regarding procedure and form, which is

The illegality in terms of form and procedure is divided into two as "material" and "immaterial."[682] The State Council has clarified this division as follows: "In administrative law, the violation of the rules of form and procedure results in the error of administrative acts and decisions. However, deficiencies of form should be divided into primary (substantive) and secondary (subsidiary) deficiencies in terms of legal effects and consequences. While primary deficiencies of form of the act result in the illegality of the act or decision and affect the validity of the act in case of non-compliance, secondary deficiencies in form do not affect the consequence and therefore the validity of the act."[683] For instance, lack of signature on an administrative act is a material error of form. Lack of signature also concerns the element of authority since the signature of authorized person is absent.[684] Moreover, such an important error may result in the act to be counted as null as in the lack of president's signature in joint decrees.[685]

On the other hand, errors like lack of date or name and surname of the owner of the signature are immaterial form errors. Immaterial errors do not result in the annulment of the act. In other words, judiciary will not rule on the illegality of the act in case of an immaterial form error. When evaluating whether the error is material or immaterial, judiciary examines several factors. On this regard, judiciary decides the materiality of the error by examining whether the violation of form concerns "the validity conditions" of the act, whether it is "in the characteristic of affecting the result" or the "legal effect of the violation upon the act."[686]

The reasoning of an administrative act also concerns the shape of the act and therefore the element of form. At this point, it should be evaluated whether the lack of reasoning on the act is a material error. The Constitution seeks for

---

pre-determined by law, are not obeyed when making an administrative act or taking a decision, comprises contrariety to law. (…) As known, the reason why the form and procedure which must be obeyed when making some acts are pre-determined by law is to provide guarantee for persons. …" SC 10th C., M. 2000/1220, D. 2001/55, 15.01.2001, www.kazanci.com.

682 Emre Can, *İdari İşlemin Şekil Unsuru* [*The Element of Form of Administrative Act*] (İstanbul: On İki Levha, 2016), 407–427.

683 SC 8th C., M. 2014/6446, D. 2015/3634, 29.04.2015, www.lexpera.com.

684 Louvaris, *Droit Administratif*, 99.

685 Sarıca, *İdari Kaza*, 148.

686 SCPSCAC, M. 1995/769, D. 1997/525, 17.10.1997, www.hukukturk.com; SCPSCAC, M. 2007/1800, D. 2011/267, 21.04.2011, www.hukukturk.com; SC 10th C., M. 2001/550, D. 2003/3963, 14.10.2003, www.hukukturk.com.

reasonings in the decisions of the courts. However, administrative acts principally do not have to comprise a written reasoning. In a dispute before State Council, it was evaluated whether the lack of reasoning on the rejection act upon an application for a press card is material: "… Since the form condition in question is not concerning the validity condition of the act, does not affect the consequence and has a characteristic that does not change the situations of the related persons, … the act should not be annulled solely for this reason."[687] Notwithstanding that, in a recent decision of State Council, it is ruled that administrative acts should also include its reasoning: "In addition to the fact that the acts established by the administration upon the applications of individuals should include a reasoning, it is a necessity to show the legal regulation, which is the basis of the act, to reveal the element of motive and enable judicial review."[688]

In addition, State Council ruled that administration should indicate the reasoning in the acts in the characteristics of a penalty that concerns fundamental rights and freedoms: "In general terms, the lack of the element of motive in the administrative act does not constitute its condition of form… However, the administration must comply with the obligation to present reasoning in the acts that have the characteristics of administrative penalty, considering that these acts will have serious consequences for the governed, in acts that limit the fundamental rights and freedoms and interfere with them, and in acts that revoke a given right, permission or authority."[689]

On the other hand, sometimes laws may have a provision which necessitates the administrative act to be reasoned. For instance, according to the article 12 of the Law on Right to Information, in case that an application to obtain information is rejected, the reasoning thereof should be provided. In case that laws oblige the reasoning of administrative acts to be indicated, incompliance with this rule will be counted as a material error and the judiciary will annul the act.[690] It seems that a bylaw would not be sufficient for this outcome since SCPSCAC has ruled that the lack of reasoning in an administrative act is not a material error where the obligation to show reasoning is envisaged in a bylaw.[691]

---

687 SCPSCAC, M. 1995/769, D. 1997/525, 17.10.1997, www.hukukturk.com.
688 SC 6th C., M. 2015/11741, D. 2017/11713, 25.12.2017, www.kazanci.com.
689 SCPSCAC, M. 2007/1800, D. 2011/267, 21.04.2011, www.hukukturk.com.
690 Atay, "Kuvvetler Ayrılığı İlkesi," 134.
691 SCPSCAC, M. 1995/769, D. 1997/525, 17.10.1997, www.kazanci.com.

While it is not obligatory to indicate the reasoning in an administrative act, the administration must inform judiciary on the reasoning of the act in an annulment case.[692]

1.3.2.2. Procedure

In some cases, a procedure that should be followed is set forth in law for the declaration of the intent which is the basis of the administrative act. The procedure element refers to ways or methods that should be followed.

As in the element of authority, the principle of parallelism also governs the element of procedure.[693] Accordingly, in case that the law does not prescribe another method, the procedure followed when an administrative act is established should also be followed on the withdrawal or removal of the act. For instance, a law may envisage voting method for the establishment of an act and may be silent on the withdrawal or abolishment of this act. In this case, abolishment or withdrawal of the act should also be carried out according to the voting method.

Another important issue regarding procedure is that the errors in procedure are also subject to the division of material and immaterial errors. The administrative act shall not be annulled in case of immaterial errors of procedure. On this regard, for instance, not obtaining the defense of the related person during a disciplinary penalty should be counted as a material error.[694] On the other hand, disobedience to the time limits which are envisaged for the administration to decide fast, disobedience to the procedures which only benefits administration itself and not dressing the academic gown during a PhD qualifying exam are examples of immaterial errors.

1.3.3. Motive

The motive of an administrative act may be defined as the incidents, designated by objective rules of law, that come before and impel the administration to establish an act.[695] The objectiveness of the motive excludes the incidents which reflect the thoughts and choices of the person establishing the act. In other words, motive is a material fact or reason that objective rules of law set, and which is irrespective with the person establishing the act.[696]

---

692 SC 10th C., M. 1993/1403, D. 1994/5633, 10.11.1994, www.hukukturk.com.

693 Emre, *İdari İşlemin*, 429–435.

694 Odyakmaz and Kaymak, *İdare Hukuku*, 73.

695 Günday, *İdare Hukuku*, 138.

696 Özay, *Günışığında*, 455.

According to another definition in the doctrine, the element of motive is the factual and legal incidents that impel administration to establish an act.[697] These incidents occur before the act and remain outside of the act.[698] According to State Council, the element of motive is "actual or legal factors which necessitate an administrative act to be established."[699] Therefore, a motive is comprised of "legal factors" and "actual factors." This division leads to another division as "legal basis of the element of motive" and "factual basis of the element of motive."

The legal basis of the element may be found in a law, a PD or another administrative act. The administrative act that is the legal basis for the subsequent administrative act may be an individual act[700] or a regulatory act. The legal basis of a regulatory administrative act may be a law[701] or a PD.

In case that the legal basis of an administrative act is an administrative act as well, the judiciary will scrutinize both acts in terms of legality. In other words, during the review of the second act, the first act—which is the basis of the second act—will also be reviewed. In case that the first act is illegal, the element of motive of the second act may as well be illegal. According to the State Council, "'The element of motive' of an administrative act is the factual and legal incidents that are determined in advance in the legislation that is the basis of the establishment of the act and that impel the administration to establish that act. Therefore, in cases where an administrative act is the cause of another administrative act, the legality review of the first act, which is the basis, should also be made during the legality review of the second act."[702]

The factual basis of the element of motive is related to the facts which impel the administration to establish the act. An error in the factual basis may emerge

---

697 Odyakmaz and Kaymak, *İdare Hukuku*, 80.

698 Sarıca, *İdari Kaza*, 65; Gözler, *İdare Hukuku V. I*, 1008; Sancakdar, Önüt, Doğan, Turhan, and Seyhan, *İdare Hukuku*, 339.

699 SCPSCAC, M. 1995/769, D. 1997/525, 17.10.1997, www.kazanci.com.

700 In a case before the State Council, the dispute was related to the short payment of the administration to a person. State Council ruled that the legal dimension/basis of the act related to the short payment (second act) was the act (first act) of the administration in which the performance of the person was calculated incorrectly. See SC 11th C., M. 2005/2069, D. 2007/9757, 17.12.2007, www.kazanci.com.

701 SC 13th C., M. 2012/678, D. 2015/4618, 17.12.2015, www.hukukturk.com; SC 8th C., M. 2012/6113, D. 2015/998, 19.02.2015, www.hukukturk.com; SC 8th C., M. 2010/9072, D. 2014/5707, 25.06.2014, www.hukukturk.com.

702 SC 11th C., M. 2005/2069, D. 2007/9757, 17.12.2007, www.kazanci.com.

where the fact in question is "not real"[703] or when the administration is mistaken at the "qualification of the fact."[704]

To explain the element of motive, an example can be given. According to the Public Servants Law numbered 657, servants who "use official equipment or similar property on their private use" are punished with reprimand. The legal basis of the element of motive in our example is the provision which prohibits the private use of the property of the state. In case such a provision did not exist, and administration gave a disciplinary punishment for the private use of an official equipment, the legal basis of the punishment act would be faulty. On the other hand, if another servant used the official equipment and not the servant who was punished, the factual basis of the motive would be faulty.

A fault in factual or legal basis of motive leads the administrative act to be unlawful in terms of the element of motive and the act will be annulled by the administrative court. When an annulment case is brought before the court, the court will investigate the legal basis of the act. Regarding the factual basis, the court will ask the administration to prove that sufficient conditions emanated and they are real. In case that administration cannot prove such conditions, the act will be annulled.[705]

---

703 Sarıca, *İdari Kaza*, 72. The author explains the subject with this example: In France, a governor has the authority to discharge a municipality mayor according to law. The law did not envisage any reasoning for the discharge. Thereof, a governor decided to dismiss a mayor who attended to a funeral of a famous person on the grounds that the mayor disrespected the deceased (perhaps due to the hostility between the deceased and the mayor). The governor stated that the deceased had entered the cemetery not through the door, but through a hole in the wall and that it was difficult for the deceased to be buried because the grave was narrow. However, the reality was different. The mayor proved that in reality, the deceased was inserted through the hole in the wall as the cemetery gate was rendered unusable due to a heavy rain. Moreover, the hole was a passage that had been used before. At the same time, as a result of an examination, it was understood that the cemetery was excavated in a regular manner. As can be seen, the factual basis of the motive of the act was faulty.

704 For instance, in a disputed case, administration decided that the action of leaving the teachers' board meeting was an action which "disturbs the working environment" and concluded that this action required the change of the teacher's place of duty. The Court decided that the act of the administration was unlawful since the administration made a mistake at the qualification of the action. See DAC 1st APC., M. 2016/205, D. 2016/194, 10.11.2016, www.kazanci.com.

705 Akyılmaz, Sezginer, and Kaya, *Türk İdare Hukuku*, 426.

In one of its decisions, the Military High Administrative Court (MHAC)[706] summarized the subject with the following words: "In case where the motive that is the basis of the administrative act is clearly indicated in the legislation, in order for the administrative act to be lawful, the administrative act must be based on this motive and this must be shown in the decision and there must be proof to show the existence of the motive."[707]

In some cases, the motive of the administrative act is not prescribed by the law explicitly. The law may incorporate that the administration may establish acts with general motives like "public interest," "public order," "general morality" and "national security." As seen, these expressions are ambiguous and unclear. For instance, according to the Law for Provincial Administration, the governor "take necessary measures to protect public order and security." In these cases, "ambiguous motives" grant administration with the discretionary power. Sometimes, the law may not incorporate any motive for an administrative act to be established.

While the law may grant the discretionary power to the administration, administration cannot act arbitrarily by using "discretionary power" as an excuse due to the principle of a state governed by law. Judiciary shall scrutinize the acts of administration to a certain extent even though the administration has discretion. State Council has highlighted that "… Since the existence of discretionary power in an act does not mean that the act is groundless, the issues of whether the reasons put forward are real and justifying the establishment of the act will be scrutinized by the judicial authorities. Acceptance of the contrary may lead to arbitrary administration."[708] Therefore, in situations that the motive is prescribed with ambiguous and unclear words, judiciary has means scrutinize the act regarding arbitrariness. In another dispute before it, State Council looked for concrete proofs in order for the administration to postpone a strike with the reasonings of national security and general health: "As a result of the evaluation of the defense of the defendant administration and the information and documents in the file; considering the nature of the workplaces where the strike was carried out and the nature of the work done, it is concluded that the postponed strike did not deteriorate national security and general health in the sense envisaged in the law."[709]

706 This high court was abolished with a constitutional amendment. However we still prefer to make references to some of its important decisions.
707 MHAC 2nd C., M. 1991/378, D. 1993/95, www.kazanci.com.
708 SC 12th C., M. 2016/7880, D. 2017/3948, 27.09.2017, www.kazanci.com.
709 SC 10th C., M. 1995/6497, D. 1997/3777, 15.10.1997, www.lexpera.com.

In private law, persons can establish private law transactions with any motive or reason.[710] Private law transactions are established to realize private interest and benefits. It is assumed that the person can appreciate her benefits and harms in the best way. The law only designates the factors which will distort public order and public interest and is not interested with the motives which lead the persons to establish the transactions.[711] On the other hand, the aim is fulfillment of public interest when administrative acts are in question.[712] Public interest means procurement of peace and well-being of persons and society.[713] In this case, validity of a reason which will provide public interest is necessary for an administrative act to be established.[714] Therefore, judiciary uses the criteria of "public interest and necessities of the service" in cases where the administration is granted with discretion.[715] Thus, a limited legal review becomes possible preventing arbitrary acts of the administration under the excuse of discretion.

The same holds true when regulatory administrative acts are in question. In other words, administration must show the motive of "public interest" when the administration has discretionary power. According to State Council, administration must put forth the concrete facts which necessitate the legal provision that is going to provide public interest, when establishing the administrative act.[716] Administration has to put forth objectively the motives on why it renounces from the "consistent practice" when changing regulation.[717]

In sum, the judiciary can evaluate the legality of the act, even in cases where the motive is not prescribed in the law explicitly and the administration is granted with broad discretionary power. Through this evaluation, especially

710 Günday, *İdare Hukuku*, 138.

711 Günday, *İdare Hukuku*, 139.

712 Günday, *İdare Hukuku*, 139.

713 CC, M. 1977/1, D. 1977/20, 05.04.1977, OG 05.12.1977–16130.

714 Günday, *İdare Hukuku*, 139.

715 SCPSCAC, M. 2018/844, D. 2019/2099, 02.05.2019, www.kazanci.com.

716 SC 8th C., M. 2009/10357, D. SE, 19.04.2010, www.kazanci.com.

717 In one of its decisions, State Council found an act of Higher Education Council unlawful. Accordingly, before the Council's act, the graduates of the department of medical biological sciences could receive specialization training in medicine. The Institution abolished this practice with its act subject to the dispute. State Council highlighted that the practice applied before the act had provided administrative consistency and there was no justification for the change. See SC 8th C., M. 2009/6398, D. SE, 28.12.2009, www.kazanci.com.

constitutional principles are considered[718] such as "equality," "social state," "right to defense," "public interest"[719] or "necessities of public service." The principles of consistent administration and legal certainty should also be added to the list.[720]

Lastly, administration must show its motive when it establishes an act. However, principally, it is not obligatory to show the motive of the act in the text of the act. As we have mentioned, the lack of reasoning on the text of the act is related to the element of "form." Principally, lack of reasoning on the text is accepted to be an immaterial form error which do not necessitate the act to be annulled.[721] In this case, it may be asked how the judiciary would know the motive of administration when a suit is filed against an administrative act. According to the Administrative Judicial Procedure Act, the administration is obliged to inform and prove the motive of the act when a case is filed against the act (article 20/1).

1.3.4. Subject

The subject of an administrative act may seem to have a meaning that is related to the substance or content of the act. However, in the doctrine and precedents of administrative law, the element of subject is not used in this sense. The subject of an administrative act is "the legal consequence born." In other words, it is the change that the act made in the legal world.[722] For instance, if a public servant,

---

718 Bahtiyar Akyılmaz, "Takdir Yetkisinin Yargısal Denetimi [Judicial Review of Discretionary Power]," *Selçuk University Social Sceinces Vocational School Journal* 1, no. 1 (1998): 34, https://dergipark.org.tr/tr/pub/selcuksbmyd/issue/11287/134883.

719 Odyakmaz and Kaymak, *İdare Hukuku*, 81.

720 State Council refers to "consistent administration" principle as an element of the principle of equality: "The principle of consistent administration, which is one of the appearances of the principle of equality envisaged in the article 10 of our Constitution, is described as regulation of the areas where the administration has the authority to regulate, objectively with administrative texts such as by-laws or ordinances and maintaining legal consistency with regular practices… Therefore, administration needs to establish objective regulations to provide the lawful practice in the areas where it is authorized to regulate, and to establish consistent practices. Within this scope, leaving settled and consistent practices without a justified reason by the regulations that the administration make in the area of it's authority … will mean that the administration uses its freedom in violation of the principle of consistent administration and the principle of equality…" SC 8th C., M. 2016/3609, D. SE, 16.01.2017; www.kazanci.com.

721 For more information, see the title "Form."

722 Yayla, *İdare Hukuku*, 132; Günday, *İdare Hukuku*, 157; Odyakmaz and Kaymak, *İdare Hukuku*, 81.

who used public equipment on her private use, is sanctioned with a reprimand; "sanctioning with a reprimand" constitutes the element of subject.

Error in the element of subject may appear in several ways. In the event that the subject of administrative act is "impossible" or "illegitimate," this act will be unlawful in terms of the element of subject.[723]

In case that the subject of the act is illegitimate, and the consequence born is contrary to law, the act will be erred. In other words, when the rules necessitate a certain legal consequence to be born and the administrative act does not comply with that consequence, the act will be unlawful.[724] For instance, supposing that a bylaw is not amended even though the law which is the basis of this bylaw was amended; an individual administrative act, which is established based on this bylaw that is inconsistent with the law, will be unlawful in terms of the element of subject.[725]

It should be noted that the error in the element of subject does not only appear when the act is contrary to the law. The law which is the basis of the act may be contrary to the Constitution or international agreements. Therefore, the act should not only follow the law, but it should also follow the "legal realm."

At this point, a distinction should be made. When establishing an administrative act, the administration may have the "authority of discretion" or may be under "binding authority." Within the scope of binding authority, administration must establish the act which the law envisages when administration detects that the motive is valid. In other words, the legal consequence of the act is predetermined, and administration will establish the act which will bear this legal consequence when the motive to establish the act is realized.[726] Otherwise, the act will be erred in terms of subject.[727]

In one of its decisions, MHAC has indicated the aforementioned explanations as such: "In binding authority, the law authorizes administration with the establishment of an act and limits this authorization with regards to the elements of motive and subject. In case of acts established within binding authority, administration does not enjoy the authority of discretion in the elements of motive and

723 Günday, *İdare Hukuku*, 144; Odyakmaz and Kaymak, *İdare Hukuku*, 82.

724 Yayla, *İdare Hukuku*, 134; Some examples from the decisions of State Council: SC 10th C., M. 2007/7151, D. 2009/9037, 21.10.2009, www.hukukturk.com; SC 12th C., M. 2014/10025, D. 2017/5821, 21.11.2017, www.lexpera.com.

725 SC 10th C., M. 2014/920, D. 2016/1102, 04.03.2016, www.kazanci.com.

726 Akyılmaz, Sezginer, and Kaya, *Türk İdare Hukuku*, 127.

727 Yayla, *İdare Hukuku*, 134.

subject. Within the scope of binding authority, administration must establish the act envisaged by law when it detects the motive envisaged by law."[728]

When administration is granted with the authority of discretion, it can choose how to decide or whether to decide in case the motive prescribed in law has realized. Therefore, in the event that administration takes a decision or makes a choice in cases where it has discretion, there may be no error in terms of subject because of the result not chosen by the administration.[729]

On the other hand, the element of subject is also unlawful if administration is granted with a disproportional discretion making the legal review of judiciary considerably difficult.

The subject of an administrative act should also not be impossible. For instance, the subject will be unlawful when a deceased person is assigned as a public servant.[730]

In light of this general rule, we may handle some appearances of subject errors. At first, it should be mentioned that administration is bound with its own acts.[731] Within this scope, individual administrative acts must be consistent with the regulatory administrative acts. Individual administrative act which is contrary to regulatory administrative act is erred in terms of the element of subject.[732] An individual administrative act might as well depend on and should be compliant to another individual administrative act. For instance, the act of the inferior is bound with the act of the superior. If the act of the inferior is contrary to the act of the superior, the act will be unlawful in terms of its subject.[733]

Binding effect might as well be valid where a hierarchical order is not in question or between the two acts of the same administration. In case that the posterior act is enforced without abolishing the first act, the motive and subject of the posterior act will be erred.[734] For instance, in a dispute before the State Council, while administration determined that the dwelling houses built by a cooperative is a social dwelling (social housing) in the first act, in the second act it imputed additional tax since the taxpayer could not prove that the dwellings were social dwellings. As seen, administration sought for the cooperative to prove a concrete

728 MHAC, 1st C., M. 2006/582, D. 2007/1132, 27.11.2007, www.legalbank.net.
729 Yayla, *İdare Hukuku*, 134.
730 Günday, *İdare Hukuku*, 158.
731 Pertev Bilgen, *İdare Hukuku*, 104.
732 Yayla, *İdare Hukuku*, 134.
733 Yayla, *İdare Hukuku*, 134.
734 Yayla, *İdare Hukuku*, 134.

subject which it confirmed earlier. State Council highlighted that two administrative acts which regulate the same subject and which are contradictory cannot be accepted in a state governed by law. According to the Council, an act should be withdrawn, abolished or amended in case that the administrative act is not accurate. In case that administration establishes an inconsistent act with the prior act, the element of subject will be erred.[735]

In another dispute before State Council, administration decided to demolish a building which is constructed in compliance with the building license granted by the administration itself. State Council decided that the demolishment act is unlawful, and administration should compensate the damage of the claimant.[736]

Another appearance of subject error is when the administrative act violates decisions of judiciary.[737] Since administration shall comply with court decisions according to article 138 of Constitution, the act which is not compliant with the decisions of judiciary is unlawful in terms of the element of subject. When administration does not establish an act that the judicial decision requires, or when it establishes an act that possess the errors of the prior annulled act, the act will be unlawful.[738] In addition, in case that administration establishes an act just to appear like it is implementing the court decision, this act will be unlawful, too.[739] For instance, in one of the disputes before State Council, the claimant won the case she filed against an act which removed her from office. After this court decision, administration appointed the claimant to her previous office for "one day" and then removed her from the office again. The High Court ruled that the latter act was unlawful.[740] As seen, the appointment act for one day was only to give the impression that the administration implemented the court decision.

Moreover, administrative acts principally cannot be established in a retrospective manner.[741] Otherwise, act will be unlawful in terms of the element of subject.[742] According to State Council, "Although the administrations always

---

735 SC 9th C., M. 1987/936, D. 1988/1667, 25.04.1988; reciter Yayla, *İdare Hukuku*, 134, footnote 307.

736 SC 6th C., M. 1968/2692, D. 1970/3395, 24.12.1970; reciter Yüksel Esin, *Danıştay'da Açılacak*, 267.

737 Akyılmaz, Sezginer, and Kaya, *Türk İdare Hukuku*, 436.

738 Yayla, *İdare Hukuku*, 134; Gözler, *İdare Hukuku V. I*, 1053.

739 Akyılmaz, Sezginer, and Kaya, *Türk İdare Hukuku*, 436.

740 SC 5th C., M. 1988/1600, D. 1991/2176, 20.11.1991, www.kazanci.com.

741 Muhammed Göçgün, *İdari İşlemin Konu Unsuru* [*The Element of Subject of Administrative Act*] (İstanbul: On İki Levha, 2017), 266–267.

742 Yayla, *İdare Hukuku*, 135; Günday, *İdare Hukuku*, 146.

have the authority to change the administrative acts for the public interest, it is one of the fundamental principles of administrative law that administrative acts are not retroactive."[743] However, administration may be obliged to establish acts in a retrospective manner to implement court decisions.[744] In this situation, since the court decision is retrospective (the court decision abolishes the act with its whole terms and consequences from the moment it was established), the "retroactivity" emerges due to court decision. When this is the case, retrospective act is not erred in terms of the element of subject.[745]

In addition, Constitutional Court ruled that the acts which are in favor of persons can be established in a retrospective manner: "It is one of the general principles of law that the laws coming into force do not influence the past and legal situations which have gained a 'final' character. However, there is no doubt that legislator has discretion to establish legal regulations that provide rights in favor of individuals with retrospective effect."[746] Therefore, it may be concluded that administration may as well establish acts in favor of individuals retrospectively for the retrospective law to be implemented.[747]

The element of subject will also be unlawful when the legal provisions available for the persons in a status are implemented to persons who are not within this status.[748]

It should be stressed that there is a close relationship, a lien of causality, between the elements of motive and subject. When this lien of causality between the mentioned elements is not pursued, the act may be unlawful in terms of the element of subject.[749] In other words, "in most of the time," an act which is unlawful in terms of the element of motive will also be unlawful in terms of subject.

For instance, in a dispute before State Council, a driver who parked his car involved in a fight when heading to the market. This person who was taken to police station was also subjected to a breath test (alcohol examination) and her driving license was forfeited due that she was under the influence of alcohol. In the related provisions, "driving" car when under the influence of alcohol is subjected to penalties. However, it is not detected that the person was driving a car

---

743 SC 10th C., M. 1985/1132, D. 1985/2134, 17.12.1985, www.hukukturk.com.

744 Yayla, *İdare Hukuku*, 135; Günday, *İdare Hukuku*, 146; Göçgün, *İdari İşlemin*, 274.

745 Günday, *İdare Hukuku*, 146.

746 CC, M. 2014/194, D. 2015/55, 17.06.2005, OG 26.06.2015–29398.

747 We will detail "withdrawal of an act" in the title "Withdrawal of Administrative Acts."

748 Günday, *İdare Hukuku*, 145.

749 Gözler, *İdare Hukuku V. I*, 1054; Sancakdar, Önüt, Doğan, Turhan, and Seyhan, *İdare Hukuku*, 354.

while intoxicated. Therefore, the element of motive is erred in the concrete case. The error in the element of motive also led to the element of subject to be erred since the legal consequence of "revocation of the license" emerged even though the person was not driving while intoxicated.[750]

While an error in one of the elements of subject or motive leads the error of the other element most of the times, exceptionally only the element of subject or motive may be unlawful. We may explain these situations with an example. Suppose that administration sentenced a public official who came to the office under the influence of "drugs" with stay of promotion which is the penalty envisaged for the action of "coming to office intoxicated," since the disciplinary action of "coming into office under the influence of drugs" is not explicitly regulated and administration is authorized to sanction the same penalties to the quasi actions. In case that administration sentences the person with a heavier penalty such as removal from public office, only the element of subject will be unlawful. In case that administration sanctions the person due to coming to office under the influence of drugs, but the person was under the influence of alcohol, solely the element of motive will be unlawful. The element of subject is lawful since the same penalty is envisaged for both actions.

In the second situation—where the motive is erred—judiciary may annul the act due that the factual basis of the motive is erred. It is a matter of concern whether the judiciary may choose not to annul the act, since the consequence of the act is not erred. In case that judiciary chooses not to annul the act, the person would be labeled as if she used drugs. This is an extremely inconvenient situation in a state governed by the rule of law. However, judiciary may choose not to annul the act, by declaring that the penalty is based on the usage of alcohol instead of drugs in its decision. This is called "substitution of motive." MHAC has explained the motive substitution with these expressions: "In administrative judiciary, substitution of motive is available, administration can make an act with another motive negligently or confusedly when it was supposed to establish the same act based on the motive prescribed by law. When a suit is brought against this act, judiciary shall reject the case due that the consequence of the act is lawful by declaring the motive prescribed by law for this act, in cases where judiciary could detect the legal motive from the file and the motive based by administration is illegitimate or legally invalid."[751]

750 SC 8th C., M. 2008/5065, D. 2011/3982, 19.09.2011, www.kazanci.com.
751 MHAC 2nd C., M. 1992/329, D. 1993/374, www.kazanci.com.

1.3.5. Aim (Distortion of Procedure, Distortion of Authority)

The element of aim is the final consequence which the legislator intend to achieve and seek with the administrative act.[752] The authority of administration to use public force is based on the idea of public interest and public service.[753] Administration can only establish acts to realize this idea.[754] Activities and acts which are performed in order to obtain a result other than and distant from public interest are unlawful from the perspective of the element of aim.[755] In cases where the element of aim is not satisfied, administration has a subjective aim rather than the aim of public interest. Briefly, an unlawful aim is subjective.

Positive law basis of the element of aim[756] may be found in the Constitution. Accordingly, the principle of equality before law has two results. Firstly, it necessitates nondiscrimination based on political thoughts. Secondly, it brings along the principle of equal benefitting from public services offered by administration.

In a decision of State Council, it was indicated that "... When making judicial review related to the element of aim of an administrative act, the aim pursued when making this act should be determined, and this aim is public interest in all administrative acts. Within this scope, it is important to examine the real aim other than the aim or reasons in sight which influence the administration to execute this aim, to designate whether authority and duty granted to establish this act was distorted and whether the authority was misused. Unlawfulness in the element of aim may emerge in regulatory acts as well as individual acts. The aim of regulatory acts should be to maintain norms (like laws and bylaws) to be implemented in the direction of their aims."[757]

Accordingly, two important points are apparent in the decision. First, an administrative act which is performed based on an aim other than public interest is unlawful. Secondly, the element of aim may be breached both in individual administrative acts and regulatory administrative acts.

Even though the aim is public interest in general, in some situations laws may require a specific public interest for the establishment of an act.[758] State Council also indicated that a specific aim may be envisaged by law: "... One of the reasons

---

752 Günday, *İdare Hukuku*, 146.
753 Yayla, *İdare Hukuku*, 140; Odyakmaz and Kaymak, *İdare Hukuku*, 83.
754 Onar, *İdare Hukukunun Umumi Esasları V. I*, 318.
755 Yayla, *İdare Hukuku*, 140; Özay, *Günışığında*, 501.
756 Özay, *Günışığında*, 502.
757 SC 6th C., M. 1997/4439, D. 1998/5786, 24.11.1998, www.danistay.gov.tr.
758 Yayla, *İdare Hukuku*, 141; Akyılmaz, Sezginer, and Kaya, *Türk İdare Hukuku*, 439.

to annul an administrative act is illegality on the element of aim and the general aim of all administrative acts is public interest, other than the specific aim envisaged by law for administrative acts."[759] Then, targeting general public interest instead of specific aim prescribed in the law also violates the element of aim.[760] For instance, when the law pursued public interest concerning "public morality" for the establishment of an act and administration has used its authority to establish the act to protect "public health," the element of aim will be erred.[761] In a dispute before the State Council, the court evaluated an act regarding contribution to Quran (Koran) courses and dormitories. The Council found the act to be unlawful, since the "specific aim" prescribed in the Municipal Law was not targeted.[762]

As we have mentioned, aims other than "public interest" causes the act to be unlawful. Then, how can we define an ambiguous and broad notion as public interest? We cannot. Judiciary will make a determination in each case considering the concrete features of the case. However, both doctrine and judiciary agree that in some cases mentioned below the element of aim is unlawful.

Targeting a personal aim is one of the cases where the act is unlawful in terms of the element of aim. For instance, if a senior officer assigns a low-ranking officer to another office out of hostility, a personal aim rather than public interest is targeted. The aim element of such an act will be unlawful. However, when the act, established in consequence of personal aim, also coincides with the objective aim specified in law, there will not be an error. In other words, public interest may as well emerge coincidentally by targeting personal aim.[763]

Administration may also establish acts to protect or benefit for a third person instead of public interest. In this case, the element of aim will also be unlawful. For instance, this will be the situation where a municipality gives a firm belonging

---

759 SC 8th C., M. 2008/7089, D. 2008/7331, 11.11.2008, www.kazanci.com.

760 Gözler, *İdare Hukuku V. I*, 1099; However, it should be indicated that in case a specific aim is prescribed by law, public interest is inherent in this specific aim. See Akyılmaz, Sezginer, and Kaya, *Türk İdare Hukuku*, 439.

761 To give another example, we may cite a decision of the State Council: "On the other hand, since Act no 4046 targets to provide efficiency in economy and decrease in public expenditures through privatization practices, … judicial review should be made … on whether the aim specified in the law is realized in the concrete case." SCPSCAC, M. 2008/770, D. 2008/2337, 25.12.2008, www.kazanci.com.

762 SC 8th C., M. 2008/7089, D. 2008/7331, 11.11.2008, www.kazanci.com.

763 Yayla, *İdare Hukuku*, 142.

to a person close to the mayor unfair advantage to win a tender, the tender act will be unlawful.

Unlawful aim is also evident when the act is established for a political purpose. For instance, when the ruling party establishes act to set up its own cadre in public offices, the act will be unlawful in terms of aim.[764]

Lastly, it is important to explain the notions of "distortion of authority" and "distortion of procedure." Distortion of authority has the same meaning with illegality in terms of the element of aim.[765] Distortion of authority emerges when an administrative office uses authorities for different aims other than the one that it must use for.[766] Since administration uses the authority it possesses, it is hard to prove that authority is used to realize a different aim. In these cases, it is extremely difficult to reveal the true intent of the administration from available evidence. The fact that the evidence which will prove the true intent is within the hands of administration makes it even harder to reveal the error in the element of aim. However, as a reflex, administrative judiciary may take notice of any kind of evidence. For instance, in a case before State Council, a ministry's explanations to the public were taken as evidence to prove the error in the element of aim.[767]

When administration does not follow the legal procedure that it should have and follows another procedure which bears the same legal consequences to facilitate the proceedings, the element of aim is unlawful.[768] For instance, administration should follow "expropriation procedure" to obtain the property that it needs to use for public service. In case that administration follows the procedures of

---

764 SC 5th C., M. 1997/13, D. 1998/515, 25.02.1998, www.kazanci.com.

765 Sarıca, *İdari Kaza*, 152.

766 Lebreton, *Droit Administratif Général*, 496 ff; Gözler, *İdare Hukuku V. I*, 1106; State Council also uses the term "distortion of authority": "Through the legal evaluation of administrative act from the perspective of the element of aim, it is important to designate the true intent other than the apparent aim, whether the duty and authority granted to administration is distorted and whether the authority is misused." SC 6th C., M. 1997/4439, D. 1998/5786, 24.11.1998, www.kazanci.com.

767 The related part of the decision is as follows: "… the non-extension of the plaintiff's duty, by failing to take account the suggestions made by the Ministry of Foreign Affairs regarding the extension of the duty of the Attaché who was understood to have rendered successful services as the Cultural Attaché of the Embassy in order to carry out the cultural activities in …, has an arbitrary nature in the face of the public statements of the Minister of Culture of the period." SC 5th C., M. 1997/1422, D. 1997/2952, 10.12.1997, www.kazanci.com.

768 Yayla, *İdare Hukuku*, 141.

"occupation" or "urgent expropriation" to avoid expropriation procedure, which is more expensive and laborious compared to others, the element of aim would be erred due to distortion of procedure.

A famous decision regarding distortion of procedure was taken by State Council regarding "Sweeping of Haliç." Municipality back then aimed to protect Haliç from the buildings and facilities which polluted environment and distorted appearance. Instead of expropriating the properties, municipality used the demolition procedure. State Council ruled that "While administration should have achieved its aim by expropriating in due form, the fact that administration chose to demolish the construction … constitutes distortion of procedure."[769]

As a concluding remark, it is possible to refer to a decision of MHAC summarizing the elements of administrative acts: "Each administrative act should be established by the legally authorized person in compliance with the form conditions sought for in law and should be evaluated as being lawful in terms of elements of motive, subject and aim. The element of motive of an administrative act represents the factor that leads the administrative act to be established, the element of subject represents the consequence of the act, the element of aim represents the purpose targeted from the act and error in one of these elements results in the unlawfulness of the act."[770]

1.4. Termination of Administrative Acts

Administrative acts may be terminated in several ways. Firstly, an administrative act may terminate on its own motion. For instance, a law may determine the time limit of a specific act or oblige administration to set a time limit when establishing an act.[771] Acts regarding allowances or licenses covering a specific period may be examples on this regard. Likewise, the existence of an administrative act may be conditioned. For instance, according to the article 29 of the Construction Law, the time to start construction is two years from the date of the license. In case that the construction is not started in two years or it is not completed in five years, the license becomes invalid. It is also possible that the subject of an administrative act may cease its existence. For instance, in case that the lake, for

769 SC 6th C., M. 1987/451, D. 1987/590, 27.05.1987, www.hukukturk.com.

770 MHAC 1st C., M. 1995/274, D. 1995/472; www.kazanci.com.

771 Akyılmaz, Sezginer, and Kaya, *Türk İdare Hukuku*, 451.

which an allowance is granted to operate a beach, dries, the act regarding allowance terminates.[772]

Secondly, an administrative act may be terminated through an annulment decision of administrative courts. When courts annul an administrative act, the act is cancelled retroactively. In other words, in case of annulment, the act is removed with all of its consequences as of the moment it is made.[773]

It is also possible for administration to terminate its acts. While administration itself may terminate an act on its own, it can also terminate an act after a request of the related persons. Article 11 of the Administrative Judicial Procedure Act has a special provision on this regard. According to the Act, "before bringing an action, related persons may request abolishment, withdrawal, alteration of the administrative act or establishment of a new act from the superior office, if there is no superior office, from the office which established the act within the term of administrative litigation."

In this title, we will detail the cases where administration itself terminates its own act. Administration may either retroactively or prospectively terminate an administrative act. While prospectively termination of an act refers to the abolishment of the act, retroactively termination refers to the withdrawal of the act.[774]

1.4.1. Abolishment of Administrative Acts

Abolishment of an administrative act refers to the situations in which administration terminates the legal existence of an act prospectively.[775] Alteration of an administrative act also amounts to the abolishment of the act most of the times. For instance, when a provision of a bylaw is altered, the prior provision is abolished.[776]

The rules governing the abolishment of an administrative act differ. Within this scope, abolishment of an individual act and a regulatory act should be

---

772 Turgut Tan, *İdari İşlemin Geri Alınması* [*Withdrawal of Administrative Act*] (Ankara: Sevinç Matbaası, 1970), 1.

773 Gözler, *İdare Hukuku V. I*, 1209.

774 Gözler, *İdare Hukuku V. I*, 1214.

775 Akyılmaz, Sezginer, and Kaya, *Türk İdare Hukuku*, 455; Odyakmaz and Kaymak, *İdare Hukuku*, 91.

776 However, it is clear that when a totally new provision is adopted in the bylaw, this alteration does not amount to abolishment. Akyılmaz, Sezginer, and Kaya, *Türk İdare Hukuku*, 456.

handled separately. Administration can always abolish a regulatory act as a consequence of a legal or factual change, since a regulatory act does not directly create an acquired right for persons or an individual legal situation that should be protected. Surely, related persons have a right to benefit from the advantages which a regulatory act in force provides. However, related persons do not have a right to ask for this regulatory act not to be changed or abolished.[777]

When a regulatory act is abolished, the legal effect of this abolishment to the individual acts established by being based on this regulatory act should also be questioned. As we will also mention below, principally, the legal situation of individual acts based on an abolished regulatory act do not change due to the principles of acquired rights and non-retroactivity.[778] However, due to the reasons of public order or public interest, exceptionally, these individual acts may also be abolished.

Within the scope of the abolishment of an individual act,[779] it should be first highlighted that the acts, which do not cause any right for persons, can always be abolished.[780] For the acts which create advantageous legal situations for the related persons, a distinction should be made between unlawful acts and lawful acts. Such lawful individual acts principally cannot be abolished.[781] In some situations, the existence of such acts may be terminated with an "opposite act."[782] For instance, dismissal of a public servant due to disciplinary sanction is an opposite act.[783] The opposite act bears the same legal consequences with the abolishment of an act.

777 Akyılmaz, Sezginer, and Kaya, *Türk İdare Hukuku*, 458.

778 Gözler, *İdare Hukuku V. I*, 1219.

779 It should be indicated that abolishment of some individual acts is not meaningful. Some individual acts deplete when implemented. For instance, allowance act to an event depletes when implemented. Abolishment of such an act does not serve to any purpose. See Akyılmaz, Sezginer, and Kaya, *Türk İdare Hukuku*, 459.

780 Gözler, *İdare Hukuku V. I*, 1217.

781 Erdoğan Bülbül, *İdari İşlemin Yürürlükten Kaldırılması* [*Abolishment of Admnistrative Act*] (İstanbul: Beta, 2010); Gözler, *İdare Hukuku V. I*, 1217; Odyakmaz and Kaymak, *İdare Hukuku*, 91.

782 Odyakmaz and Kaymak, *İdare Hukuku*, 91.

783 Derya Deviner Erguvan, *Yargı Kararları Işığında İdari İşlemin Geriye Yürümezliği İlkesi ve Geri Alma İstisnası* [*The Principle of Non-retroactivity of Administrative Acts and the Exception of Withdrawal within the Scope of Judicial Decisions*] (Ankara: Adalet, 2017), 272.

However, there may be instances where a right is lawfully obtained at the time, but it was understood that this right may distort public order or have negative effects on public interest. For instance, allowance act to importation of a product which is afterward realized to have negative effects on public health may be abolished.[784] Therefore, while the act of allowance may be evaluated to be an "acquired right"[785] for the related persons, in obligatory situations where public order and public interest requires so, lawful acts may as well be abolished.[786]

On the other hand, principally, unlawful administrative acts may be abolished by administration.[787] This is because, unlawful individual acts do not give rise to acquired rights for the related persons.[788] For instance, in one dispute before State Council, a student was unlawfully rewarded with a scholarship due that the administration thought the student had the highest grades. In this case, State Council ruled that "it is clear that administration can abolish the act regarding the scholarship … which is detected to be unlawful with a later assessment."[789] It should be highlighted that this part of the decision concerns the future installments of the scholarship, since abolishment of an act does not have an effect on the past. That is to say, as we have indicated, abolishment of an act terminates the act prospectively.

Notwithstanding that unlawful individual acts principally can be abolished, these acts can as well bear advantageous legal situations for the related persons. In these cases, it is a matter of wonder if and in what conditions administration can abolish such acts. Since the decisions of administrative courts are not in line,[790] it is hard to reach a conclusive conclusion on this regard. Notwithstanding that, the notion of "personal gains" has been found place both in the

784 Murat Ekinci, *İdari İstikrar İlkesi* [*Administrative Stability Principle*] (Ankara: Adalet, 2021), 112.

785 We will detail the notion of acquired rights in the title of "Withdrawal of Administrative Acts."

786 Ekinci, *İdari İstikrar İlkesi*, 112.

787 Akyılmaz, Sezginer, and Kaya, *Türk İdare Hukuku*, 458; In doctrine, Gözler indicates that abolishment of an unlawful act is possible within the litigation term. According to the author, the rules governing abolishment of an individual unlawful act are the same with the ones governing withdrawal of such an act. Gözler, *İdare Hukuku V. I*, 1223.

788 Akyılmaz, Sezginer, and Kaya, *Türk İdare Hukuku*, 460.

789 SCPSCAC, M. 2021/1172, D. 2021/1713, 11.10.2021, reciter Akyılmaz, Sezginer, and Kaya, *Türk İdare Hukuku*, 460.

790 Akyılmaz, Sezginer, and Kaya, *Türk İdare Hukuku*, 464.

doctrine and judicial decisions. In one of its decisions, State Council ruled that "in case that the status gained due to an unlawful administrative act and the acts and actions based on this status bear effects and consequences to the public, this status will not be protected; however, personal gains will not be touched obtained by the related person until the wrongful act is corrected."[791] Therefore, in each case, "personal gains" and "public interest and public order" should be balanced.

1.4.2. Withdrawal of Administrative Acts

Withdrawal of an administrative act refers to the situations where an administrative act is deleted from the legal sphere as of the moment it is established.[792] In other words, the prior situation before the withdrawn act is achieved when the act is withdrawn.

The most important difference between withdrawal and abolishment of an administrative act is the effect of these on time.[793] Withdrawal act cancels the withdrawn act retroactively.[794] From this perspective, withdrawal of an act by administration resembles annulment of an act by judiciary.[795] On the other hand, unlike withdrawal, when an act is abolished, the abolishment act's affect is only prospective.[796]

Since withdrawal of an act may violate prescribed rights of the related persons, it should be researched whether and in what terms administrative acts can be withdrawn. Here, it should be first indicated that an act which bears obligations to the related persons (instead of rights) can always be withdrawn,[797] since this withdrawal will not violate acquired rights. On the other hand, for the acts which give rise to interests of the related persons, withdrawal is more problematic.

---

791 SC 5th C., M. 1994/7834, D. 1997/2030, 09.10.1997, www.hukukturk.com.

792 Tan, *İdari İşlemin Geri Alınması*, 5.

793 Akyılmaz, Sezginer, and Kaya, *Türk İdare Hukuku*, 465.

794 Özge Aksoylu, "Yargıcın Bakış Açısıyla İdare Hukukunda 'Kazanılmış Hak' Kavramı [The Notion of 'Acquired Right' From the Eye of Judge in Administrative Law]," *Yıldızhan Yayla'ya Armağan, Galatasaray Üniversitesi Yayınları* Armağan Serisi 4 (2003): 67; Odyakmaz and Kaymak, *İdare Hukuku*, 86.

795 Aksoylu, "Yargıcın Bakış," 67.

796 Akyılmaz, Sezginer, and Kaya, *Türk İdare Hukuku*, 465; Tan, *İdari İşlemin Geri Alınması*, 5.

797 Karahanoğulları, *İdare Hukuku*, 134; Erguvan, *Yargı Kararları Işığında*, 123.

Within this scope, the decision on the unification of conflicting judgments of State Council is noteworthy. In this decision of 1952, the general conditions governing withdrawal is not mentioned; however, the Court drew a limit on this regard. The Court noted that unlawful promotion act should be protected in case that more than one promotion acts are established after the establishment of the first unlawful act.[798]

Court of Cassation, in its decision on the unification of conflicting judgments, ruled on the general conditions of withdrawal of an act for the first time in 1973. In this decision, the Court determined whether administration can take back the overpayments basing on a wrongful adaptation act. In this decision, the Court first ruled that administrative law should be implemented. Afterward, the Court set the general framework by indicating that "it is not possible to withdraw the lawful acts retroactively... When it comes to unlawful, wrongful acts, ... the general principle of administrative law is that an administrative act cannot be retroactive. However, withdrawal of an act, just like the annulments, bear consequences retroactively. ... Here, public interest in the withdrawal of a wrongful act of administration and protection of legal situations which is created by the wrongful act in favor of persons (the principle of stability) is in conflicting positions. However, this confliction is only on the surface, since public interest is also inherent in the protection of the stability... The acceptance that established situations can always be canceled retroactively disturbs the feeling of confidence and stability even though these established situations are born as a consequence of fault and do not constitute a right. ... Therefore, it should be accepted that legal situations should be protected after a time has passed..." Basing on these thoughts, the Court ruled that "administration can withdraw its wrongful act (especially wrongful adaptation acts) only within the litigation term, or in the time if the law prescribes a special time limit, or until the end of litigation in case an action is brought, excluding the cases of non-existence, absolute nullity, and in condition that the act is the consequence of false statement or fraud of the person."[799]

State Council, too, in its decision on the unification of conflicting judgments in 1973, ruled that unlawful acts of administration can principally be withdrawn within the litigation term. The Court indicated that in case of nullity, manifest

---

798 SC, General Assembly on the Unification of Judgements, M. 1952/15, D. 1952/244, 26.09.1952.

799 Court of Cassation, General Assembly on the Unification of Judgements, M. 1972/6, D. 1973/2, 27.01.1973, OG 04.04.1973–14497.

error, false statement or fraud of the servant, administration can always withdraw unlawful promotion act and overpayment basing on this act without searching for a time limit.[800]

As seen in these decisions, the courts have targeted to balance the principle of prescribed rights and administrative stability[801] with the lawfulness of administration. In brief, some conclusions may be reached: First of all, the acts which bear obligations for the related persons, instead of rights, may be withdrawn all the time. In contrast with this, for the acts which create advantageous situations for the related persons, two conditions are sought for the withdrawal of an act. Firstly, the administrative act should be contrary to law.[802] Secondly, withdrawal should be within the term of litigation. As for the second condition, in case of nullity, manifest error, false statement or fraud of the related person, administration can always withdraw the unlawful act.

1.5. Administrative Acts Which Are Null and Void

Within the scope of administrative acts, "nullity" appears in two forms. First, material nullity appears in case of nonexistence of the administrative act and nonexistence of any records that such an act is established. Legal nullity, on the other hand, is a situation of nullity that is a legal notion which emerges in consequence of severe errors which necessitate this act to be considered as not legally born. MHAC explained these two appearances with these words: "Within the scope of nullity, two aspects of administrative acts may be mentioned. These are material nullity (absolute nullity) and legal nullity (to be accepted null and void). 'Material nullity' means that the administrative act, which is thought to exist, does not have any material existence, and clearly does not exist in the physical realm. On the other hand, 'accepting null and void' means that an administrative act that exists materially is unlawful because of 'severe and obvious errors.'"[803]

---

800 SC, General Assembly on the Unification of Judgements, M. 1968/8, D. 1973/14, 22.12.1973, www.hukukturk.com.

801 In doctrine, Yılmaz indicates that the principle of administrative stability is mostly implemented in the cases concerning withdrawal of an act. Harun Yılmaz, "Danıştay Kararları Işığında İdari İstikrar İlkesinin İdari Yargılama Hukukuna Önemli Yansımaları [Important Reflections of the Administrative Stability Principle on the Administrative Jurisdiction Law in the Light of the Decisions of the Council of State]," *Court of Jurisdictional Disputes Journal*, no. 17 (2021): 528, https://dergipark.org.tr/tr/download/article-file/1844508.

802 Odyakmaz and Kaymak, *İdare Hukuku*, 87.

803 MHAC, 1st C., M. 2003/21, D. 2004/1570, www.kazanci.com.

Here, the notion of legal nullity should be touched upon. In some cases, the error in administrative act is so severe that it is accepted as being null and void. While nullity can arise in a severe error in the element of authority ("usurpation of power," "usurpation of authority" and "serious and obvious trespassing of authority"), it may as well arise in an error in the element of subject (such as administrative act emerges a legal consequence which the law forbids).[804] For instance, when administration establishes an act which is in the area of legislature, the act is null and void (usurpation of power). For another example, in one of the disputes before State Council, a person who was elected to be headman of a village was removed from office by district administration council due to her prior criminal record. However, the authority to evaluate whether the person possesses the requirements to be a headman is granted to the "election board," since in Turkey acts regarding elections are made under the supervision of judiciary. Election Boards are accepted to be under the organization of the judiciary, not in the administration. In this case, State Council ruled that the act of the district administration council is null and void due to severe error on the element of authority.[805]

It is accepted that an act which is null and void does not bear any legal consequence and the act shall not be executed. In addition, nullity can be pleaded by anyone and in any time.[806] However, administration can try to execute the act nevertheless. Therefore, judiciary must deliver a judgment on the nullity.

On the other hand, declaratory action is not available in the administrative jurisdiction. There are only two types of lawsuits: action of annulment and full remedy action. Therefore, against an act which is null and void, an action of annulment may be brought.[807] In the action of annulment, judiciary

---

804 In doctrine, there are authors expressing that an error in the element of motive may as well lead nullity. See Sarıca, *İdari Kaza*, 65–67.

805 SC 8th C., M. 1985/157, D. 1985/575, 06.06.1985, www.kazanci.com.

806 Sarıca, *İdari Kaza*, 56.

807 Halil Kalabalık, *İdari Yargılama Usulü Hukuku* [*Administrative Judicial Procedure Law*] (Konya: Sayram, 2015), 147; Rightfully, Sarıca expresses that in case of nullity there is not any act available referable to administration. Therefore, the author indicates that nullity of administrative act may also be detected by the civil courts. Sarıca, *İdari Kaza*, 56; Çağlayan on the other hand states that nullity should be determined by administrative jurisdiction due that administrative jurisdiction relies on principles different from private law. Çağlayan, *İdare Hukuku Dersleri*, 425.

will decide on nullity of administrative act.[808] Technically, judiciary will reject the case since the act does not exist, but also rule the nullity.[809] Since there is no administrative act, there is no case to be heard.

808 "There are such administrative acts which are called to be null and void acts in administrative law, of which the errors are very severe, and which are accepted to be never born in the legal sphere. These 'null' acts do not take effect on the related persons, do not create changes in the legal situations, since they are thought to have never existed. When an administrative act is explicitly contrary to the law or it is one of the acts that should have never been established by administration, a null administrative act will be in question. There is no need to bring an action against an act which is null and void before administrative jurisdiction. However, in case the administration continues to enforce the act by not accepting it as null, the related person may be in need to bring action. In such cases, if administrative court determines that the act in question is null and void and resolves the dispute, it will also be complying with the principle of 'State Governed by Rule of Law,' which requires all acts and actions of administration to be subject to judicial review. In practice, declaratory action is filed with the purpose to designate whether a legal relation or fact exists and are precursors of the actions for performance. The case reviewed is a case which should have been heard in the form of an annulment action since an explicitly unlawful act is requested to be determined as null and void … rather than a request on determination of an abstract fact via a judicial decision." SC 10th C., M. 1995/397, D. 1997/1911, 20.05.1997, www.kazanci.com.

809 Kalabalık, *İdari Yargılama Usulü*, 508.

2. Agreements of Administration

Administration establishes unilateral administrative acts most of the time when carrying out its duties. Sometimes, administration may as well conduct agreements which emerge with the mutual will of the parties. For instance, administration may need certain goods and services to carry out public service. Providing these goods and services may not be possible with a unilateral act. Moreover, it may not be always possible for the public to benefit from public services through unilateral acts.

In this section, firstly we will explain the criteria of administrative acts since administration may as well be a party of a private law agreement. Secondly, we will explain the mostly conducted types of administrative agreements. Thirdly, we will assess how administrative acts are terminated. Fourthly, the principles of *fait du prince* and unpredictability will be examined which govern administrative acts. Lastly, we will touch upon private law agreements of administration.

2.1. The Notion and Criteria of Administrative Agreements

"Administrative agreements" and "agreements of administration" are two distinct notions. All kinds of agreements, of which administration is a party, are not administrative agreements. Some agreements of administration are subject to private law.[810] Since administration has legal capacity, it can make private law agreements like other persons.[811] Administration may make such agreements with private law persons as well as with other administrations. For instance, when administration wills to rent its real estate, this rental agreement will be subject to private law agreement.[812] Disputes arising from these agreements are reviewed by civil jurisdiction.[813]

According to State Council, "While administration may conduct administrative agreements basing on superior rights and authorities in public nature to

---

810 Akyılmaz, Sezginer, and Kaya, *Türk İdare Hukuku*, 481; Gözler, *İdare Hukuku V. II*, 9.

811 Özay, *Günışığında*, 508.

812 Gözler, *İdare Hukuku V. II*, 60.

813 Özay, *Günışığında*, 508; In another example, State Council ruled that a preliminary real estate contract between municipality and building contractor is a private law agreement which is based on the mutual equality of interests. SC 6th C., M. 1995/6502, D. 1995/4568, 15.11.1995, www.kazanci.com.

provide a public service, it may as well conduct private law agreements by using its general capacity and pursuing freedom of contract and equality of parties. In administrative agreements, administration determines the subjects and conditions of the agreement in principal on the other hand, in private law agreements, parties bind themselves legally on designated subjects via their mutual, compliant, and free declarations of intent."[814] However, it should be noted that a total freeness is not possible for administration even in private law agreements.[815] Administration has to obey several procedural rules when making private law agreements. Accordingly, administration cannot freely designate the other contracting party and the subject of the agreement like private law persons.[816] This is because, administration spends the money comprising of taxes gathered from public which it cannot waste. Administration needs to obey objective rules prescribed by law when choosing the party that it will make an agreement with.[817] In addition, while administration may make private law agreements, it may establish unilateral acts especially till the agreement is concluded. Disputes arising from such acts are subject to the review of administrative jurisdiction.

On the other hand, some agreements of administration are subject to the rules of administrative law. These agreements are called administrative agreements. Last paragraph of article 47 of the Constitution lays down that "Investments and services carried out by State, state economic enterprises and other public corporate bodies, which could be performed by or delegated to persons or corporate bodies through private law agreements, shall be determined by law."[818] Accordingly, a law may as well provide an agreement to be an administrative agreement.[819] The contrary is also possible. Namely, in case that the law designates that an agreement of administration is a private law agreement, then the agreement shall be subject to private law. In case that the law does not designate the

814 SC 15th C., M. 2015/9987, D. 2015/9042, 22.12.2015, www.kazanci.com.

815 Duran, *İdare Hukuku Ders*, 427.

816 Akyılmaz, Sezginer, and Kaya, *Türk İdare Hukuku*, 482.

817 Atay, *İdare Hukuku*, 532.

818 This article may as well be interpreted that when the law does not specifically lay down the agreement to be a private law agreement, this agreement will be deemed to be administrative. However, as will be noted, this is not how judiciary handles the subject.

819 Özay, *Günışığında*, 511; Çağlayan, *İdare Hukuku Dersleri*, 466; Gözler, *İdare Hukuku V. II*, 10.

characteristic of the agreement, following criteria are applied to specify whether the agreement is administrative.[820]

Firstly, at least one of the parties to the agreement should be administration.[821] When both parties are administration, the agreement between them may also be either an administrative or a private law agreement.[822] In such a case, the context of the agreement should be evaluated to make a conclusion. If the context concerns the law of obligations, the agreement should be deemed as a private law agreement. Exceptionally, an agreement of which the parties are both private law persons may as well be accepted as an administrative agreement. To reach such a conclusion, the agreement should be related to the undertaking of a public service and at least one of the parties should possess public power privileges.[823]

Secondly, administration which is the party of the agreement should possess superior rights and authorities compared to the other party. Since public interest is prior than personal interest, administration is granted with prior authorities to provide and secure public interest.[824] It may be challenging to designate the authorities or rights which are prior. Provisions which cannot be included in a private law agreement by their nature (such as exemption from taxes), or authorities which indicate the imbalance between the parties (such as authorities regarding supervision) may be counted as "superior authorities or rights."[825]

Lastly, the agreement should be related to the provision of a public service. However, an agreement is deemed to be administrative only when the private law person "directly undertakes the exercise of public service" or a real person "directly participates in public service" via this agreement. In other words, all agreements that are related to a public service are not administrative in character.[826] For instance, an agreement related to the purchasing of the equipment needed in public service will not be accepted as an administrative agreement.

---

820 İsmet Giritli, Pertev Bilgen, Tayfun Akgüner, and Kahraman Berk, *İdare Hukuku* [*Administrative Law*] (İstanbul: Der, 2015), 1308 ff; Özay, *Günışığında*, 511–512; Çağlayan, *İdare Hukuku Dersleri*, 467 ff.

821 Atay, *İdare Hukuku*, 523; Gözler, *İdare Hukuku V. II*, 19.

822 Akyılmaz, Sezginer, and Kaya, *Türk İdare Hukuku*, 493.

823 Atay, *İdare Hukuku*, 526–529; On the other hand, in doctrine Gözler states that this criterion is absolute in Turkey since the author has not coincide with any judicial decision which brings exception to this criterion. Gözler, *İdare Hukuku V. II*, 43.

824 Akyılmaz, Sezginer, and Kaya, *Türk İdare Hukuku*, 495.

825 Akyılmaz, Sezginer, and Kaya, *Türk İdare Hukuku*, 495.

826 Gözler, *İdare Hukuku V. II*, 44.

This is because, the other party to the agreement does not directly participate in or undertake a public service.

It should be indicated that the second and the last criterion are alternatives. In other words, to conclude that an agreement is an administrative agreement, the first criterion should be realized with one of the other two criteria.

Constitutional Court references these criteria: "As also accepted in doctrine, for an agreement to be qualified as an administrative agreement, one of the parties to the agreement should be public administration, institution or establishment; the agreement should be related to performance of public service and the administration should be granted with the authorities exceeding private law authorities."[827] State Council also refers to these criteria: "For an agreement to be an administrative agreement, administration should prepare it depending on its public authorities and the agreement should be prescribed relating to the performance of a continuous public service by granting privileges and superiority to the administration."[828]

The importance of the distinction appears on the designation of applicable law and the jurisdiction of courts. First, as already mentioned, private law agreements of administration are subject to law of obligations. On the other hand, administrative law is applied to administrative agreements since through these agreements, administration aims to realize public interest and acts as a representative of public interest rather than as a private law person. Due that public interest is superior to private benefits, administration is the party that is superior.

---

827 CC, M. 1994/71, D. 1995/23, 28.06.1995, OG 20.03.1996–22586.

828 SC 8th C., M. 1999/2852, D. 1999/7533, 13.12.1999, www.kazanci.com. State Council reaches a conclusion by considering abovementioned criteria in disputes arising from agreements. For instance, High Court used these criteria when examining whether "system usage agreement" is an administrative agreement: "System Usage Agreements are subject to a regime exceeding the provisions of administrative law and the agreement incorporates articles exceeding private law, when considering that the system usage agreement is prepared by TEİAŞ and confirmed by EPDK, the articles of the agreement is also laid down in the secondary legislation enforced by EPDK, distribution company has to sign the agreement in order to carry out the activity that is subject to a license and therefore freedom of agreement is not available, EPDK has the authority to unilaterally change the provisions of agreements, the amounts that is needed to be paid is designated by EPDK, in case of delayed payment, interest will be charged pursuant to the Law no 6183, EPDK is authorized to solve the disputes arising from the agreement (as optional), the decisions of EPDK regarding dispute resolution are binding..." SC 13th C., M. 2015/3731, D. 2018/3338, 26.11.2018, www.kazanci.com.

As for the jurisdiction of courts, disputes arising from private law agreements are handled in civil jurisdiction.[829] On the other hand, administrative agreements are within the jurisdiction of administrative courts. The decisions of the courts are in the same vein: "All disputes arising from establishment, implementation, interpretation and termination of administrative agreements are within the jurisdiction of administrative courts as in administrative acts."[830]

Within the administrative judiciary, annulment actions cannot be brought against administrative agreements. This is because, first, these agreements are not unilateral acts. Secondly, administrative acts bear subjective rights and obligations between the parties. Third persons cannot file a case for rights and obligations which only concerns the parties. Since Administrative Judicial Procedure Act only recognizes two actions (annulment and full remedy actions) and annulment action is not suitable for disputes regarding administrative agreements, full remedy (plain action: "plein contentieux" in French) action remains at hand.[831] According to doctrine, actions brought against administrative agreements are also full remedy actions.[832] State Council also defined full remedy actions as involving "actions arising from administrative agreements."[833] However, in one of its decisions, State Council evaluated administrative agreements as administrative acts and concluded that action of annulment should be brought against them. Moreover, High Court was of the view that the evaluation of administrative agreements may as well be carried out by dealing with the elements of administrative acts.[834]

829 "When assessing the agreement between the defendant administration and plaintiff, it is understood that this agreement is based on the free wills of the parties and is in a commercial character. Public law and therefore public power is not within this agreement. In this case, the dispute arising from the termination of the agreement … should be handled in civil jurisdiction in accordance with private law provisions." SC 6th C., M. 1997/2708, D. 1998/2270, 06.05.1998, www.hukukturk.com.

830 SC 10th C., M. 1991/1, D. 1993/1752, 29.04.1993, www.hukukturk.com.

831 We preferred the term "full remedy" because all actions that are not in the character of annulment actions are counted as full remedy actions. Simply, these actions are a remedy for any dispute that is not possible to be resolved by an annulment action.

832 Çağlayan, *İdare Hukuku Dersleri*, 510 ff.

833 "Full remedy actions may be defined as actions filed by related persons with the purpose of reparation of rights and violations arising from nonfulfillment of administrative action, act or agreement or decisions of administrative courts." SC 8th C., M. 2004/596, D. 2004/3110, 29.06.2004, www.kazanci.com.

834 SC 10th C., M. 1991/1, D. 1993/1752, 29.04.1993, www.hukukturk.com.

As an exception, in some cases, even though administrative agreements cannot be subject to action of annulment, unilateral acts that are related to the agreement or which can be separable from the agreement may be requested to be annulled. According to the "separable act doctrine," administrative acts which are separable from the agreement may be subject to an annulment action.[835] Indeed, administration may establish unilateral acts before establishment or during implementation of an agreement. Related persons can bring action to these acts which can be separable from the agreement.[836]

In administrative agreements, while there may be provisions in contractual characteristics, there may be "regulatory" provisions prepared by administration unilaterally. For instance, a provision, stating that the activity subject to the agreement should be carried out pursuant to public service principles, could be such a provision. These provisions are also in the characteristics of administrative acts and may be subject to an action of annulment.

---

835 Özay, *Günışığında*, 541.

836 Sancakdar, Önüt, Doğan, Turhan, and Seyhan, *İdare Hukuku*, 633. In one decision, State Council ruled that the decision of tender committee, which was held before the agreement concerning the sale of TÜPRAŞ via privatization procedure, is a separable unilateral administrative act. SC 10th C., M. 2004/8257, D. 2004/7618, 22.06.2004, www.kazanci.com.tr. In another decision, a private law agreement was before State Council. State Council ruled that "As known, in tenders, while the cases filed with the request of annulment of administration's acts or decisions taken until the agreement phase … should be handled in administrative jurisdiction, disputes arising from implementation of the agreement or cases concerning the agreement should be handled in civil jurisdiction according to private law provisions…" In doctrine, Sezginer pointed out that due to separable act doctrine, the administrative decision on whether agreement should be established, is also a separable act, according to Turkish and French judiciary. See Sezginer, *Ayrılabilir İşlem Kuramı*, 152. For instance, the act of municipality on not selling a private estate to a private law person may be regarded as an administrative act. In our opinion, private law provisions should be implemented when administration does not exceed the rules of private law agreement by using public power (when administration stays in the borders of private law). In other words, if the agreement, which administration avoids signing, would not be signed supposedly between two private law persons, avoidance of administration to sign the agreement should be evaluated as if administration is a private law person. However, in case administration uses public force, then separable act doctrine may be applicable. For instance, in case that administration decides that an already signed private law agreement will be counted as unsigned, this decision may be subject to separable acts doctrine.

The effect of annulment of separable act to the agreement may change depending on concrete cases.[837] There is difference between the acts which is the basis of the agreement, and which has small influence on it. In the first situation, it is accepted that the agreement is also terminated. In the second situation, a conclusion should be made depending on how the agreement is affected. Consequently, the agreement may be terminated, renewed or continues to be implemented without amendment.[838]

2.2. The Types of Administrative Agreements

There are no limits regarding the types of administrative agreements. Administration may get into agreements on any subject and type in line with its needs. In this title, we only mention two types of these agreements which mostly appear: public service concession agreements and administrative service agreements.

2.2.1. Public Service Concession Agreements

It may be hard and costly for administration to establish and operate a public service which requires establishment of facilities, qualified personnel and technological equipment. Therefore, administration may choose to have private persons establish public service and allow them to operate until they make a reasonable profit. Public service concession agreements are agreements which allow private law persons to carry out public service. In order to provide public service, private law person undertakes to construct the buildings, hire professional personnel, fulfill technological needs and pay for other costs of the service. Private law person gets the return for these investments from the beneficiaries of the service.[839] Administration, on the other hand, scrutinize the private law person to ensure that public service is carried out in line with the public service principles.[840] At the end of the term of the

837 For detailed explanations, see Sezginer, *Ayrılabilir İşlem Kuramı*, 164–179.

838 Çağlayan, *İdare Hukuku Dersleri*, 514.

839 Akyılmaz, Sezginer, and Kaya, *Türk İdare Hukuku*, 498; Gözler, *İdare Hukuku V. II*, 72.

840 "Agreements which are established, to have real or legal persons outside the administration perform public service or have them participate in the exercise of the service or with the purpose of procurement of money, property and personnel needed for providing the service, and which have extraordinary terms and conditions in favor of administration, are called 'administrative agreements' in doctrine. Responsibility of

agreement, the service, which is established and operated, is transferred to administration.[841]

Constitutional Court, in one of its decisions, explained public service concession agreements with these expressions:

> The notion of concession in administrative law is accepted to be a method of providing public service. It is called concession when public service is carried out by private law persons which undertakes capital, profit, damage and loss of public service, in accordance with a generally extremely long-term "administrative agreement", under the supervision and scrutinization of administration. The multitude of administration's duties and difficulties in finding resources sometimes necessitate application of this method and allow public service to be performed by private enterprises. Agreements on transfering the establishment and/or operation of public service are defined as "public service concession agreements."
>
> Public service concession agreements possess all of the characteristics of administrative agreements in that the subject of the agreement is establishment and/or operation of a public service, the agreement grants the providers of the service with authorities based on public power to execute the service, and administration is authorized to supervise and scrutinize to ensure that the service is carried out regularly and stable.[842]

As understood from the definition, the subject of concession agreements does not have to involve establishment of facilities. Administration can also transfer the facilities that exist to the service provider.

In a decision of State Council, differences of concession agreements from other administrative agreements are explained: "Public service will be carried out with a concession method if the fulfillment of a public service task is transferred to a private entrepreneur with an administrative agreement. The fact that the price to be collected from the beneficiaries of the public service during the concession period will be launched over a tariff to be determined by law and that this transfer of service is made for a long and specific period are the features that distinguish public service concession agreements from other administrative agreements."[843]

---

administration in terms of provision of the public service that is subject to administrative agreement continues and therefore administration is granted with supervision and scrutinization authorities to ensure that public service is carried out in a regular and stable manner." CC, M. 2005/110, D. 2005/111, 29.12.2005, OG 26.07.2006–26240.

841 Gözler, *İdare Hukuku V. II*, 72.

842 CC, M. 1994/43, D. 1994/42-2, 09.12.1994, OG 24.01.1995–22181.

843 SC 10th C., M. 1991/1, D. 1993/1752, 29.04.1993, www.hukukturk.com.

In order to determine the regime of concession agreements, the provisions of Constitution shall be considered. According to the fourth paragraph of article 47, "Those investments and services carried out by State, state economic enterprises and other public corporate bodies, which could be performed by or delegated to persons or corporate bodies through private law agreements, shall be determined by law." According to the article 125, "Recourse to judicial review shall be available against all actions and acts of administration. As to concession conditions and contracts concerning public services, it may be envisaged that the disputes can be settled through national or international arbitration. Only those disputes involving foreign element may be submitted to international arbitration." Lastly, according to article 155/2 of Constitution, "State Council..., give its opinion within two months on the conditions and contracts under which concession is granted concerning public services ..."

Considering the provisions of Constitution, it is understood that legislature is free to designate the legal order and the jurisdiction that the agreement is subject to.[844] Consequently, there are two types of concession agreements: classical concession agreements and concession agreements that are subject to private law and arbitration. It is also understood that there may be agreements which relate to public service, but do not possess the title of "concession."

Lastly, common rights and obligations of the parties of concession agreements may be of mention. Parties to the concession agreement are "owner of concession" (private person) and "concessionaire" (administration). Rights of the owner of concession are to request compliance with the agreement, to demand financial balance of the agreement not to be disturbed and to file suits against disputes arising from the agreement. Obligations of the owner of concession are to carry out the service continuously and regularly, to adapt the service and to personally execute the agreement.

On the other hand, rights of the concessionaire are to supervise and scrutinize the owner of concession, to implement sanctions and to make unilateral

---

844 Legislature may as well prescribe that an activity can only be carried out by private persons via a concession agreement. In the article 15/2 of Law numbered 4046, it is envisaged that some activities should be counted as concession and agreements and conditions regarding these activities are concession agreements. State Council ruled that the agreement which concern having private persons perform activities of DHMİ can only be concession agreement. SC 13th C., M. 2014/35, D. 2017/691, 17.03.2017, www.kazanci.com.

amendments to the agreement. Obligations of concessionaire are to abide by the agreement and to pay compensation in case the financial balance is disturbed.

2.2.2. Administrative Service Agreements

Administration may employ persons with service agreements. These agreements between administration and its employees may be subject to either private law or public law. Agreements conducted between public employee (who are not in the status of an [civil] employee) and administration are administrative agreements.[845] These agreements are called administrative service agreements[846] and they are subject to public law.

The distinction between administrative service agreements and private law service agreements is essential. Disputes arising from administrative service agreements are reviewed by administrative courts. On the other hand, civil courts have jurisdiction on private law service agreements of administration. Then, how can we decide that a service agreement is administrative? The answer to this question lies in the article 128 of the Constitution. As we have already mentioned, according to this article, the fundamental and permanent functions required by the public services that public corporate bodies assigned to perform in accordance with principles of general administration shall be carried out public employees. In case that public corporate bodies have an agreement with an employee which carries out such services, the agreement shall be deemed as administrative.[847]

The characteristics of service agreements between foundation universities (which are also public corporate bodies) and faculty members have been disputed. In one of its decisions, Court of Jurisdictional Disputes ruled that "the plaintiff, who works in the university's fundamental and permanent public service, is a public employee within the scope of Administrative Law when the plaintiff's status, induction, rights and powers are considered… Within this context, compensation request arising from administrative act regarding termination of the agreement of the plaintiff … should be reviewed by administrative courts."[848]

---

845 Duran, *İdare Hukuku Ders*, 428.

846 We have mentioned in the title of "Public Employees" that the bond between public employees and administration may be provided either via an assignment act or an agreement.

847 Gözler, *İdare Hukuku V. II*, 77.

848 CJD, Law Branch, M. 2019/603, D. 2019/818, 23.12.2019, www.hukukturk.com.

To give another example, according to State Council, "Agreements between associations, boards and unions—whose purpose of establishment is public interest and whose area of activity is public service, which possess superior and privileged public force compared to private law persons and whose personnel are also subject to public law since they create new legal situations via unilateral acts—and their personnel are in an administrative character."[849]

2.3. Termination of Administrative Agreements

There are several ways that administrative agreements may terminate. First, the term of the agreement may expire. Secondly, the deed that is the subject of the agreement may be fulfilled. Thirdly, judiciary may decide on termination of the agreement upon the request of one party. Fourthly, administration and private party may decide on termination of the agreement.

Besides these situations, administration may terminate the agreement unilaterally. Two cases may emerge in this situation. Firstly, in case that the party other than administration has gross fault, administration will not be obliged to pay compensation. However, administration may as well terminate the agreement when public interest requires, even though the private party does not have any fault. In this situation, administration is obliged to pay compensation to the private party.[850]

2.4. The Principles of Fait Du Prince, Unpredictability (Imprevision) and Force Majeure

During the operation of administrative agreements, due to acts of administration or events that cannot be predicted and avoided, financial balance of the other party may be disturbed. In these situations, if the conditions are met, two theories may be implemented: *fait du prince* and unpredictability theories.

Fait du prince, which is a French expression, is hard to be translated. Perhaps, the expressions of "action of public force" or "action of governor" may be preferred. On some occasions, administration may disturb the financial balance of the agreement with its acts or actions to the detriment of the other party. In this situation, if this administration (owner of the act or action) is also the party to the agreement, it is obliged to compensate the damage of the other party in

849 SC 8th C., M. 2005/1337, D. 2005/4464, 28.10.2005, www.hukukturk.com.

850 Duran, *İdare Hukuku Ders*, 446.

accordance with the principle of *fait du prince*.[851] If the administration whose acts or actions disturbed the financial balance is another administration that is not party to the agreement, then the damage of the other party is not covered. However, if conditions are met, the principle of unpredictability may be applicable in the second situation.

Financial balance of the agreement may also be disturbed as a consequence of unpredictable and unavoidable incidents such as war, natural disaster and severe economic crisis. In this situation, pursuant to the principle of unpredictability, while private party has to carry on performing the service, administration is obliged to pay compensation.[852] This compensation may be lower than the total damage of the private party, considering that the private party may have gained profit from this service in the past.[853]

Here, it should be taken into consideration that the agreement is operable with the help of administration despite extraordinary conditions. However, force majeure will be in question when unpredictable and unavoidable incident, that emerges outside the will of the parties, makes the agreement inapplicable for either one of the parties or both.[854] In case of force majeure, parties will be relieved of their contractual obligations.

Force majeure will be applicable when these conditions are fulfilled together: First, the incident which disturbs the financial balance of the agreement should not be predictable for the parties and should realize outside of their will.[855] Second, due to this incident, the conditions of the private person should be aggravated to such an extent that it would not be fair to expect the implementation of the agreement.[856] In other words, it is not sufficient that the private person cannot gain profit or lose money to a certain extent. Judiciary will evaluate whether this condition is met according to the circumstances of the concrete case.

2.5. Private Law Agreements of Administration

Agreements regarding purchasing equipment, leasing or all construction and public works are private law agreements of administration. Even though these

---

851 Gaudemet, *Traité De Droit Administratif*, 712.
852 Lombard, Dumont, and Sirinelli, *Droit Administratif*, 291–292.
853 Duran, *İdare Hukuku Ders*, 445.
854 Gözler, *İdare Hukuku V. II*, 178.
855 Duran, *İdare Hukuku Ders*, 444.
856 Duran, *İdare Hukuku Ders*, 444–445.

agreements are subject to private law, freedom to enter into an agreement of administration is limited to a certain extent. Administration shall make these agreements according to certain procedures. Even though the agreement is not an administrative agreement, administrative law should partly be implemented due that public money is being spent and public interest is aimed in these agreements too.

Firstly, administration does not have the authority to designate the other party and subject of the agreement freely. To briefly explain, process of entering into a private law agreement begins with a preparation process. Thereafter, upon a public notice, applications of contractors are gathered. The following phase in which the best offer is determined and party for the agreement is to be chosen, four procedures may be applied depending on the circumstances: sealed bid method, auction method, negotiation method and contestation method. After the best party and offer are chosen, the decision on tender is taken and the agreement enters into force.

As for the jurisdiction of the courts, pre-agreement phase is wholly subject to administrative jurisdiction.[857] On the other hand, disputes concerning the agreement, and which arise after an agreement has entered into force, are subject to civil jurisdiction.

Depending on the subject of the agreement, either Public Procurement Law numbered 2886 or Public Tender Act numbered 4734 will be applied to the private law agreements of administration. With a brief distinction, it may be stated that while Law numbered 2886 is applied when administration enters into an agreement to generate income, agreements that require expenditure of the administration are according to law numbered 4734.

There are also basic principles governing private law agreements of administration. According to publicity principle, administration should inform related persons about the acts regarding tender process, or these acts should be accessible. This way, it is aimed to avoid negative results such as corruption.[858]

According to free competition principle, a competitive process should be provided to choose the best offer with the best-qualified person. Pursuant to this principle, provisions are adopted providing competition and punishing anticompetitive conducts in the related laws.[859] Of course, free competition is only

857 Akyılmaz, Sezginer, and Kaya, *Türk İdare Hukuku*, 511.

858 Atay, *İdare Hukuku*, 536; Akyılmaz, Sezginer, and Kaya, *Türk İdare Hukuku*, 519; Gözler, *İdare Hukuku V. II*, 117.

859 Atay, *İdare Hukuku*, 536.

available when administration is impartial. Thus, some authors add "impartiality principal" to the competition principle.[860]

Lastly, principle of seeking a certain talent in the person who wills to make an agreement should be mentioned. Accordingly, an agreement should not be signed with a person, who will not be able to fulfill obligations prescribed in the agreement or who will not provide the quality standards, since the tender relates to public interest. Therefore, the features such as "financial power," "technical sufficiency" and "experience" of the applicants are evaluated during tender process.[861]

The principles governing private law agreements of administration is not limited with the mentioned principles. In the related laws, principles, such as "confidentiality," "equal treatment," "public scrutiny" and "obtaining an environmental assessment report"—depending on the subject of the agreement—are also prescribed.

---

860 For instance, Gözler believes that in accordance with the free competition principle, the acquaintances of the public employees who carry out the tender and these employees themselves cannot participate in the tender. Gözler, *İdare Hukuku V. II*, 118.

861 Atay, *İdare Hukuku*, 536–537.

Section IV: Administrative Liability

Abstract
Article 125 of the Constitution lays down that administration shall be liable to compensate the damages resulting from its actions and acts. While the general conditions may be inferred from this article, the determination of types and other matters of liability is left to the judiciary. In this section, after handling the general conditions of liability, we will touch upon the types of administrative liability, which are fault-based liability that is the prime liability of administration and absolute liability. While fault is principally sought to held administration liable, the damages born from lawful acts of administration may be compensated due to the concerns on equity.

Compensation liability of public employees should also be assessed. In Turkish administrative law, compensation suits concerning damages born due to faults of public employees in the exercise of their duties shall be compensated by administration. We will handle the scope of "exercise of a duty" and whether a public employee would be held liable.

Fourthly, in some cases, lien of causality between the act or action of administration and the damage may be disturbed. Force majeure, unexpected cases, fault of the damaged and fault of a third person are such cases. In this section, lastly, we will see how these cases effect the administrative liability.

Keywords: administrative liability, fault-based liability, principle of equality before public burdens, principle of risk, principle of social risk, force majeure, unexpected cases

1. The Notion of Administrative Liability

According to the last subparagraph of article 125 of the Constitution, "The administration shall be liable to compensate for damages resulting from its actions and acts." As seen, in this norm and in any other norm of the Constitution, the elements of liability (e.g., service fault and absolute liability) besides lien of causality are not laid down. In the reasoning of the related article in the Constitution dated 1961, it was indicated that designation of the other elements of liability is left to judiciary by the lawmaker. In other words, it is envisaged that determining the types and other matters of liability shall be determined by judicial practices. Consequently, until this day, the subject of administrative liability emerged and evolved via judiciary decisions.

In the aforementioned article 125 of the Constitution, it is highlighted that administration is liable to compensate damages "born" from its "own" actions and acts. In other words, an act or an action of administration should be in question, a damage should be born from this act or action and a lien of causality should be valid between the damage and act or action.[862] Before examining the liability of administration in detail, it should be indicated that obligation of administration to compensate the damage it caused by its acts and actions is an institution of law. As clearly indicated in the decisions of State Council, it is not a "grace" or a "grant."[863]

It is also important to note that administration cannot be excluded from liability even though the damage is born from the activities of private law persons performing under the supervision and scrutinization of administration. In one of the disputes before State Council, the High Court dealt with the damage of

---

862 Peiser, *Droit Administratif*, 230–231.

863 SC 10th C., M. 2007/3301, D. 2008/2939, 29.04.2008, www.hukukturk.com; SC 13th C., M. 2014/5316, D. 2015/1709, 04.05.2015, www.hukukturk.com; SC 15th C., M. 2013/4471, D. 2016/2461, 11.04.2016, www.hukukturk.com; SC 15th C., M. 2013/4524, D. 2016/3302, 09.05.2016, www.hukukturk.com; SC 15th C., M. 2013/4536, D. 2016/2825, 25.4.2016, www.hukukturk.com. In the last-mentioned decision, it is stated: "Legal liability of administration is not a principal concerning payment of a certain amount of money with the feelings of grace and grant, it is a legal consequence of the relationship between administration and individuals in a democratic society order. Within this regard, administrative judiciary has to designate the area and reasons of administrative liability with its practices by implementing principles and rules of administrative law."

a touristic facility because of the explosives used by a private enterprise during road widening and improving works which was assigned to the enterprise as a result of a private law agreement made with General Directorate of Highways. State Council ruled: "The fact that administration has private and legal persons carry out public service, which the administration has to provide, and the damage is born during the performance of this public service, does not change the public service qualification of the service and does not eliminate the liability of the administration."[864]

We have mentioned that for the administration to be liable, "damage" is a condition.[865] State Council has also evolved some specifications for damage. First, damage may be material or moral. Secondly, the damage should be "real." Damages which are not realized yet, but are likely to realize, are not sufficient for compensation. That is to say, the fault of administration which does not cause any damage will not give rise to administrative liability.[866] However, if the damage will definitely be realized, the condition of damage being real would be satisfied. That is, in such a case, the damage that will be realized should be compensated. In a decision of State Council, it was stated that "… in order for the administration to be held liable from the damage, the damage should have occurred, or will certainly occur. Therefore, it is clear that damages which will likely to occur do not give rise to the liability of the administration."[867] In another decision, it was indicated that "… the administration can be held liable for compensation only if a material damage has definitely emerged and has become evident. In case that the material damage, which is defined as the loss and decreases in the material property of the person against her will, and the lack of the possibility of increases, has not yet emerged, it is not possible to resort to the compensation liability of the administration at this stage."[868]

Thirdly, the damage should be "special and extraordinary." Special damage can be defined as a damage which does not spread throughout the public, in other words, which does not become a "general burden."[869] For instance, economic

---

864 SC 10th C., M. 2002/7475, D. 2003/5193, 16.12.2003, www.hukukturk.com. Court of Jurisdictional Disputes also has decisions to this effect, for an example, see CJD, Law Branch, M. 2016/106, D. 2016/152, 14.03.2016, www.kazanci.com.

865 In doctrine, Gözler states that all victimizations are not damages. The author notes that the notion of victimization is broader than the notion of damage. Gözler, *İdare Hukuku V. II*, 1321.

866 Gözler, *İdare Hukuku V. II*, 1323.

867 SC 10th C., M. 2008/1506, D. 2012/4467, 28.09.2012, www.kazanci.com.

868 SCPSCAC, M. 2008/909, D. 2011/278, 28.04.2011, www.kazanci.com.

869 Odyakmaz and Kaymak, *İdare Hukuku*, 136.

crisis affects all citizens. For this reason, damage born from economic crisis that every citizen equally suffer from shall not be compensated. However, damages from which certain people suffer more than the others, that is, damages that become "special," can be subject to compensation.

Extraordinary damage, on the other hand, is the type of damage that is not possible to be expected from persons to be endured during performance of the public service. For instance, having waited for a long time for the bus due to a traffic jam and missing a job interview does not amount to an extraordinary damage. However, being injured in an accident as a result of the faulty action of the bus driver can exemplify extraordinary damage.

According to State Council, "Although all kinds of measures are taken by the administration to prevent any damage arising from the cause and effect of the performance of the public service, it is not possible for the administration to compensate the loss arising from a general and ordinary burden on the beneficiaries of the service, which arises as a natural and compulsory result of the service, in accordance with the principle of equality before public burdens. In order for a damage arising from the performance of a public service to be compensated by the administration in accordance with the principle of equality before public burdens, the alleged damage must go beyond a public burden and become special and extraordinary for the beneficiaries of the service."[870]

However, on some occasions, general public burdens may as well be attributed to administration. For instance, people may not have the chance to take necessary precautions, since administration omits to inform about the general burden. In such a case, administration may be held liable for this damage. In one of its decision, State Council ruled that "In the events that concern the general benefit of the public, only the special damages suffered by the individuals can be compensated, those concerned have to bear general burdens. In this respect, it is not possible to compensate for the general damages suffered by those involved in agriculture in this region due to water retention in the dam lake for the general benefit of the society. However, it is the duty of the administration to announce to the farmers in a timely manner that water will be retained in the dam area. Since it is clear that, upon the announcement, farmers can reduce the damage which they will bear, by taking precautions regarding their agricultural activities, it is undisputable that the farmers, who could not take the necessary precautions

870 SC 10th C., M. 2008/188, D. 2012/934,16.03.2012, www.kazanci.com.

due to the failure to make announcements, and therefore the faulty operation of the service, should be compensated for the damages of a special nature."[871]

Fourthly, the damaged person does not always have to be a beneficiary of the service. When those who carry out the service, that is, public employees get damaged, administration undoubtedly will be liable if conditions are met.

871 SC 10th C., M. 2007/5777, D. 2008/6696, 16.10.2008, www.kazanci.com.

2. The Types of Administrative Liability

As we have mentioned above, the Constitution has not provided an explicit provision on the types of liability. Therefore, this field of Turkish administrative law has progressed by the case law of administrative jurisdiction. Under this title, we will mention fault-based liability and absolute liability (strict liability) below according to the case law.

2.1. Fault-Based Liability (Service Fault)

The notion of fault-based liability occurs where the administration is obliged to compensate the damage it caused via its faulty actions or acts.[872]

In the case law, the "fault" within the notion of fault-based liability is also referred as "service fault" with the same meaning.[873] It should be indicated that the "service" in the notion of "service fault" also covers the policing activities of the administration. Since policing is within the broader meaning of public service, service fault will also be in question regarding policing acts and actions. For instance, in case that a civilian is injured during an armed conflict between the police and suspects due that the police officer omits to constitute a security strip and to take necessary precautions, the policing is deemed to be operated in a faulty manner.

According to the case law, service fault is defined as objective defect or failure in the establishment or functioning of a public service.[874] From this definition, some conclusions may be reached.

---

872 Gözler, *İdare Hukuku V. II*, 1083.

873 Gözler, *İdare Hukuku V. II*, 1084.

874 "... Damages arising from administrative acts and actions are compensated in accordance with the principles of service fault or absolute liability within the framework of administrative law. Service fault, which can be defined as an objective defect, failure, or deficiency in the establishment, organization or functioning of a service, takes place in the event that the service performs poorly, late or does not perform at all, and arises the of compensation obligation of administration." SC 10th C., M. 2011/1371, D. 2011/1607, 26.04.2011, www.hukukturk.com.

First, defect or failure may be in the establishment of the service.[875] In other words, sufficient organization, personnel or other elements may not be provided for proper functioning of the service.[876]

Secondly, defect or failure may be in the functioning of the service. That is, the service may not be provided properly even though the organization, personnel and other components are sufficient.

Thirdly, defect or failure in the service fault is objective. Objective is the reverse of subjective. The notion of "objective" means that the liability cannot be attributed to one person or particular persons in every instance. Sometimes, detection of the person who caused the damage may be possible. For instance, when a public employee is detected to use force unproportionally from the camera recordings, the situation is as such.

However, sometimes, damage may emerge as a consequence of union of acts or actions of multiple persons. In this situation, the damage cannot be attributed to only one person or one administration. For instance, a pregnant woman, who was about to have a troubled birth and was constantly losing blood because of a complication, was taken from home by an ambulance to be transported to the hospital, which was a long distance. On the way when it became dark it was realized that the headlights of the ambulance were not working and it was not

875 It may be discussed whether the notion of "establishment"—of a public service—includes the activities of legislature regarding the establishment of the service. If the answer is affirmative, while administration may be faulty, legislature may also be liable in the establishment of the service. A public service can only be established with a law or with an administrative act based on the authority granted by a law. In case that legislature did not enact the law for the establishment of a service, was too late for such enactment on this subject or the law was insufficient for the establishment of a public service (even though liability of administration cannot be in question since legislature is outside of administration but inside the state), "liability belonging to state" may be in question. For instance, according to the related provisions regarding social and economic rights and duties of the Constitution, some public services are to be established compulsorily. In case that a defect or failure arises in the establishment of one of these services due to activities of legislature, state liability due to legislative activity may arise.

876 In one of the decisions of the State Council, it is emphasized that a service which is established with insufficient organization involves service fault: "… it is necessary that administration must compensate damages arising from the faults in the establishment (organization-structure) and/or functioning of a public service which administration has duty to carry out." SC 11th C., M. 2003/2027, D. 2005/5962, 19.12.2005, www.kazanci.com.

possible to continue. Another ambulance was called, but this time two tires of the second ambulance went flat. After arrival at the hospital with the help of a car passing by, it was seen that the only doctor had gone to the cinema leaving the workplace. Then the doctor was found, but the cabinet containing the medicine to be injected to the patient was locked, and the key was missing. Due to all these events, the patient was not treated in time and lost her life. In this example, it is extremely hard to detect the liable person and whose act or action is the only cause of the damage. That is, damage is born with the unification of the faulty actions and neglects. So, the notions of "objectiveness" and "anonymousness"[877] are used to refer to this feature of service fault.

2.1.1. Appearances of Service Fault

Appearances of service fault may be subject to a distinction: the service functions "badly" or the service functions "not at all."[878] When the service functions badly, the service is established and functioning. However, damage is born since administration omits to fulfill a certain obligation. In case law and administrative law books, "delayed service" is also included in the distinction. However, we do not prefer triple distinction, since "late" functioning is also a type of "bad" functioning.

As an example of "bad functioning," a decision of State Council can be cited. In its decision, State Council ruled: "It is indisputable that the aforementioned building was built with 8 floors instead of 4 floors in violation of the license, contrary to science and construction techniques, that the defendant administration did not fulfil their inspection obligations for a long time, thus causing damage due to the late functioning of the service."[879]

In another decision, State Council reached the following conclusion: "It is evident that on the second day of 4th Pir Sultan Abdal Cultural Events the defendant administration failed in attempts to disperse and neutralize the crowd, could not take preventive policing measures, did not have tools and equipment ready to disperse the crowd for nearly seven hours from the start of the protest actions to hotel arson, in sum, disputed damage emerged due to late and bad functioning of the service."[880]

---

877 Odyakmaz and Kaymak, *İdare Hukuku*, 127.

878 Turan Yıldırım, "İdarenin Sorumluluğu [Liability of Administration]," in *İdare Hukuku*, ed. Turan Yıldırım (İstanbul: On İki Levha, 2022), 773.

879 SC 6th C., M. 2008/10988, D. 2010/9590, 19.10.2010, www.kazanci.com.

880 SC 10th C., M. 1994/7359, D. 1995/3559, 12.07.1995, www.kazanci.com.

Service fault also appears when the service does not function at all. In this situation, even though administration which can provide the public service properly is present, one cannot benefit from it at all. For instance, when a person, who received serious blows to his body during police intervention in a social event was sent home from the hospital to rest without necessary examinations made and died at home as a result of internal bleeding, the service did not function at all.

2.1.2. Principle of Service Fault as Prime Liability

Prime liability principle stands for the necessity to firstly examine whether there is "service fault" when a damage occurs as a result of an administrative act or action. In other words, according to this principle, the courts shall initially examine if service fault is present in the case. State Council quashes the decisions of the courts of first instance when this court rules on "absolute liability" without initially examining whether there is service fault.

Indeed, usually service fault is detected with a thorough examination in cases that administration appears to have no fault at first glance. For instance, an elementary school student brought a nail to school that she found in the street and hurt her friend's eye with it. With a preliminary evaluation at this stage, service fault liability of administration is not obvious. However, as a result of thorough investigation, if it is found that a teacher saw that the kids were playing with a nail and did not intervene during the break before the incident, administration would be liable according to service fault.

As seen, existence of "intelligence" or "information or notification on the likelihood of the emergence of the incident" and omittance of administration to take necessary precautions can turn non-liability or absolute liability of the administration to service fault liability.

At this point, we can mention a decision of State Council. In the incident, a person who received threats applied to the police to get protection. After a long time, measures were taken to protect the person by the police. Eventually, the measures taken were terminated because a long time had passed without any incident. But soon after that, the person was injured due to an armed attack. Dispute arising from this incident was reviewed by the State Council. The High Court concluded that the request for "material" compensation should be rejected since the incident took place after necessary precautions were taken. However, the Court also ruled that service fault was evident since the precautions were taken after a long time passed from the date of the request and highlighted that compensation for moral damage should be ruled due to the sadness and distress felt for the delay in paying due attention to the safety of life.[881]

If the Court had reached the conclusion that the administration was responsible according to absolute liability, the material damage could have been compensated. However, since service fault is the prime liability, it was obligatory for the court to rule on service fault. This outcome is closely associated with another principle accepted by State Council. Accordingly, administration cannot be held liable for both service fault and absolute liability.[882] Then, it is not possible to consider the disputes arising from damages in a single incident partially and determine the type of responsibility for one part as service fault and other part as absolute liability.

2.1.3. Severe (Gross) Service Fault

In some judicial decisions, service fault is detected to be severe. For instance, nonobedience of administration to judicial decisions is accepted to be severe service fault.[883] Administrative judiciary sometimes uses this term to indicate the intensity of the fault.[884]

However, in some disputes, the severity of service fault is sought as a condition to rule on liability by the courts.[885] That is, in some of the disputes regarding the activities of administration (especially in dangerous activities), an approach evolved in judiciary that administration is not liable unless there is severe service fault of administration. For instance, due that "health" public service is risky, and complications may occur during a treatment, the courts decide that administration is only liable in case of severe service fault.[886] At this point, a basic

---

881 SC 10th C., M. 2007/4863, D. 2010/9105, 23.11.2010, www.kazanci.com.

882 "... While determining the compensation liability of the defendant administration by the administrative court, the principles of both service fault liability and absolute liability was based on. However, it is not legally possible for the administration to be liable for compensation based on both service fault and absolute liability. It is necessary to determine the compensation liability of the administration by examining the occurrence of the event and nature of the damage, first investigating the service fault, and examining whether the principle of absolute liability can be applied if there is no service fault." SC 10th C., M. 1995/2388, D. 1996/5893, 08.10.1996, www.kazanci.com.

883 SC 10th C., M. 2004/13990, D. 2007/739, 27.02.2007, www.kazanci.com.

884 Gözler, *İdare Hukuku V. II*, 1130.

885 Gözler, *İdare Hukuku V. II*, 1110; Tan, and Bayazıt, *İdare Hukuku*, 446.

886 "... According to the principles of administration law and settled precedents of State Council, in cases where the damaged person is the beneficiary of the service and the service bears a risky nature, the damage should occur as a result of gross service defect

distinction is made between "medical intervention" and "other health services." While severe service fault is sought for responsibility in case of the prior, basic fault is sufficient for the latter.[887]

2.2. Absolute Liability (Strict Liability, Liability Without Fault)

Apart from the fact that the service fault is the primary liability principle, it is accepted that administration may as well be held liable for the special and extraordinary damages caused as a result of an administrative act or action if the other conditions are fulfilled.

Absolute liability of administration is based on three sub-principles, namely, the principle of risk, the principle of equality before public burdens and the principle of social risk.[888]

2.2.1. The Principle of Risk

The principle of risk is based on the idea that some activities of administration are dangerous.[889] In fact, activities of administration, such as policing,[890]

---

of administration for the compensation liability of administration to arise. In cases that beneficiaries of health service, which embodies risk, get damaged, compensation of this damage is only possible where gross service fault of administration exists." SCPSCAC, M. 2007/2113, D. 2011/1468, 24.11.2011, www.kazanci.com.

887 Ahmet Kürşat Ersöz, "Sağlık Hizmetleri Açısından Hizmet Kusurunun Ağırlığı ve İspat Problemi [Severity of Service Fault from the Perspective of Health Services and the Problem of Proof]," *İl Han Özay'a Armağan, İstanbul Law Review* 69, no. 1–2 (2011): 930 ff.

888 In French Administrative Law, the latter principle is called "La responsabilité pour rupture d'égalité devant les charges publiques." A translation of this to English would be "responsibility for rupture of equality before public burdens." We preferred to call the principle "equality before public burdens." We think that the term "equal sacrifice" can also be used referring to this principle.

889 Peiser, *Droit Administratif,* 224 ff; Ramazan Çağlayan, "Risk İlkesi Gereğince İdarenin Kusursuz Sorumluluğu [Absolute Liability of Administration Pursuant to the Principle of Risk]," *Sorumluluk Ve Tazminat Hukuku Sempozyumu* (2009): 457, https://webftp.gazi.edu.tr/hukuk/sorumluluk/s_22.pdf; Odyakmaz and Kaymak, *İdare Hukuku,* 132–133.

890 In one of its decisions, State Council ruled that security services embody risk in it. SC 10th C., M. 2009/6665, D. 2013/9317, 23.12.2013, www.legalbank.net.

nuclear energy generation[891] and developing vaccine for a dangerous virus, are dangerous. During the performance of these services, there is a possibility of an accident to emerge, that is, an incident to occur which is not predictable and preventable, even though all necessary cautions have been taken. Administration, which cannot be determined responsible for fault, since it took all the precautions, is obliged to compensate this damage pursuant to the principle of risk when the dangerous activity results in a damage.

For instance, assuming that during a theft crime chase, the police car receives gun shots from the car that the suspects are in. The police officer shoots a gun aiming the tire of the suspects' car, but the bullet ricochets off the tire and kills a person sitting in front of a store. In this incident a fault cannot be attributed to the police. However, since police activities are "dangerous," material and moral damage of the relatives of the deceased should be compensated pursuant to the "principle of risk."

Likewise, based on the principle of risk, State Council ruled on compensation of the material and moral damage of the inheritors of the police officer who worked at the bomb disposal bureau and died upon an explosion: "Depending on the developing technology and growing needs, it is observed that some of the public services performed by administration carry structural risks. Due to the activities in which there is a risk arising from the nature of the service, the damages incurred by the administration agents carrying out this activity, the beneficiaries of the service or the third persons are required to be compensated according to the principle of absolute liability."[892]

We think that the cases that the principle of risk is implemented are "unexpected cases" (which remove the service fault of administration) that is explained under the title of "Factors Effecting Administrative Liability."

2.2.2. The Principle of Equality Before Public Burdens

A damage can also result from an activity of administration which is not dangerous.[893] If other conditions are also fulfilled, administration shall be liable even though it has no fault. For instance, compensation is awarded for damages incurred during the performance of public works within the scope of the principle of equality before public burdens. State Council in one of its decisions ruled on compensation depending on this principle to the owner of the building which

891 Tan and Bayatız, *İdare Hukuku*, 427.

892 SC 10th C., M. 1997/3996, D. 1997/2544, 23.06.1997, www.kazanci.com.

893 Yıldırım, "İdarenin Sorumluluğu," 778; Odyakmaz and Kaymak, *İdare Hukuku*, 135.

lost value because of staying below the road level due to the construction of a bridge.[894]

Likewise, a lawful act of administration may cause a special and extraordinary damage. In these situations, again, the principle of equality before public burdens is implemented. In one decision of MHAC, it was highlighted: "If acts made in accordance with law in order to realize public interest damages some persons extraordinarily, it is necessary to share the damage with the public and not leave it on these persons, therefore, to equalize the sacrifice between the persons who suffered special and extraordinary damage and the rest of the public."[895]

2.2.3. The Principle of Social Risk (Social Damage)

The principle of social risk is a principle which is implemented by judiciary for the compensation of damage suffered due to terrorist activities and social incidents.

2.2.3.1. Application of the Principle in Case of Damages Caused by Terrorist Activities

According to the principle of social risk, it is not always possible to foresee and prevent the damage caused by terrorist activities.[896] Consequently, individuals can get damaged due that they are a part of the society, and this damage should be compensated by the rest of the public.

Following expressions, used by State Council in the decisions that the principle of social risk is implemented, are of importance:

> With the principle of social risk…, it is aimed to compensate by sharing with the society the special and extraordinary damages which occurred in the field of activity of administration, but not the direct consequence of the public service, and which are realized as a consequence of social risk and incurred only because of being a member of the society…
>
> According to its stated nature, for the principle of social risk to be implemented, the event shall be related to the whole society, the damage shall occur as a result of the realization of a social risk, and the event and the damage shall not be the direct consequence

---

894 SC 12th C., M. 1969/801; reciter Esin, *Danıştay'da Açılacak*, 141–142.

895 MHAC, M. 1993/98, reciter Şeref Gözübüyük and Turgut Tan. *İdare Hukuku* [*Administrative Law*], Vol. II (Ankara: Turhan, 2014), 671–672.

896 Odyakmaz and Kaymak, *İdare Hukuku*, 134.

> of the public service, that is, lien of causality cannot be established between the damage and administrative action.[897]

In another decision of State Council, these expressions draw attention: "This principle called social risk is based on the conception of objective liability which grants the compensation of damages that the administration is obliged to prevent but could not, without seeking the conditions of the fault and lien of causality..."[898]

Two expressions draw attention in the decision of State Council. First, State Council's expression of "being obliged to prevent, but could not" is curious. From this expression, "failure," "nonfulfillment of an obligation" or "inability to carry out policing activities" may be inferred. In other words, this expression can be interpreted that "service fault" exists. This contradicts with the fact that social risk principle constitutes a subcategory of absolute liability.

Secondly, State Council states that lien of causality is not sought to implement the principle of social risk. In fact, the damages that occur due to terrorist activities do not result from administrative acts or actions. They are the results of the actions of a terrorist organization. This understanding is open to criticism since it ignores lien of causality which has been a ground principle of law for centuries.[899] It is also questionable to accept that a third person's act may remove liability due that it cuts off the lien of causality while liability is settled without lien of causality in case of social risk. In order to rule out these controversial points, a different solution is necessary.

We believe that this contradiction may be eliminated with two different approaches. First, administration may either be held liable due to service fault because of not being able to prevent the damages caused by terrorist activities. In this situation, lien of causality can be established between the damage and "neglect" of administration. Or it can be concluded that there is no lien of causality and administration is not liable. In this case, in order to achieve equality before public burdens, a law can be enforced which envisages the compensation of the damages due to terrorist activities.

It can be stated that a third approach was preferred by the legislature. According to Law on Compensation of Damages Arising from Terror And Counter-Terror Activities (Law no. 5233) that came into force in 2004, persons damaged by terrorist activities have the right to apply to "Damage Determination

---

897 SC 15th C., M. 2012/189, D. 2012/7048, 18.10.2012, www.kazanci.com.
898 SC 10th C., M. 2009/5172, D. 2009/11183, 29.12.2009, www.hukukturk.com.
899 Çağlayan, *İdare Hukuku Dersleri*, 682.

Commissions" within the administration. Upon the application, the commission determines the damage caused by terrorist activities and tries to reach a settlement with the damaged. If a settlement is reached, the administration pays the compensation. Otherwise, a "dispute report" is issued and the damaged persons have the right to file a lawsuit against the administration before administrative judiciary.

In case a lawsuit is to be filed against the administration, State Council rules that administrative courts are primarily obliged to determine if "service fault" or "absolute liability besides social risk" is applicable respectively given that lien of causality exists between the damage and administrative action.[900] If lien of causality does not exist, then Law no. 5233 shall be applied by the administrative courts.[901]

It should be stressed that Law no. 5233 only prescribes the compensation of "material damages" and excludes "moral damages." Besides, Law no. 5233 provides a unique calculation method for the compensation of material damages which is different than the method traditionally used by administrative judiciary.

Consequently, regarding "material damages," either the compensation amount is calculated by the administration according to Law no. 5233 and paid to the damaged persons if a settlement is reached or otherwise the compensation shall be calculated by administrative judiciary if a lawsuit is filed. State Council rules that if a lawsuit is filed against the administration, administrative courts are obliged to calculate the amount of compensation according to the method envisaged by Law no. 5233.[902]

For the compensation of moral damages caused by terrorist activities, it is only possible to file a case against administration before administrative judiciary. State Council ruled that in such a case responsibility of administration depends

---

900 SC 10th C., M. 2019/11405, D. 2021/1583, 05.04.2021, www.lexpera.com.tr; SC 10th C., M. 2019/5888, D. 2021/1300, 23.03.2021, www.lexpera.com; SC 10th C., M. 2019/5785, D. 2021/1294, 23.03.2021, www.lexpera.com; SC 10th C., M. 2019/7473, D. 2021/1589, 05.04.2021, www.lexpera.com.

901 CC, M. 2006/79, D. 2009/97, 25.06.2009, OG 13.11.2009–27407. According to the High Court, Law no. 5233 provides the compensation of damages caused by terrorist activities in case lien of causality cannot be established between the damage and administration.

902 SC 10th C., M. 2019/9964, D. 2020/6323, 15.12.2020, www.lexpera.com; SC 10th C., M. 2020/890, D. 2020/6270, 15.12.2020, www.lexpera.com; SC 10th C., M. 2019/11405, D. 2021/1583, 05.04.2021, www.lexpera.com.tr; SC 10th C., M. 2018/5536, D. 2020/6315, 15.12.2020, www.lexpera.com.

on the principle of "social risk" and the amount of compensation shall be calculated according to the traditional method.[903]

Lastly, social risk principle requires administration to also compensate damages to "goods" pursuant to the principle of social risk. In a case filed by a person whose car was burned by the members of a terrorist organization, State Council ruled that the damage should be compensated according to social risk principle.[904]

2.2.3.2. Application of the Principle in Case of Damages Caused by Other Social Incidents

As mentioned above, Law no. 5233 is solely applicable to the compensation of damages resulting from terrorist activities. Additionally, State Council has the tendency to apply social risk principle to disputes arising from damages caused by terrorist activities and prefers to use the term "equality before public burdens" when ruling for the compensation of damages arising from social incidents besides terrorist activities.[905] Rarely, application of social risk principle to disputes arising from damages caused during other social incidents by State Council is observable.[906]

As "equality before public burdens" is the foundation of absolute liability and embodies social risk, we think that ultimately it makes no difference to prefer either one of these principles.

2.2.4. Absolute Liability of Administration as a Result of Legislative and Judicial Activities

Most of the time, the laws enforced by the legislature affect the rights and interests of the governed through administrative acts or actions based on these laws. Likewise, judicial decisions also bear consequences with the implementation of these by administration. Then, it is a wonder whether administration may be held liable from the damages born due to the activities of legislature and judiciary.

Since administration is the implementer of the judicial decisions, it is hard to allege that administration acted unlawfully or with fault. Therefore, within

903 SC 10th C., M. 2016/998, D. 2021/1570, 05.04.2021, www.lexpera.com.

904 SC 10th C., M. 1996/9012, D. 1997/6164, 25.12.1997, www.kazanci.com.

905 Ahmet Yayla, *İdarenin Kusursuz Sorumluluğu* [*Absolute Liability of Administration*] (İstanbul: On İki Levha, 2015), 95.

906 SCPSCAC, M. 2009/3035, D. 2013/2056, 27.05.2013, www.lexpera.com.

the scope of judicial decisions, the discussion is on whether administration can be held liable pursuant to absolute liability principle. However, administrative courts rule that administration cannot be held liable due to "judicial activity."[907] So, it is hard to conclude that administration can be liable due to judicial activity from the perspective of positive law unless the courts change their approach.

On the other hand, in Turkish Legal System, not administration but the "state" is liable from damages caused by judicial activities. According to the 46th article of Civil Procedure Law no. 6100, it is possible to file a compensation case against the "state" for harms caused by judges in the course of judicial function. Last paragraph of article 46 provides that state shall recourse to the responsible judge after paying the compensation.

Additionally, European Court of Human Rights (ECHR) may find the "state" liable and rule for compensation regarding unlawful decisions of the judiciary.

Consequently, administration may be regarded as a tool only making the payment of the compensation from the public safe on behalf of the state. As there is no fault attributable to administration, we think that responsibility of administration in this case can, if necessary, only be determined as "absolute liability."

What is meant by the liability of administration due to legislative activity is the liability of administration for the damages caused directly by a law, without any administrative act that implements the law. In case that there is an administrative act, the general rules on administrative liability is applicable. However, in this particular situation, damage may be born just because of a law that is enacted. For instance, in the past, all casinos were closed down by a new law. With the enactment of this law, business establishments such as hotels which have casinos incurred a loss without any need to an administrative act for implementation.

---

907 SC 1st C., M. 1992/224, D. 1992/1600, 22.12.1992, reciter Serdar Özgüldür, *Askeri Yüksek İdare Mahkemesi Kararları Işığında Tam Yargı Davaları* [*Full Remedy Actions In Light of the Decisions of Military High Administrative Court*] (Ankara: Yetkin, 1996), 148–152. In one of the decisions of the State Council, it is understood that only acts of prosecution that are not judicial in character can be brought before administrative courts: "In addition, the case against the Ministry of Justice should be heard by administrative judiciary, since the removal of the decision of detention in absentia from the records, which was annulled by a court, is an administrative duty for the security units, as well as an administrative task for public prosecutors, other than the judicial function." SC 10th C., M. 2006/6131, D. 2008/4559, 18.06.2008, www.danistay.gov.tr. Also see Yayla, *İdare Hukuku*, 349–351; Ramazan Cengiz Derdiman, *İdare Hukuku* [*Administrative Law*] (Aktüel, 2015), 498.

Thus, the following question is to be answered: Can administration be held liable due to legislative activity?

In doctrine, Zabunoğlu alleges that administration cannot be held liable for pure legislative activities.[908] Since a fault attributable to administration is absent, it is hard to allege that administration is liable from the damages born due to legislative activity within the scope of service fault. On the other hand, absolute liability may be possible.[909]

An exemplary case has also been brought before Turkish administrative judiciary. In the case, with an explicit provision of a law enacted by TBMM, applicant's employment in a public corporate body was terminated. However, Constitutional Court annulled this provision of the law. Upon this annulment, those concerned whose term of office had not expired before the termination filed a lawsuit before administrative court. The approach of State Council in this case was as follows:

> … French State Council decided in 1938 that special and extraordinary damages incurred on persons due to the implementation of a law which was accepted to bear public interest should be compensated even though there is not any law due to the principle of equality before public burdens.
>
> In the case, it is explicit that the office of the plaintiff has ended as a result of the implementation of the rule by the administration which is: "… the employment of the board members terminate on the date of the enactment of this Law".
>
> In its decision, Constitutional Court indicated that the laws should be general, abstract and objective in a constitutional state but the provision of the Law did not possess these features, and highlighted specifically that legislative acts shall not violate legal security of persons assigned to a status without any amendment in this status. As the Constitutional Court's decision ultimately reveals that the plaintiff's termination of employment is unlawful even though prescribed by law, the material damage born due to this provision should be compensated by the defendant administration according to the principle of service fault due to the necessities of constitutional state.[910]

As it can be seen, High Court accepted that the law did not incur a direct damage. The court ruled on administrative liability based on the assumption that there is an administrative act regarding the implementation of this law. However, related provision of law clearly provides that termination of employment is realized at the moment the law was enacted.

908 Zabunoğlu, *İdare Hukuku*, 711.
909 Louvaris, *Droit Administratif Général*, 237.
910 SCPSCAC, M. 2009/901, D. 2010/903, 29.04.2010, www.kazanci.com.tr.

Thus, State Council has not yet accepted liability due to pure legislative acts. However, the French State Council's decision referred by Turkish State Council grants administrative liability due to pure legislative acts.

Additionally, State Council implemented the principle of "service fault" in its decision. We believe that it is not possible to rule that administration, which implements the explicit law provision, and which does not have discretionary power, has "fault." In our opinion, the principle of absolute liability should have been applied.

We reckon that responsibility from damages caused by pure legislative acts should be accepted for the reason that in these situations pure legislative act disturbs equality before public burdens.[911] Given that the administration is not faulty and does not have an act or action causing the damage, the "state" rather than "administration" may be held responsible according to absolute liability. Consequently, administration can be regarded only as a means or an instrument that pays the compensation from the public safe to the damaged.

911 On the contrary, Ülgen in doctrine indicates that service fault may be in question when a law which is contrary to the Constitution causes damage. Özen Ülgen, *Anayasa Yargısında İptal Kararlarının Etkileri* [*Effects of Annulment Decisions in Constitutional Judiciary*] (İstanbul: On İki Levha, 2016), 210.

3. Compensation Liability of The Public Employees

Principally, lawsuits cannot be brought against public employees. Paragraph 5 of article 129 of the Constitution is as follows: "Compensation suits concerning damages arising from faults committed by public servants and other public employees in the exercise of their duties shall be filed only against the administration in accordance with the procedure and conditions prescribed by law, in condition that subsequently compensation shall be recoursed to them."

The provision only comprises the compensation suits arising from faults of public employees committed "in the exercise of their duties." That is, for the faults committed outside duty (for pure personal fault),[912] compensation suit may be brought directly against the public employee.

In one of the decisions of Court of Jurisdictional Disputes, it is stated that "... acts and actions that can be separated from the duties and powers of a public employee, from his official title, in other words, act and actions that lose their administrative quality by turning into a crime form are outside of the above-mentioned Constitutional protection, and therefore, it is possible to file a lawsuit for compensation directly against a public official based on personal fault."[913]

In sum, compensation suits arising from the faults committed in the exercise of duties can only be brought against administration. Administration will pay the compensation in case that judiciary decides so. Administration shall recourse to the public employee with a lawsuit before civil courts to take back the amount of compensation.

This rule is based on two basic ideas. Firstly, there is an assumption that public employees cannot work properly being constantly under the threat of lawsuits, which eventually may cause public service to be disrupted. Secondly, and more importantly, the amount of compensation that would be ruled on is most of the time higher than the amount which a public employee can pay right away. In other words, compensation will be secured since administration undoubtedly can afford it. After administration makes the payment, it takes back this payment by obtaining a judicial decision concerning making cutoffs from the salary of the related public official.[914]

---

912 Tan and Bayazıt, *İdare Hukuku*, 427.

913 CJD, Law Branch, M. 2002/11, D. 2002/10, 25.03.2002, www.hukukturk.com.

914 It is important to note that administration cannot by its own make cutoffs without obtaining a judicial decision.

Court of Jurisdictional Disputes explains the reasoning of this rule with these expressions: "With this provision, it is aimed to protect public order by preventing public servants and other public officials from being brought before the judiciary, rightly or unjustly, due to their faulty conduct while using their authorities, and ensuring that public service is carried out without interruption; and in terms of the person who suffered the damage, a liable party (administration) with a higher solvency compared to public servants and other public officials is designated as the respondent."[915]

Before the amendment dated February 21, 2014, an exception to this rule was laid down in the Administrative Judicial Procedure Law. According to the previous provision, compensation suit could be brought against the public official who did not deliberately implement a judicial decision. In fact, this provision was brought before Constitutional Court and the Court found that the provision was in conformity with the Constitution.

After the amendment, paragraph 4 of article 28 of the Law is as follows: "If the public officials fail to fulfil the requirements of the decisions of the courts within the time limit, compensation suit can only be brought against the related administration." In this situation, it is no longer possible to bring action against the public official who does not fulfill the requirements of the court decisions. We believe that the new provision removed a remedy which could be deterrent for public officials who do not comply with the court decisions.

Then, can this negative consequence be eliminated? According to the Constitution, the rule to file a lawsuit solely against the administration is only valid when public officials use their "authorities." At this point, it can be questioned whether "not implementing the court decision" is an authority. The answer to this question is negative. Article 138 of the Constitution mandates court decisions to be implemented.

As a conclusion, since there is no authority to make a decision on not implementing a court decision, it cannot be accepted that not implementing a court decision is a fault committed in the exercise of a duty. This is a personal fault and is not within the protection of the Constitution. Therefore, we think that a compensation suit can be brought against the public official who does not implement a court decision due to personal fault.

915 CJD, Law Branch, M. 2007/6, D. 2007/117, 02.07.2007, www.hukukturk.com.

4. Factors Effecting Administrative Liability

We have mentioned that a lien of causality is necessary between the act or action of the administration and the damage to conclude that administration is liable. On some occasions, there shall be no liability due that the lien of causality is interrupted. On some other occasions, liability decreases since other persons are faulty as well as the administration. In this title, we will examine the factors where liability of administration ceases or diminishes.

4.1. Force Majeure

Both service fault and absolute liability of administration ceases in case of force majeure. The reason of this is that force majeure cuts the lien of causality. To put it more simply, in case of force majeure, the damage occurred is the result of the incident which is counted as force majeure, but not the result of the act or action of administration.

Force majeure may be defined as incidents which have no link with the activities of administration, and which comes out of the field of these activities. That is, force majeure is "exterior."[916] Furthermore, force majeure are incidents which cannot be predictable and preventable by administration.[917] Damages resulting from earthquakes, floods, avalanches and landslides can be evaluated within the scope of force majeure. Besides, social and political incidents such as revolution or war can constitute force majeure.[918] These incidents may not be predictable and preventable beforehand.

---

916 "Coercive reason (force majeure) is defined as events that are outside the perpetrator due to their origin, natural, social and legal nature, which cannot be prevented by the perpetrator, and which cannot be recognized and predicted.
According to this definition accepted both in judicial decisions and doctrine, the basic element that constitutes the concept of coercive reason is that it is 'unpreventable' and 'unpredictable' as well as 'external.'" SCPSCAC, M. 2008/11, D. 2009/3108, 17.12.2009, www.kazanci.com.

917 The conditions of "unpredictability" and "unpreventability" are cumulative. Gözler, *İdare Hukuku V. II*, 1351; Çağlayan, *İdare Hukuku Dersleri*, 709.

918 Meltem Kutlu Gürsel, "Deprem ve İdarenin Sorumluluğu [Earthquake and Liability of Administration]," *Amme İdaresi Dergisi* 32, no. 4 (1999), 20; Gözler, *İdare Hukuku V. II*, 1348.

Here, an important distinction should be made. In case that the incident which can be subject to force majeure was known to occur, but necessary cautions were not taken, administration will be liable. For instance, the location and intensity of earthquakes can be predicted, even though their exact time cannot. In case that administration permits unstable buildings to be constructed on the fault line, it will be held liable due to service fault.[919]

For instance, in a case disputed before State Council, a building which was constructed without a license was decided to be demolished, but this decision was not implemented. Afterward, this building collapsed due to an earthquake. The High Court ruled that "administration is liable due to service fault for the damages occurred as a result of nonfulfillment of the activities that should be exercised in the construction phase of the collapsed building."[920]

4.2. Unexpected Cases

Unexpected cases are also incidents which are unpredictable and unpreventable. Unlike force majeure, unexpected cases are incidents which emerge within the activities of administration.[921] That is, unexpected cases are not "exterior," but "internal."[922] They may also be expressed as the accidents related to the activities carried out by administration.

---

919 "It is undoubted that earthquake is an example to force majeure since it is 'unpredictable' and 'unpreventable.' Even though it is not possible to rule on the liability of administration when the damage is solely a result of the earthquake, it is necessary to hold administration liable, when the judiciary designates that administration aggravates the damage along with the force majeure, for the aggravated part of the damage and by taking into account the fault for the aggravated part. For instance, in the incidents where administration grants construction license contrary to the construction conditions in compliance with the earthquake regulation in an area which is designated as earthquake area, or where the fault line is opened to construction, naturally the related administrations are liable due to the damages arisen as a consequence of the earthquake at the rate of their faults. However, it is also undoubtable that administration cannot be held liable for all damages that the earthquake caused." SCPSCAC, M. 2008/11, D. 2009/3108, 17.12.2009, www.kazanci.com.

920 SC 6th C., M. 2011/8609, D. 2012/2662, 23.05.2012, www.kazanci.com.

921 The basic distinction between force majeur and unexpected cases is that while force majeur is external, unexpected cases are internal. Gözler, *İdare Hukuku V. II*, 1348.

922 Lombard, Dumont, and Sirinelli, *Droit Administratif*, 546; Kutlu Gürsel, "Deprem ve İdarenin Sorumluluğu," 19; Çağlayan, *İdare Hukuku Dersleri*, 717.

For instance, occurrence of an explosion of an arsenal in an unpredictable and unpreventable way, despite that all necessary precautions are taken, is an unexpected case. Or unexpected case will be in question when a bomb explodes after disposal.

Within the scope of unexpected cases, a fault cannot be attributed to the administration. However, administration is still obliged to compensate the damage through absolute liability. In sum, while service fault liability is removed, absolute liability continues in case of unexpected cases. As a final remark, it can be stressed that unexpected cases constitute the implementation area of the principle of risk.

4.3. Fault of The Damaged

On some occasions, the person that suffers the damage may also contribute to the formation of damage along with the administration. In these cases, two situations may be in question, namely, liability of administration may cease or diminish.[923]

In case that the act of the damaged is the only cause of the damage, that is, if lien of causality is cut off between the administrative act or action and the damage, administration will not be liable. For instance, in a case before State Council, the Court ruled that administration shall not be liable for the damages, incurred on persons who exploded the grenades that they found in a land even though they knew what a grenade is and how it explodes. According to the High Court, while service fault exists since that administration left the grenades at the land, the faults of the damaged persons cut off the lien of causality.[924] Likewise, in a case which was brought by a person who could not obtain an exam entry document due that this person omitted to fulfill the requirements that are prescribed in the guide to take the university entrance exam, State Council ruled

923 Gözler, *İdare Hukuku V. II*, 1358.

924 "In this case; in the incident, there is a service fault due to the defendant's administration's failure to conduct the security service well enough since a hand grenade is found in a regularly used area situated near residential areas; however, since the damage is caused due to the personal faults of the plaintiff and the plaintiffs friends, the acts of the damaged and third persons removed the lien of causality between the faulty service of administration and the damage. In the incident, that the lien of causality does not exist, it is not possible to admit the compensation liability of the administration." SC 10th C., M. 2005/4493, D. 2007/4199, 18.09.2007, www.kazanci.com.

that administration will not be liable due that this person could not take the exam.[925]

In a dispute subject to an individual application, the reasoning of the Constitutional Court on the issue draws attention:

> … In the incident, it is clear that the father of the applicants, who was not vulnerable to the danger for any reason, went to an area that he knew clearly posed a danger to his life with his brother, and took some sand from under the heap of sand, causing a subsidence, as a result, he lost his life under this subsidence, and therefore his action cut off the lien of causality between the damage and liability of administration.
>
> Accepting the contrary will mean accepting the liability of the state in every situation and under all circumstances, including all places that are under the jurisdiction and disposal of the State and all situations people openly expose themselves to danger, and this will be an interpretation generating overload on public offices by not taking into account the necessities and realities of the modern life, unpredictability of human actions and priorities and sources of administration.[926]

In case that administration has fault along with the damaged person, compensation that will be paid by administration diminishes. In a dispute concerning a shepherd who was injured by blasting an explosive with a lighter, State Council ruled that administration is also liable along with the shepherd by leaving the explosive in the area during military activity regarding counterterrorism and diminished the amount of compensation in proportion with the fault of the shepherd.[927]

State Council used following expressions in a decision regarding a person who died during snowboarding: "...relative of the plaintiff … also have fault on the occurrence of the incident, when taking into account that the relative of the plaintiff … moved by not having necessary and sufficient equipment by not evaluating the air conditions and ski run condition with self experience and knowledge on winter sports, acted inconsistently to the instructions of gendarmery personnel contacted after getting lost with a cellphone, complicated the search works by constantly being on move and not waiting in sheltered places even having reached to such places, endangered own life safety by putting off clothes…"[928]

Another dispute, which became subject to a lawsuit before State Council, arose from the fact that the plaintiff, who declared himself the head of the ward

---

925 SC 8th C., M. 1996/20, D. 1997/1479, 05.05.1997, www.kazanci.com.

926 CC, IA, AN 2014/2433, 04.10.2017, OG 30.11.2017–30256.

927 SC 15th C., M. 2011/9487, D. 2013/1480, 21.02.2013, www.kazanci.com.

928 SC 10th C., M. 2015/4254, D. 2016/1847, 07.04.2016, www.kazanci.com.

and smuggled a gun into the prison, was injured with the same weapon as a result of provoking another convict whom he appointed as his assistant. The High Court concluded that the fault of the damaged person cut off the lien of causality and ruled that the administration was not liable. In our opinion, this decision is open to criticism since it can be accepted that there is a lien of causality between the negligence of administration that is manifested by not taking necessary precautions to prevent the gun from being smuggled into prison and the damage.[929]

4.4. Fault of A Third Person

Act or actions of a third person or persons may intervene between the activity of administration and the damage. In case that the action of a third person cuts the lien of causality, that is, the damage is the consequence of a third person, but not of administration, administration will not be liable.[930] However, if the act or action contributes to the occurrence of the damage along with an action of a third person, the liability of administration does not cease but diminish.

In doctrine, in the context of the effect of the fault of a third person to the liability, a distinction is made between the situations in which administration is liable due to service fault and absolute liability.[931] Accordingly, in case that there is service fault, the fault of a third person will diminish the liability of administration, or if the action of the third person cuts the lien of causality, administration shall not be liable.[932] On the other hand, it is accepted that the fault of a

929 SC 10th C., M. 2003/646, D. 2006/1932, 15.03.2006, www.kazanci.com.

930 For instance, State Council ruled that administration was not liable in the accident that occurred as a result of a vehicle dropping a spare tire on the road. SC 15th C., M. 2014/605, D. 2017/781, 16.02.2017, www.kazanci.com.

931 Atay, *İdare Hukuku*, 718–7120; Gözler, *İdare Hukuku V. II*, 1366.

932 At this point, a relevant part of a decision of State Council may be mentioned: "… there cannot be an objective lien of causality between the action and the execution of the public duty, if the public official inflicts harm on the person under the influence of grudge, malice, animosity, and similar feelings for political, personal, or other feelings." If attention is paid, the High Court states that in some cases, the act of a public official will result in a complete alienation from the administration and almost becoming a third person. In a dispute related the killing of a person during military service with a gun taken from the police station due to a personal matter, the State Council concluded that the lien of causality between the administration and the damage had been cut. SC 10th C., M. 2011/985, D. 2013/7802, 06.11.2013, www.kazanci.com. However, in a decision of SCPSCAC, it was stated that "In the event of the fault of duty, which can be defined as the unlawful acts of the administrative agent, which can be attributed to him, by taking advantage of the duties, powers, and

third person does not affect the absolute liability of the administration.[933] In this case, administration can recourse to the third person, after paying the compensation.[934] We believe that in such cases the "action" of the third person shall also be taken into consideration. If the action of a third person cuts off the lien of causality, administration shall not be liable.

---

tools given to him in the service or due to the service, the liability of administration will also be in question. In this sense, fault of duty is the personal fault of the agent of the administration, which cannot be separated from service and duty." SCPSCAC, M. 2010/2740, D. 2012/194, 15.03.2012, www.kazanci.com. It can be alleged that the decision of the 10th Circuit contradicts with this decision of SCPSCAC.

933 Gözler, *İdare Hukuku V. II*, 1368.

934 Atay, *İdare Hukuku*, 720.

References

Akartürk, Ekrem Ali. "2017 Anayasa Değişikliğinin 'Parlamentosuzlaştırma' Etkisi Üzerine [About 'Deparliamentarization' Effect of Constitutional Amendment of 2017]." *Yeditepe University Law Faculty Journal* 17, no. 1 (2020): 1–25. https://www.jurix.com.tr/article/20389.

Aksoylu, Özge. "Yargıcın Bakış Açısıyla İdare Hukukunda "Kazanılmış Hak" Kavramı [The Notion of "Acquired Right" From the Eye of Judge in Administrative Law]." *Yıldızhan Yayla'ya Armağan, Galatasaray Üniversitesi Yayınları* Armağan Serisi 4 (2003): 65–82.

Akyılmaz, Bahtiyar, Murat Sezginer, and Cemil Kaya. *Türk İdare Hukuku.* Ankara: Savaş, 2022.

Akyılmaz, Bahtiyar. *İdari Usul İlkeleri Işığında İdari İşlemin Yapılış Usulü* [*Establishing Procedure of Administrative Act Within the Scope of Administrative Procedure Principles*]. Ankara: Yetkin, 2000.

Akyılmaz, Bahtiyar. "Takdir Yetkisinin Yargısal Denetimi [Judicial Review of Discretionary Power]." *Selçuk University Social Sciences Vocational School Journal* 1, no. 1 (1998): 23–57. https://dergipark.org.tr/tr/pub/selcuksbmyd/issue/11287/134883.

Ardıçoğlu, Artuk. "Cumhurbaşkanlığı Kararnamesi [Presidential Decree]," *Ankara Bar Journal*, no. 3 (2017): 21–51.

Atar, Yavuz. "Cumhurbaşkanlığı Kararnamelerinin Hukuki Rejimi ve Anayasallık Denetimi [Legal Regime and Constitutional Review of Presidential Decrees]." *Anayasa Yargısı* 36, no. 1 (2019): 241–259.

Atasayan, M. Gözde. *Kamu Hizmetlerinin Süreklilik ve Düzenlilik İlkesi* [*The Principle of Continuity and Regularity of Public Service*]. İstanbul: On İki Levha, 2012.

Atay, Ender Ethem. "Bağımsız Idari Otoriteler ve Türkiye Uygulaması [Independent Regulatory Authorities and Turkish Practice]." *Gazi University Law Faculty Journal* 10, no. 1, 2 (2006): 259–293. https://dergipark.org.tr/tr/download/article-file/789830.

Atay, Ender Ethem. *İdare Hukuku.* Ankara: Turhan, 2022.

Atay, Ender Ethem. "Kuvvetler Ayrılığı İlkesi Uyarınca Yürütme Yargı Ayrılığı ve İdari Yargı Denetiminin Niteliği [Separation of Executive and Judiciary and the Characteristics of Administrative Judicial Review Within the Scope of the Principle of Separation of Powers]." In *Danıştay ve İdari Yargı Günü 140. Yıl Sempozyumu*, 123–148. Danıştay Tasnif ve Yayın Bürosu Yayınları no. 77, Danıştay Matbaası, 2009.

Atay, Ender Ethem. "Müfettişlerin Hazırladıkları Disiplin Soruşturma Raporlarından Dolayı Sorumlu Tutulabilirliği Sorunu [The Issue of Holding the Inspectors Accountable for Disciplinary Proceedings Reports Prepared by Them]." *Court of Jurisdictional Disputes Journal*, no. 7 (2016): 167–182. https://dergipark.org.tr/tr/pub/mdergi/issue/24952/263382.

Barın, Taylan. "Cumhurbaşkanı Kararnamelerinin Normlar Hiyerarşisindeki Yeri Sorunu [The Issue of the Place of Presidential Decrees in the Hierarchy of Norms]." In *Cumhurbaşkanının İşlemleri Hukuki Niteliği, Normlar Hiyerarşisindeki Yeri ve Denetimi*, edited by Oktay Uygun and Egemen Esen, 153–198. İstanbul: On İki Levha, 2019.

Baş, Ömer Can. "Tax-Farming Procedure and Tax-Farming Contract in Administrative Law." *Marmara Üniversitesi Hukuk Fakültesi Hukuk Araştırmaları Dergisi* 26, no. 2 (2020): 1006–1046. https://dergipark.org.tr/en/download/article-file/1330752.

Bilgen, Pertev. *İdare Hukuku* [*Administrative Law*]. İstanbul: Filiz, 1996.

Bülbül, Erdoğan. *İdari İşlemin Yürürlükten Kaldırılması* [*Abolishment of Administrative Act*]. İstanbul: Beta, 2010.

Can, Emre. *İdari İşlemin Şekil Unsuru* [*The Element of Form of Administrative Act*]. İstanbul: On İki Levha, 2016.

Chapus, René. *Droit Administratif Général Tome II*. Paris: Montchrestien, 2001.

Çağlayan, Ramazan. *İdare Hukuku Dersleri* [*Administrative Law Lectures*]. Ankara: Adalet, 2022.

Çağlayan, Ramazan. "Kamulaştırma İşleminin İptali ve Mülkiyetin Akibeti [Annulment of Expropriation Act and Aftermath of the Property]." *Journal of İstanbul University Law Faculty* 69, no. 1, 2 (2011): 453–466.

Çağlayan, Ramazan. "Risk İlkesi Gereğince İdarenin Kusursuz Sorumluluğu [Absolute Liability of Administration Pursuant to the Principle of Risk]." *Sorumluluk Ve Tazminat Hukuku Sempozyumu* (2009): 451–495. https://web ftp.gazi.edu.tr/hukuk/sorumluluk/s_22.pdf.

Delvolve, Pierre. *Droit Administratif*. Paris: Daloz, 2014.

Derdiman, Ramazan Cengiz. *İdare Hukuku* [*Administrative Law*]. Aktüel, 2015.

Duran, Lütfi. *İdare Hukuku Ders Notları* [*Administrative Law Lecture Notes*]. İstanbul: İstanbul Üniversitesi Yayınları, 1982.

Ekinci, Murat. *İdari İstikrar İlkesi* [*Administrative Stability Principle*]. Ankara: Adalet, 2021.

Erguvan, Derya Deviner. *Yargı Kararları Işığında İdari İşlemin Geriye Yürümezliği İlkesi ve Geri Alma İstisnası* [*The Principle of Non-retroactivity of

Administrative Acts and the Exception of Withdrawal within the Scope of Judicial Decisions]. Ankara: Adalet, 2017.

Erkut, Celal. *İptal Davasının Konusunu Oluşturması Bakımından İdari İşlemin Kimliği* [*Identity of Administrative Acts as Constituting the Subject of Annulment Case*]. Ankara: Danıştay Yayınları no. 51, 1990.

Ersöz, Ahmet Kürşat. "Sağlık Hizmetleri Açısından Hizmet Kusurunun Ağırlığı ve İspat Problemi [Severity of Service Fault from the Perspective of Health Services and the Problem of Proof]." *İl Han Özay'a Armağan, İstanbul Law Review* 69, no. 1–2 (2011): 927–934.

Ertaş, Türker. "Yürütme Organının Asli Düzenleyici İşlem Yapma Yetkisi Bağlamında Cumhurbaşkanlığı Kararnamelerinin Karşılaştırmalı Anayasal Düzenlerdeki Benzer İşlemlerle Kıyaslanması ve Türk Hükümet Sistemine Etkisi [Comparison of Presidential Decrees with Similar Acts in Comparative Constitutional Orders within the scope of the Power of Executive to Establish Primary Regulatory Act and Its Affect on the Turkish Governmental System]." In *Cumhurbaşkanının İşlemleri Hukuki Niteliği, Normlar Hiyerarşisindeki Yeri ve Denetimi*, edited by Oktay Uygun and Egemen Esen, 9–52. İstanbul: On İki Levha, 2019.

Esin, Yüksel, *Danıştay'da Açılacak Tazminat Davaları, İkinci Kitap, Esas* [*Compensation Actions Before State Council, Second Book, Merits*]. Ankara, 1973.

Fendoğlu, Hasan Tahsin. "Cumhurbaşkanlığı Kararnameleri Mahfuz Düzenleme Alanı Mıdır? [Are Presidential Decrees Exclusive Regulatory Area?]." *Ankara Bar Journal*, no. 3 (2019): 277–310.

Gaudemet, Yves. *Traité De Droit Administratif Tome I.* Paris: LGDJ, 2001.

Giritli, İsmet, Pertev Bilgen, Tayfun Akgüner, and Kahraman Berk. *İdare Hukuku* [*Administrative Law*]. İstanbul: Der, 2015.

Gözler, Kemal. *İdare Hukuku* [*Administrative Law*]. Bursa: Ekin Basım Yayın Dağıtım, 2019.

Gözler, Kemal. "Korona Virüs Salgınıyla Mücadele İçin Alınan Tedbirler Hukuka Uygun Mu? (2) [Are the Measures Taken for the Fight Against Corona Virus Pandemic Lawful? (2)]." July 6, 2020. https://www.anayasa.gen.tr/korona-2.htm.

Göçgün, Muhammed. *İdari İşlemin Konu Unsuru* [*The Element of Subject of Administrative Act*]. İstanbul: On İki Levha, 2017.

Gözübüyük, Şeref, and Turgut Tan. *İdare Hukuku* [*Administrative Law*]. Volume I. Ankara: Turhan, 2001.

Gözübüyük, Şeref, and Turgut Tan. *İdare Hukuku* [*Administrative Law*]. Volume II. Ankara: Turhan, 2014.

Gülan, Aydın. "Borcunu Ödemeyen Devlete Karşı Ne Yapılabilir? [What Can Be Done Against the State Which Does Not Pay Its Debt]." *Journal of Administrative Law and Administrative Sciences* 13, no. 1, 11 (1995): 11–29. https://dergipark.org.tr/tr/pub/iuihid/issue/57855/14642.

Gülan, Aydın. "Kamu Mallarına İlişkin Sorunlara Uyuşmazlık Mahkemesinin Yaklaşımı [Approach of Court of Jurisdictional Disputes to the Issues Concerning Public Property]." *Journal of Administrative Law and Administrative Sciences* 11, no. 1, 3 (1990): 19–23.

Gülan, Aydın. *Maden İdare Hukukumuzun Ana İlkeleri ve Temel Müesseseleri* [*The Essential Principles and Foundations of Our Mine Administrative Law*]. İstanbul: Lamure, 2008.

Gülan, Aydın. "Kamu Malları [Public Property]." In *Günışığında Yönetim*, edited by İl Han Özay. İstanbul: Filiz, 2017.

Gülan, Aydın. "Türkiye'de Kamu Hizmetlerinin Gelişimi [Development of Public Service in Turkey]." *Journal of İstanbul University Law Faculty* 56, no. 1–4 (1998): 97–107. https://dergipark.org.tr/tr/pub/iuhfm/issue/9068/113076.

Gülan, Aydın. "Kamu Hizmeti Kavramı [The Notion of Public Service]." *Journal of Administrative Law and Administrative Sciences* 9, no. 1–3 (1988): 147–159. https://dergipark.org.tr/tr/pub/iuihid/issue/1251/14697.

Gülan, Aydın. *Kamu Mallarından Yararlanma Usullerinin Tabi Olduğu Hukuki Rejim* [*Legal Regime of the Procedures to Benefit from Public Properties*]. İstanbul: Alfa, 1999.

Günday, Metin. *İdare Hukuku* [*Adminitrative Law*]. Ankara: İmaj, 2017.

Günday, Metin, and Çiğdem Sever, "2017 Anayasa Değişiklikleri ve Uyumlaştırma Sürecinin İdare Hukukunda Yarattığı Etki Üzerine Bir Değerlendirme [An Evaluation Concerning the Effects of Constitutional Amendments of 2017 and Process of Harmonization on Administrative Law]." In *Prof. Dr. Nami Çağan Anısına Armağan*, 623–666. Atılım Üniversitesi Yayınları no. 63, 2020.

Gürsel, Esin. "Cumhurbaşkanlığı Hükümet Sisteminde Yürütmenin Düzenleme Yetkisi ve Cumhurbaşkanlığı Kararnamelerinin Anayasal Sınırı [Power to Regulate of Executive Organ in Turkey and the Constitutional Limits of Presidential Decrees]." *Ankara Social Sciences University Journal*, no. 2 (2019): 391–424.

İnanç, Mehmet. *Özel Hukuk Tüzel Kişilerinin İdari İşlemleri* [*Administrative Acts of Private Law Persons*]. İstanbul: On İki Levha, 2018.

İşbir, K. Begüm. *Kamu Tüzel Kişiliği* [*Public Corporate Body*]. Ankara: Turhan, 2017.

Kalabalık, Halil. *İdare Hukuku Dersleri* [*Lectures of Administrative Law*]. Volume 2. Konya: Sayram, 2016.

Kalabalık, Halil. *İdari Yargılama Usulü Hukuku* [*Administrative Judicial Procedure Law*]. Konya: Sayram, 2015.

Kaman, Nur. "Disiplin Soruşturması, Ceza Soruşturması, Görevden Uzaklaştırma [Disciplinary Investigation, Criminal Investigation, Removal from Duty]." In *İdare Hukuku*, edited by Turan Yıldırım, 315–346. İstanbul: On İki Levha, 2022.

Kaman, Nur. "Kamu Görevlileri [Public Employees]." In *İdare Hukuku*, edited by Turan Yıldırım, 261–313. İstanbul: On İki Levha, 2022.

Kaman, Nur. "Kamu Malları [Public Properties]." In *İdare Hukuku*, edited by Turan Yıldırım, 363–404. İstanbul: On İki Levha, 2022.

Kanadoğlu, Korkut. "Cumhurbaşkanlığı Kararnamesi [Presidential Decree]." *Galatasaray University Law Faculty Journal*, no. 2 (2018): 637–650.

Karahanoğulları, Onur. *İdare Hukuku* [*Administrative Law*]. Ankara: Turhan, 2022.

Karahanoğulları, Onur. *Kamu Hizmeti* [*Public Service*]. Ankara: Turhan, 2015.

Karslı, Mehmet Rauf. *İdare Hukukunda Kamu Görevlisi Kavramı* [*The Notion of Public Employee in Administrative Law*]. İstanbul: On İki Levha, 2016.

Kaya, Cemil. "Danıştay İçtihatlarında Hükümet Tasarrufu Teorisinden Devletin Hükümranlık / Egemenlik Hakkı Teorisine [From the Act of State Theory within the Council of State Jurisprudence through to the State Sovereignty Theory]." *Court of Jurisdictional Disputes Journal*, no. 7 (2016): 637–663. https://dergipark.org.tr/tr/download/article-file/229918.

Kutlu Gürsel, Meltem. "Deprem ve İdarenin Sorumluluğu [Eartquake and Liability of Administration]." *Amme İdaresi Dergisi* 32, no. 4 (1999): 15–27.

Kutlu Gürsel, Meltem. *Kamulaştırma Hukuku* [*Expropriation Law*]. Ankara: Seçkin, 2009.

Lebreton, Gilles. *Droit Administratif Général*. Paris: Dalloz, 2013.

Lombard, Martine, Gilles Dumont, and Jean Sirinelli, *Droit Administratif*. Paris: Dalloz, 2013.

Louvaris, Antoine. *Droit Administratif*. Paris: PUF, 2011.

Odyakmaz, Zehra, and Ümit Kaymak. *İdare Hukuku* [*Administrative Law*]. Ankara: Seçkin, 2022.

Oğurlu, Yücel. *Karşılaştırmalı İdare Hukukunda Ölçülülük İlkesi* [*Principle of Proportionality in Comparative Administrative Law*]. Ankara: Seçkin, 2002.

Okay Tekinsoy, Özge. "Kolluk Faaliyetleri [Policing Activities]." In *İdare Hukuku*, edited by Turan Yıldırım, 609–672. İstanbul: On İki Levha, 2022.

Onar, Sıddık Sami. *İdare Hukukunun Umumi Esasları* [*General Principles of Administrative Law*]. İstanbul: Hak Yayınevi İsmail Akgün Matbaası, 1999.

Özay, İl Han, ed. *Günışığında Yönetim* [*Administration in the Sunshine*]. İstanbul: Filiz, 2017.

Özdemir, H. Eyüp. "Kamulaştırma [Expropriation]." In *İdare Hukuku*, edited by Turan Yıldırım, 735–789. İstanbul: On İki Levha, 2022.

Özgüldür, Serdar. *Askeri Yüksek İdare Mahkemesi Kararları Işığında Tam Yargı Davaları* [*Full Remedy Actions in Light of the Decisions of Military High Administrative Court*]. Ankara: Yetkin, 1996.

Özsoy Boyunsuz, Şule. "Regime Cycles, Constitution Making, and the Political System Question in Ottoman and Turkish Constitutional Developments." In *The Failure of Popular Constitution Making in Turkey*, edited by Felix Petersen and Zeynep Yanaşmayan, 84–117. Cambridge: Cambridge University Press, 2020.

Peiser, Gustave. *Droit Administratif*. Paris: Dalloz, 2014.

Sancakdar, Oğuz, Lale Burcu Önüt, Eser Us Doğan, Mine Kasapoğlu Turhan, and Serkan Seyhan. *İdare Hukuku Teorik Çalışma Kitabı* [*Administrative Law Theorical Study Book*]. Ankara: Seçkin, 2022.

Sarıca, Ragıp. *İdari Kaza* [*Administrative Jurisdiction*]. İstanbul: Kenan Matbaası, 1942.

Sever, Çiğdem. "Cumhurbaşkanının Teşkilatlanma Konusundaki Yetkileri ya da 'Panthenogenesis' Olmak [The Powers of the President on Organization or Being 'Panthenogenesis')." In *Cumhurbaşkanının İşlemleri Hukuki Niteliği, Normlar Hiyerarşisindeki Yeri ve Denetimi*, edited by Oktay Uygun and Egemen Esen, 353–388. İstanbul: On İki Levha, 2019.

Sezer, Abdullah. "Normlar Hiyerarşisi ve Cumhurbaşkanlığı Kararnameleri (Çok Boyutlu Normlar Piramidi Yaklaşımı) [Hierarchy of Norms and Presidential Decrees (Multidimensional Pyramid of Norms Approach)]." *Anayasa Yargısı* 36. no. 1 (2019): 353–412.

Sezginer, Murat. *Ayrılabilir İşlem Kuramı*. Ankara: Yetkin, 2000.

Sezginer, Murat. "İdari İşlem-İcrailik-Ayrılabilir İşlem-Yargısal Denetim [Administrative Act—Executability—Separable Act—Judicial Review]." *İl Han Özay'a Armağan, İstanbul Law Review* 69, no. 1–2 (2011): 241–250.

Solmaz, Eren. *Kamulaştırma Hukukunda Malikin Geri Alma Hakkı* [*Right of the Owner to Reclaim in Expropriation Law*]. İstanbul: On İki Levha, 2016.

Şahin, Cenk. *Acele Kamulaştırma* [*Urgent Expropriation*]. İstanbul: On İki Levha, 2018.

Şahin, Zeynep. "Pandemi Dönemindeki Kısıtlamaların Hukukiliği [Legality of Restrictions During Pandemics]." *KHAS Hukuk Bülteni*, June 17, 2021. https://hukukbulteni.khas.edu.tr/bulten/89.

Tan, Turgut. *İdari İşlemin Geri Alınması* [*Withdrawal of Administrative Act*]. Ankara: Sevinç Matbaası, 1970.

Tan, Turgut, and Bahar Bayazıt. *İdare Hukuku* [*Administrative Law*]. Ankara: Turhan Kitabevi, 2021.

Tanör, Bülent, and Necmi Yüzbaşıoğlu. *1982 Anayasasına Göre Türk Anayasa Hukuku* [*Turkish Constitutional Law According to 1982 Constitution*]. İstanbul: Beta, 2020.

Tutal, Erhan. "Kamulaştırmasız El Atma Davalarında Yargılama Sürecindeki Son Gelişmeler [Recent Developments in Prosecution Process of Cases of Confiscation Without Expropriation Cases]." *Court of Jurisdictional Disputes Journal*, no. 7 (2016): 1107–1132. https://dergipark.org.tr/tr/download/article-file/229933.

Ulu, Güher. *İdari İşlemin Yetki Unsuru* [*The Element of Authority of Administrative Acts*]. Ankara: Seçkin, 2012.

Ulusoy, Ali. "Cumhurbaşkanlığı Kararnameleri: Varoluşsal, Yapısal ve Hukuksal Bir Değerlendirme [Presidential Decrees: An Existential, Structural and Legal Consideration)." *Anayasa Yargısı* 37, no. 2 (2020): 31–66.

Ulusoy, Ali. *Kamu Hizmeti İncelemeleri* [*Reviews of Public Service*]. İstanbul: Ülke, 2004.

Ulusoy, Ali. "Regülasyon Kurumları Hakkında Genel Bir Değerlendirme [A General Evaluation on Regulation Institutions]." In *Günışığında Yönetim*, edited by İl Han Özay. İstanbul: Filiz, 2017.

Ülgen, Özen. *Anayasa Yargısında İptal Kararlarının Etkileri* [*Effects of Annulment Decisions in Constitutional Judiciary*]. İstanbul: On İki Levha, 2016.

Yasin, Melikşah. "Cumhurbaşkanlığı Kararnamelerinin Türk İdari Teşkilat Hukukuna Etkileri [Effects of Presidential Decrees on Turkish Administrative Organization Law]." *Anayasa Yargısı* 37, no. 2 (2020): 315–345.

Yasin, Melikşah. "Kamu Hizmeti [Public Service]." In *İdare Hukuku*, edited by Turan Yıldırım, 525–592. İstanbul: On İki Levha, 2022.

Yaşar, Hasan Nuri. *İdare Hukuku: Genel Esaslar* [*Administrative Law: General Principles*]. İstanbul: Der, 2016.

Yavuzdoğan, Seçkin. "Tehlikeli Salgın Hastalık Sebebiyle Alınan Sokağa Çıkma Yasağı Kararları Üzerine Birkaç Not [A Few Notes on Curfew Decisions Due to Dangerous Epidemic Diseases]." *Adalet Dergisi* 1, no. 2 (2020): 125–139. https://dergipark.org.tr/tr/download/article-file/1205205.

Yayla, Ahmet. *İdarenin Kusursuz Sorumluluğu* [*Absolute Liability of Administration*]. İstanbul: On İki Levha, 2015.

Yayla, Ahmet. *Türk İdare Hukukuna Göre İstimvalin Rejimi* [*The Regime of Requisition Pursuant to Turkish Administrative Law*]. Ankara: Yetkin, 2016.

Yayla, Yıldızhan. *İdare Hukuku* [*Administrative Law*]. İstanbul: Beta, 2009.

Yeniay, Lokman and Yeniay, Gülden, "Türk Hukukunda Yürütme Organının Düzenleme Yetkisi ve Cumhurbaşkanlığı Kararnamesi [Regulatory Authority of the Executive Branch and Presidential Decree in Turkish Law]." *Anayasa Yargısı* 36, no. 1 (2019): 105–138.

Yenice, Kazım. "Sıkıyönetim İlanı Kararı ve Yargısal Denetim Sorunu [Declaration of Martial Law and the Problem of it's Judicial Review]." *State Council Journal* 1, no. 2 (1971): 18–35, https://www.danistay.gov.tr/assets/pdf/yayinlar/dergi/2021-02-24-11-59-8164234.pdf.

Yıldırım, Ramazan. *Türk İdari Rejimi Dersleri* [*Turkish Administrative Regime Lectures*]. Konya: Mimoza, 2014.

Yıldırım, Turan. "Genel Kuramlar ve Anayasal İlkeler [General Theories and Constitutional Principles]." In *İdare Hukuku*, edited by Turan Yıldırım, 3–65. İstanbul: On İki Levha, 2022.

Yıldırım, Turan. "İdarenin Sorumluluğu [Liability of Administration]." In *İdare Hukuku*, edited by Turan Yıldırım, 759–789. İstanbul: On İki Levha, 2022.

Yıldırım, Turan. "İdari İşlemler [Administrative Acts]." In *İdare Hukuku*, edited by Turan Yıldırım, 407–526. İstanbul: On İki Levha, 2022.

Yıldız, Hayrettin. "İdare Hukukunun Kısa Tarihçesi [Short History of Administrative Law]." *Ankara Hacı Bayram Veli Üniversitesi Hukuku Fakültesi Dergisi* 22, no. 4 (2008): 197–223. https://dergipark.org.tr/tr/download/article-file/685872.

Yılmaz, Dilşat. *İdari İşlemin İcrailik Özelliği* [*The Feature of Executability of Administrative Act*]. Ankara: Astana, 2014.

Yılmaz, Halit. "Cumhurbaşkanlığı Kararnamelerinin Konu Bakımından Yetki Sınırları [Constitutional Limitations on the Subject of Presidential Decrees]." *İstanbul Law Review* 78, no. 1 (2020): 225–263.

Yılmaz, Harun. "Danıştay Kararları Işığında İdari İstikrar İlkesinin İdari Yargılama Hukukuna Önemli Yansımaları [Important Reflections of the Administrative Stability Principle on the Administrative Jurisdiction Law in the Light of the Decisions of the Council of State]." *Court of Jurisdictional Disputes Journal*, no. 17 (2021): 523–546. https://dergipark.org.tr/tr/download/article-file/1844508.

Yumuşak, Hakan. "İdari İşlemin Kaldırılması ve Geri Alınması [Abolishment and Withdrawal of Administrative Act]." Master's thesis, İstanbul Medipol University Social Sciences Institute, 2018.

Zabunoğlu, Yahya Kazım. *İdare Hukuku*. Ankara: Yetkin, 2012.

Zeybek Cebeci, Ebru. *Kamu Hizmetlerinin Gördürülmesine İlişkin Sözleşmeler: (Kamu Hizmeti Anlayışındaki Değişim Ekseninde) [Agreements Regarding Making Public Service Performed: (From the Perspective of Changes in Public Service Understanding)]*. Ankara: Seçkin, 2021.

www.ingramcontent.com/pod-product-compliance
Ingram Content Group UK Ltd.
Pitfield, Milton Keynes, MK11 3LW, UK
UKHW041823031026
15587UKWH00002B/535

9 783631 898987